LATER MANUSCRIPTS

The Cambridge
JANE AUSTEN

VOLUMES IN THIS SERIES

1. Childhood Writings

2. Northanger Abbey

3. Sense and Sensibility

4. Pride and Prejudice

5. Mansfield Park

6. Emma

7. Persuasion

8. Later Manuscripts

With prefaces and notes by Janet Todd

JANE AUSTEN

Later Manuscripts

The Collector's Edition

With prefaces and notes by
JANET TODD

CAMBRIDGE
UNIVERSITY PRESS

Shaftesbury Road, Cambridge CB2 8EA, United Kingdom

One Liberty Plaza, 20th Floor, New York, NY 10006, USA

477 Williamstown Road, Port Melbourne, VIC 3207, Australia

314–321, 3rd Floor, Plot 3, Splendor Forum, Jasola District Centre,
New Delhi – 110025, India

103 Penang Road, #05–06/07, Visioncrest Commercial, Singapore 238467

Cambridge University Press is part of Cambridge University Press & Assessment,
a department of the University of Cambridge.

We share the University's mission to contribute to society through the pursuit of
education, learning and research at the highest international levels of excellence.

www.cambridge.org
Information on this title: www.cambridge.org/9781009432818

DOI: 10.1017/9781009432825

© Cambridge University Press & Assessment 2025

This publication is in copyright. Subject to statutory exception and to the provisions
of relevant collective licensing agreements, no reproduction of any part may take
place without the written permission of Cambridge University Press & Assessment.

When citing this work, please include a reference to the DOI 10.1017/9781009432825

First published 2025

Cover design, illustration and frontispieces by Lauren Downing
Text design by Lyn Davies Design

Printed in the United Kingdom by CPI Group Ltd, Croydon CR0 4YY

A catalogue record for this publication is available from the British Library

Library of Congress Cataloging-in-Publication Data
Names: Austen, Jane, 1775–1817, author. | Todd, Janet, 1942– editor.
Title: Later manuscripts / with preface and notes by Janet Todd.
Description: The collector's edition. | Cambridge ; New York, NY :
  Cambridge University Press, 2025. | Series: CCJA the Cambridge Jane
  Austen | Includes bibliographical references and index.
Identifiers: LCCN 2024017716 | ISBN 9781009432818 (hardback) | ISBN
  9781009432825 (ebook)
Subjects: LCSH: Austen, Jane, 1775–1817 – Manuscripts. | Austen, Jane,
  1775–1817 – Literary collections.
Classification: LCC PR4032 .T64 2025 | DDC 828/.709–dc23/eng/20240429
LC record available at https://lccn.loc.gov/2024017716

ISBN 978-1-009-43281-8 Hardback

Cambridge University Press & Assessment has no responsibility for the persistence
or accuracy of URLs for external or third-party internet websites referred to in this
publication and does not guarantee that any content on such websites is, or will remain,
accurate or appropriate.

The texts in this edition are based on
The Cambridge Edition of the Works of Jane
Austen (2005–8), with grateful acknowledgement. Readers
interested in a more detailed textual account and in further
exploration of the novels and their publication history should
consult those volumes. The present edition contains explanatory
endnotes: under thematic headings, they provide information
on a cultural, historical and literary context that might be
unfamiliar to a modern reader. A few footnotes indicate
words that have changed meaning between
Austen's time and our own.

CONTENTS

The Manuscript Novels

PREFACE TO THE MANUSCRIPT NOVELS	*3*
PREFACE TO 'LADY SUSAN'	*7*
Lady Susan	*9*
NOTES TO 'LADY SUSAN'	*74*
PREFACE TO 'THE WATSONS'	*81*
The Watsons	*83*
NOTES TO 'THE WATSONS'	*131*
PREFACE TO 'SANDITON'	*139*
Sanditon	*141*
NOTES TO 'SANDITON'	*202*

Jane Austen on Fiction

PREFACE TO JANE AUSTEN'S WRITINGS ON FICTION	*213*
To Mrs. Hunter of Norwich	*215*
NOTES TO 'TO MRS. HUNTER OF NORWICH'	*215*
Letters on Fiction to Anna Lefroy	*217*
NOTES TO LETTERS ON FICTION	*225*
Plan of a Novel, according to hints from various quarters	*227*
NOTES TO 'PLAN OF A NOVEL'	*229*

Poems and Charades

PREFACE TO THE POEMS AND CHARADES *233*

Poems *235*
Charades *255*

THE MANUSCRIPT NOVELS

PREFACE TO
THE MANUSCRIPT NOVELS

AFTER FINISHING her teenage writings and before she began publishing her early novels Jane Austen wrote two extraordinary works. Both remained unpublished until the twentieth century. The first, 'Lady Susan', exists in a fair untitled copy and is set within the aristocracy. The second, 'The Watsons', a much-corrected fragment, describes characters from the lower middle class. Neither rank appears centrally in the six published novels.

A novella in letter form, 'Lady Susan' cannot be dated securely but family consensus places it close to an early version of *Sense and Sensibility*, about 1795, although it may have been altered later. Austen did not seek to publish it, but she made and kept a fair copy. 'The Watsons' most likely dates from around 1804; like the earlier realist fragment, 'Catharine, or the Bower', it was neither concluded nor destroyed and Jane Austen might have intended to return to it in later life. Her nephew James Edward Austen-Leigh thought his aunt abandoned 'The Watsons' when she realised she had placed her main characters too low down the social scale; a more likely factor was her father's sudden death in 1805, which must have brought the story of impoverished spinster daughters of a country vicar rather close to home.

Jane Austen died in July 1817 after a long illness. She used her last months to compose the beginning of a final novel, 'Sanditon', an exaggerated, comic work in some ways closer in style to her teenage skits than to the six novels. It is set not in the usual country house or village but in a developing seaside resort on the south coast of England. Austen's increasing weakness made it sometimes difficult for her to cope with a pen and she wrote a few passages first in pencil. There is however no sign of any falling-off in imagination. At the end of the fragment Austen entered the date on which she stopped composing: 18 March 1817.

LADY SUSAN

PREFACE TO 'LADY SUSAN'

AFTER JANE AUSTEN's death, her family were reluctant to publish 'Lady Susan' and it does indeed come as a shock to those who read it after the mature novels. Certainly the heroine, a handsome widow, is the most finished portrait of clever, charming malice that Austen ever penned. Lady Susan's brisk immorality emerges in her vivacious letters as she tunes her words to her duped recipients. She is a gambler in society, enjoying the process of the game as much as the winning, and she is prepared to risk everything for another chance at a prize.

The power that Lady Susan exerts over others is a function of her power over language. Aware that eloquence is the greatest asset a woman can have, she exploits it to control men's desire. In this novella Austen comes as close to presenting sex and sexual enjoyment as she could for the time. But Lady Susan's love of control usually outweighs her need to satisfy her physical desire. Under cover of feminine performance, she pursues the traditionally masculine aim of seducing to enjoy sexual and psychological mastery: 'There is exquisite pleasure in subduing an insolent spirit', she remarks. She wants men to respond completely and irrationally to her, and the closer she comes to imposing a vision of herself on them, the more energetic and excited she becomes.

In her mature novels Austen controls the reader's moral point of view with narrative irony, but in this epistolary novella she allows the energy of the character almost to defeat the reader's probable moral expectation. In the closing pages a narrator is introduced to point out Lady Susan's lack of 'conscience', a powerful word that leaps out of its cynical context. However, if we exclude the monstrous treatment of her meek daughter, Lady Susan has perhaps some defence for her selfishness. In a patriarchal world where 'Propriety & so forth' are stacked against women who have neither property nor status in themselves, such energy as hers has nothing to do but devour others and itself.

LADY SUSAN

LETTER I.

Lady Susan Vernon to Mr Vernon.—

Langford, Dec.^r—

My dear Brother

 I can no longer refuse myself the pleasure of profitting by your kind invitation when we last parted, of spending some weeks with you at Churchill, & therefore if quite convenient to you and Mrs. Vernon to receive me at present, I shall hope within a few days to be introduced to a sister,[*] whom I have so long desired to be acquainted with.—My kind friends here are most affectionately urgent with me to prolong my stay, but their hospitable & chearful dispositions lead them too much into society for my present situation & state of mind; & I impatiently look forward to the hour when I shall be admitted into your delightful retirement. I long to be made known to your dear little Children, in whose hearts I shall be very eager to secure an interest.—I shall soon have occasion for all my fortitude, as I am on the point of separation from my own daughter.—The long illness of her dear Father prevented my paying her that attention which Duty & affection equally dictated, & I have but too much reason to fear that the Governess to whose care I consigned her, was unequal to the charge.—I have therefore resolved on placing her at one of the best Private Schools in Town, where I shall have an opportunity of leaving her myself, in my way to you. I am determined you see, not to be denied admittance at Churchill.—It would indeed give me most painful sensations to know that it were not in your power to receive me.—Y.^r most obliged & affec: Sister

S. Vernon.—

---

[*] **Sister**: here means sister-in-law.

LETTER 2.^D

Lady Susan to M^{rs}. Johnson

Langford

You were mistaken my dear Alicia, in supposing me fixed at this place for the rest of the winter. It greives me to say how greatly you were mistaken, for I have seldom spent three months more agreably than those which have just flown away.—At present nothing goes smoothly.—The Females of the Family are united against me.—You foretold how it would be, when I first came to Langford; & Manwaring is so uncommonly pleasing that I was not without apprehensions myself. I remember saying to myself as I drove to the House, "I like this Man; pray Heaven no harm come of it!"—But I was determined to be discreet, to bear in mind my being only four months a widow, & to be as quiet as possible,—and I have been so;—my dear Creature, I have admitted no one's attentions but Manwaring's, I have avoided all general flirtation whatever, I have distinguished no Creature besides of all the Numbers resorting hither, except Sir James Martin, on whom I bestowed a little notice in order to detach him from Miss Manwaring. But if the World could know my motive <u>there</u>, they would honour me.—I have been called an unkind Mother, but it was the sacred impulse of maternal affection, it was the advantage of my Daughter that led me on; & if that Daughter were not the greatest simpleton on Earth, I might have been rewarded for my Exertions as I ought.—Sir James did make proposals to me for Frederica—but Frederica, who was born to be the torment of my life, chose to set herself so violently against the match, that I thought it better to lay aside the scheme for the present.—I have more than once repented that I did not marry him myself, & were he but one degree less contemptibly weak I certainly should, but I must own myself rather romantic in that respect, & that Riches only, will not satisfy me. The event of all this is very provoking.—Sir James is gone, Maria highly incensed, and M^{rs}. Manwaring insupportably jealous;—so jealous in short, & so enraged against me, that in the fury of her temper I should not be surprised at her appealing to her Guardian if she had the liberty of addressing him—but there your Husband stands my friend, & the kindest, most amiable action of his Life was his throwing her off* forever on her Marriage.—Keep up his resentment therefore I charge you.—We are now in a sad state; no house was ever more altered; the whole family are at war, & Manwaring scarcely dares speak to me. It is time for me to be gone; I have therefore determined on leaving them, and shall spend I hope a comfortable day with you in Town within this week.—If I am as little in favour with M.ʳ Johnson as ever, you must come to me at N.º 10 Wigmore S.ᵗ—but I hope this may not be the case, for as M.ʳ Johnson with all his faults is a Man to whom that great word "Respectable" is always given, & I am known to be so intimate with his wife, his slighting me has an awkward Look.—I take Town in my way to that insupportable spot, a Country Village, for I am really going to Churchill.—Forgive me my dear friend, it is my last resource. Were there another place in England open to me, I would prefer it.—Charles Vernon is my aversion, & I am afraid of his wife.—At Churchill however I must remain till I have something better in veiw. My young Lady accompanies me to Town, where I shall deposit her under the care of Miss Summers in Wigmore Street, till she becomes a little more reasonable. She will make good connections there, as the Girls are all of the best Families.—The price is immense, & much beyond what I can ever attempt to pay.—Adeiu. I will send you a line, as soon as I arrive in Town.—Yours Ever,

S. Vernon.

LETTER 3.

M.ʳˢ Vernon to Lady De Courcy.

Churchill

My dear Mother

I am very sorry to tell you that it will not be in our power to keep our promise of spending the Christmas with you; & we are prevented

---

* **Throwing her off**: disowning her.

that happiness by a circumstance which is not likely to make us any amends.—Lady Susan in a letter to her Brother, has declared her intention of visiting us almost immediately—& as such a visit is in all probability merely an affair of convenience, it is impossible to conjecture it's length. I was by no means prepared for such an event, nor can I now account for her Ladyship's conduct.—Langford appeared so exactly the place for her in every respect, as well from the elegant & expensive stile of Living there, as from her particular attachment to M^{rs}. Manwaring, that I was very far from expecting so speedy a distinction, tho' I always imagined from her increasing friendship for us since her Husband's death, that we should at some future period be obliged to receive her.—M^r. Vernon I think was a great deal too kind to her, when he was in Staffordshire. Her behaviour to him, independant of her general Character, has been so inexcusably artful & ungenerous since our marriage was first in agitation, that no one less amiable & mild than himself could have overlooked it at all; & tho' as his Brother's widow & in narrow circumstances it was proper to render her pecuniary assistance, I cannot help thinking his pressing invitation to her to visit us at Churchill perfectly unnecessary.—Disposed however as he always is to think the best of every one, her display of Greif, & professions of regret, & general resolutions of prudence were sufficient to soften his heart, & make him really confide in her sincerity. But as for myself, I am still unconvinced; & plausibly as her Ladyship has now written, I cannot make up my mind, till I better understand her real meaning in coming to us.—You may guess therefore my dear Madam with what feelings I look forward to her arrival. She will have occasion for all those attractive Powers for which she is celebrated, to gain any share of my regard; & I shall certainly endeavour to guard myself against their influence, if not accompanied by something more substantial.—She expresses a most eager desire of being acquainted with me, & makes very gracious mention of my children, but I am not quite weak enough to suppose a woman who has behaved with inattention if not unkindness to her own child, should be attached to any of mine. Miss Vernon is to be placed at a school in Town before her Mother comes to us, which I am glad of, for her sake & my own. It must be to her advantage to be separated from her Mother; & a girl of sixteen who has received so wretched an education would not be a very desirable companion here.—Reginald has long wished I know to see this captivating Lady Susan, & we shall depend on his joining our party soon.—I am glad to hear that my Father continues so well, & am, with best Love &c, Cath Vernon.—

LETTER 4.

M.^r De Courcy to M^{rs}. Vernon.

Parklands

My dear Sister

I congratulate you & Mr Vernon on being about to receive into your family, the most accomplished coquette in England.—As a very distinguished Flirt, I have been always taught to consider her; but it has lately fallen in my way to hear some particulars of her conduct at Langford, which prove that she does not confine herself to that sort of honest flirtation which satisfies most people, but aspires to the more delicious gratification of making a whole family miserable.—By her behaviour to Mr Manwaring, she gave jealousy & wretchedness to his wife, & by her attentions to a young Man previously attached to Mr Manwaring's sister, deprived an amiable girl of her Lover.—I learnt all this from a Mr Smith now in this neighbourhood—(I have dined with him at Hurst and Wilford)—who is just come from Langford, where he was a fortnight in the house with her Ladyship, & who is therefore well qualified to make the communication.—What a Woman she must be!—I long to see her, & shall certainly accept your kind invitation, that I may form some idea of those bewitching powers which can do so much—engaging at the same time & in the same house the affections of two Men who were neither of them at liberty to bestow them—& all this, without the charm of youth.—I am glad to find that Miss Vernon does not come with her Mother to Churchill, as she has not even manners to recommend her, &

according to M.̲ Smith's account, is equally dull & proud. Where Pride & Stupidity unite, there can be no dissimulation worthy notice, & Miss Vernon shall be consigned to unrelenting contempt; but by all that I can gather, Lady Susan possesses a degree of captivating Deceit which it must be pleasing to witness & detect. I shall be with you very soon, & am your affec. Brother

R De Courcy.—

LETTER 5.

Lady Susan to M.̲ʳˢ Johnson

Churchill

I received your note my dear Alicia, just before I left Town, & rejoice to be assured that M.̲ Johnson suspected nothing of your engagement the evening before; it is undoubtedly better to deceive him entirely;—since he will be stubborn, he must be tricked.—I arrived here in safety, & have no reason to complain of my reception from M.̲ Vernon; but I confess myself not equally satisfied with the behaviour of his Lady.—She is perfectly well bred indeed, & has the air of a woman of fashion, but her manners are not such as can persuade me of her being prepossessed in my favour.—I wanted her to be delighted at seeing me—I was as amiable as possible on the occasion—but all in vain—she does not like me.—To be sure, when we consider that I <u>did</u> take some pains to prevent my Brother-in-law's marrying her, this want of cordiality is not very surprising—& yet it shews an illiberal & vindictive spirit to resent a project which influenced me six years ago, & which never succeeded at last.—I am sometimes half disposed to repent that I did not let Charles buy Vernon Castle when we were obliged to sell it, but it was a trying circumstance, especially as the sale took place exactly at the time of his marriage—& everybody ought to respect the delicacy of those feelings, which could not endure that my Husband's Dignity should be lessened by his younger brother's having possession of the Family Estate.—Could Matters have been so arranged as to prevent the necessity of our leaving the Castle, could we have lived with Charles & kept him single, I should have been very far from persuading my husband to dispose of it elsewhere;—but Charles was then on the point of marrying Miss De Courcy, & the event has justified me. Here are Children in abundance, & what benefit could have accrued to me from his purchasing Vernon?—My having prevented it, may perhaps have given his wife an unfavourable impression—but where there is a disposition to dislike a motive will never be wanting; & as to money-matters, it has not with-held him from being very useful to me. I really have a regard for him, he is so easily imposed on!

The house is a good one, the Furniture fashionable, & everything announces plenty & elegance.—Charles is very rich I am sure; when a Man has once got his name in a Banking House he rolls in money. But they do not know what to do with their fortune, keep very little company, & never go to Town but on business.—We shall be as stupid as possible.—I mean to win my Sister in law's heart through her Children; I know all their names already, & am going to attach myself with the greatest sensibility to one in particular, a young Frederic, whom I take on my lap & sigh over for his dear Uncle's sake.—

Poor Manwaring!—I need not tell you how much I miss him—how perpetually he is in my Thoughts.—I found a dismal Letter from him on my arrival here, full of complaints of his wife & sister, & lamentations on the cruelty of his fate. I passed off the letter as his wife's, to the Vernons, & when I write to him, it must be under cover to you.—

Yours Ever, S V.—

LETTER 6.

*M*ʳˢ *Vernon to M*ʳ *De Courcy*

Churchill

Well my dear Reginald, I have seen this dangerous creature, & must give you some description of her, tho' I hope you will soon be able to form your own judgement. She is really excessively pretty.—However you may chuse to question the allurements of a Lady no longer young, I must for my own part declare that I have seldom seen so lovely a woman as Lady Susan.—She is delicately fair, with fine grey eyes & dark eyelashes; & from her appearance one would not suppose her more than five & twenty, tho' she must in fact be ten years older.—I was certainly not disposed to admire her, tho' always hearing she was beautiful; but I cannot help feeling that she possesses an uncommon union of Symmetry, Brilliancy & Grace.—Her address to me was so gentle, frank & even affectionate, that if I had not known how much she has always disliked me for marrying M:̣ Vernon, and that we had never met before, I should have imagined her an attached friend.—One is apt I beleive to connect assurance of manner with coquetry, & to expect that an impudent address will necessarily attend an impudent mind;—at least I was myself prepared for an improper degree of confidence in Lady Susan; but her countenance is absolutely sweet, & her voice & manner winningly mild.—I am sorry it is so, for what is this but Deceit?—Unfortunately one knows her too well.—She is clever & agreable, has all that knowledge of the world which makes conversation easy, & talks very well, with a happy command of Language, which is too often used I beleive to make Black appear White.—She has already almost persuaded me of her being warmly attached to her daughter, tho' I have so long been convinced of the contrary. She speaks of her with so much tenderness & anxiety, lamenting so bitterly the neglect of her education, which she represents however as wholly unavoidable, that I am forced to recollect how many successive Springs her Ladyship spent in Town, while her daughter was left in Staffordshire to the care of servants or a Governess very little better, to prevent my beleiving whatever she says.

If her manners have so great an influence on my resentful heart, you may guess how much more strongly they operate on M:̣ Vernon's generous temper.—I wish I could be as well satisfied as he is, that it was really her choice to leave Langford for Churchill; & if she had not staid three months there before she discovered that her friends' manner of Living did not suit her situation or feelings, I might have beleived that concern for the loss of such a Husband as Mr Vernon, to whom her own behaviour was far from unexceptionable, might for a time make her wish for retirement. But I cannot forget the length of her visit to the Manwarings, & when I reflect on the different mode of Life which she led with them, from that to which she must now submit, I can only suppose that the wish of establishing her reputation by following, tho' late, the path of propriety, occasioned her removal from a family where she must in reality have been particularly happy. Your friend Mr Smith's story however cannot be quite true, as she corresponds regularly with M^rs. Manwaring; at any rate it must be exaggerated;—it is scarcely possible that two men should be so grossly deceived by her at once.—Yrs &c Cath Vernon.

LETTER 7.

Lady Susan to M^rs. Johnson

Churchill

My dear Alicia

You are very good in taking notice of Frederica, & I am grateful for it as a mark of your friendship; but as I cannot have a doubt of the warmth of that friendship, I am far from exacting so heavy a sacrifice. She is a stupid girl, & has nothing to recommend her.—I would not therefore on any account have you encumber one moment of your precious time by sending for her to Edward S.^t, especially as every visit is so many hours deducted from the grand affair of Education, which I really wish to be attended to, while she remains with Miss Summers.—I want her to play & sing with some portion of Taste, & a good deal of assurance, as she has <u>my</u> hand & arm, & a tolerable voice. <u>I</u> was so much indulged in my infant years that I was never obliged to attend to anything, & consequently am without those accomplishments which are now necessary to finish a pretty Woman. Not that I am an advocate for the prevailing fashion of acquiring a perfect knowledge in all the Languages Arts & Sciences;—it is throwing time away;—to be Mistress of French, Italian, German, Music, Singing, Drawing &c will gain a Woman some applause, but will not add one Lover to her list. Grace & Manner after all are of the greatest importance. I do not mean therefore that Frederica's acquirements should be more than superficial, & I flatter myself that she will not remain long enough at school to understand anything thoroughly.—I hope to see her the wife of Sir James within a twelvemonth.—You know on what I ground my hope, & it is certainly a good foundation, for School must be very humiliating to a girl of Frederica's age; & by the bye, you had better not invite her any more on that account, as I wish her to find her situation as unpleasant as possible.—I am sure of Sir James at any time, & could make him renew his application by a Line.—I shall trouble you meanwhile to prevent his forming any other attachment when he comes to Town;—ask him to your House occasionally, & talk to him about Frederica that he may not forget her.—

Upon the whole I commend my own conduct in this affair extremely, and regard it as a very happy mixture of circumspection & tenderness. Some Mothers would have insisted on their daughter's accepting so great an offer on the first overture, but I could not answer it to myself to force Frederica into a marriage from which her heart revolted; & instead of adopting so harsh a measure, merely propose to make it her own choice by rendering her thoroughly uncomfortable till she does accept him. But enough of this tiresome girl.—

You may well wonder how I contrive to pass my time here—& for the first week, it was most insufferably dull.—Now however, we begin to mend;—our party is enlarged by M^{rs}. Vernon's brother, a handsome young Man, who promises me some amusement. There is something about him that rather interests me, a sort of sauciness, of familiarity which I shall teach him to correct. He is lively & seems clever, & when I have inspired him with greater respect for me than his sister's kind offices have implanted, he may be an agreable Flirt.—There is exquisite pleasure in subduing an insolent spirit, in making a person pre-determined to dislike, acknowledge one's superiority.—I have disconcerted him already by my calm reserve; & it shall be my endeavour to humble the Pride of these self-important De Courcies still lower, to convince M̲ʳˢ̲ Vernon that her sisterly cautions have been bestowed in vain, & to persuade Reginald that she has scandalously belied me. This project will serve at least to amuse me, & prevent my feeling so acutely this dreadful separation from You & all whom I love. Adeiu.

                Yours Ever
                 S. Vernon.

LETTER 8.

M̲ʳˢ̲ Vernon to Lady De Courcy.

                 Churchill

My dear Mother

You must not expect Reginald back again for some time. He desires me to tell you that the present open weather induces him to accept M̲ʳ̲ Vernon's invitation to prolong his stay in Sussex that they may have some hunting together.—He means to send for his Horses immediately, & it is impossible to say when you may see him in Kent. I will not disguise my sentiments on this change from you my dear Madam, tho' I think you had better not communicate them to my Father, whose excessive anxiety about Reginald would subject him to an alarm which might seriously affect his health & spirits. Lady Susan has certainly contrived in the space of a fortnight to make my Brother like her.—In short, I am persuaded that his continuing here beyond the time originally fixed for his return, is occasioned as much by a degree of fascination towards her, as by the wish of hunting with M̲ʳ̲ Vernon, & of course I cannot receive that pleasure from the length of his visit which my Brother's company would otherwise give me.—I am indeed provoked at the artifice of this unprincipled Woman. What stronger proof of her dangerous abilities can be given, than this perversion of Reginald's judgement, which when he entered the house was so decidedly against her?—In his last letter he actually gave me some particulars of her behaviour at Langford, such as he received from a Gentleman who knew her perfectly well, which if true must raise abhorrence against her, & which Reginald himself was entirely disposed to credit.—His opinion of her I am sure, was as low as of any Woman in England, & when he first came it was evident that he considered her as one entitled neither to Delicacy nor respect, & that he felt she would be delighted with the attentions of any Man inclined to flirt with her.

Her behaviour I confess has been calculated to do away such an idea, I have not detected the smallest impropriety in it,—nothing of vanity, of pretension, of Levity—& she is altogether so attractive, that I should not wonder at his being delighted with her, had he known nothing of her previous to this personal acquaintance;—but against reason, against conviction, to be so well pleased with her as I am sure he is, does really astonish me.—His admiration was at first very strong, but no more than was natural; & I did not wonder at his being struck by the gentleness & delicacy of her Manners;— but when he has mentioned her of late, it has been in terms of more extraordinary praise, & yesterday he actually said, that he could not be surprised at any effect produced on the heart of Man by such Loveliness & such Abilities; & when I lamented in reply the badness of her disposition, he observed that whatever might have been her errors, they were to be imputed to her neglected Education & early Marriage, & that she was altogether a wonderful Woman.—

This tendency to excuse her conduct, or to forget it in the warmth of admiration vexes me; & if I did not know that Reginald is too much at home at Churchill to need an invitation for lengthening his visit, I should regret Mr Vernon's giving him any.—

Lady Susan's intentions are of course those of absolute coquetry, or a desire of universal admiration. I cannot for a moment imagine that she has anything more serious in veiw, but it mortifies me to see a young Man of Reginald's sense duped by her at all.—I am &c.

           Cath Vernon.—

LETTER 9.

*M*ʳˢ *Johnson to Lady Susan*

Edward Sᵗ—

My dearest Friend

I congratulate you on Mʳ De Courcy's arrival, & advise you by all means to marry him; his Father's Estate is we know considerable, & I beleive certainly entailed.—Sir Reginald is very infirm, & not likely to stand in your way long.—I hear the young Man well spoken of, & tho' no one can really deserve you my dearest Susan, Mʳ De Courcy may be worth having.—Manwaring will storm of course, but you may easily pacify him. Besides, the most scrupulous point of honour could not require you to wait for his emancipation.—I have seen Sir James,—he came to Town for a few days last week, & called several times in Edward Street. I talked to him about you & your daughter, & he is so far from having forgotten you, that I am sure he would marry either of you with pleasure.—I gave him hopes of Frederica's relenting, & told him a great deal of her improvements.—I scolded him for making Love to Maria Manwaring; he protested that he had been only in joke, & we both laughed heartily at her disappointment, & in short were very agreable.—He is as silly as ever.—Yours faithfully

Alicia.—

LETTER 10.

*Lady Susan to M*ʳˢ *Johnson*

Churchill

I am much obliged to you my dear Friend, for your advice respecting Mʳ De Courcy, which I know was given with the fullest conviction of it's expediency, tho' I am not quite determined on following it.—I cannot easily resolve on anything so serious as Marriage, especially as I am not at present in want of money, & might perhaps till the old Gentleman's death, be very little benefited by the match. It is true that I am vain enough to beleive it within my reach.—I have made him sensible of my power, & can now enjoy the pleasure of triumphing over a Mind prepared to dislike me, & prejudiced against all my past actions. His sister too, is I hope convinced how little the ungenerous representations of any one to the disadvantage of another will avail, when opposed to the immediate influence of Intellect & Manner.—I see plainly that she is uneasy at my progress in the good opinion of her Brother, & conclude that nothing will be wanting on her part to counteract me;—but having once made him doubt the justice of her opinion of me, I think I may defy her.—

It has been delightful to me to watch his advances towards intimacy, especially to observe his altered manner in consequence of my repressing by the calm dignity of my deportment, his insolent approach to direct familiarity.—My conduct has been equally guarded from the first, & I never behaved less like a Coquette in the whole course of my Life, tho' perhaps my desire of dominion was never more decided. I have subdued him entirely by sentiment & serious conversation, & made him I may venture to say at least half in Love with me, without the semblance of the most common-place flirtation. M^{rs}. Vernon's consciousness of deserving every sort of revenge that it can be in my power to inflict, for her ill-offices, could alone enable her to perceive that I am actuated by any design in behaviour so gentle & unpretending.—Let her think & act as she chuses however; I have never yet found that the advice of a Sister could prevent a young Man's being in love if he chose it.—We are advancing now towards some kind of confidence, & in short are likely to be engaged in a kind of platonic friendship.—On my side, you may be sure of its' never being more, for if I were not already as much attached to another person as I can be to any one, I should make a point of not bestowing my affection on a Man who had dared to think so meanly of me.—

Reginald has a good figure, & is not unworthy the praise you have heard given him, but is still greatly inferior to our friend at Langford.—He is less polished, less insinuating than Manwaring,

& is comparatively deficient in the power of saying those delightful things which put one in good humour with oneself & all the world. He is quite agreable enough however, to afford me amusement, and to make many of those hours pass very pleasantly which would be otherwise spent in endeavouring to overcome my sister in law's reserve, & listening to her Husband's insipid talk.—

Your account of Sir James is most satisfactory, & I mean to give Miss Frederica a hint of my intentions very soon.—Yours &c

S. Vernon.

LETTER 11

Mrs *Vernon to Lady De Courcy.*

I really grow quite uneasy my dearest Mother about Reginald, from witnessing the very rapid increase of Lady Susan's influence. They are now on terms of the most particular friendship, frequently engaged in long conversations together, & she has contrived by the most artful coquetry to subdue his Judgement to her own purposes.—It is impossible to see the intimacy between them, so very soon established, without some alarm, tho' I can hardly suppose that Lady Susan's veiws extend to marriage.—I wish you could get Reginald home again, under any plausible pretence. He is not at all disposed to leave us, & I have given him as many hints of my Father's precarious state of health, as common decency will allow me to do in my own house.—Her power over him must now be boundless, as she has entirely effaced all his former ill-opinion, and persuaded him not merely to forget, but to justify her conduct.—Mr Smith's account of her proceedings at Langford, where he accused her of having made Mr Manwaring & a young Man engaged to Miss Manwaring distractedly in love with her, which Reginald firmly beleived when he came to Churchill, is now he is persuaded only a scandalous invention. He has told me so in a warmth of manner which spoke his regret at having ever beleived the contrary himself.—

How sincerely do I greive that she ever entered this house!—I always looked forward to her coming with uneasiness—but very far was it, from originating in anxiety for Reginald.—I expected a most disagreable companion to myself, but could not imagine that my Brother would be in the smallest danger of being captivated by a Woman, with whose principles he was so well acquainted, & whose Character he so heartily despised. If you can get him away, it will be a good thing.

Y^{rs} affec:^{ly},
Cath Vernon.

LETTER 12

Sir Reginald De Courcy to his Son

Parklands

I know that young Men in general do not admit of any enquiry, even from their nearest relations, into affairs of the heart; but I hope my dear Reginald that you will be superior to such as allow nothing for a Father's anxiety, & think themselves privileged to refuse him their confidence & slight his advice.—You must be sensible that as an only son & the representative of an ancient Family, your conduct in Life is most interesting to your connections.—In the very important concern of Marriage especially, there is everything at stake; your own happiness, that of your Parents, & the credit of your name.—I do not suppose that you would deliberately form an absolute engagement of that nature without acquainting your Mother & myself, or at least without being convinced that we should approve your choice; but I cannot help fearing that you may be drawn in by the Lady who has lately attached you, to a Marriage, which the whole of your Family, far & near, must highly reprobate.

Lady Susan's age is itself a material objection, but her want of character is one so much more serious, that the difference of even twelve years becomes in comparison of small account.—Were you not blinded by a sort of fascination, it would be ridiculous in me to repeat the instances of great misconduct on her side, so very generally known.—Her neglect of her husband, her encouragement of other Men, her extravagance & dissipation were so gross & notorious, that no one could be ignorant of them at the time, nor can now have forgotten them.—To our Family, she has always been represented in softened colours by the benevolence of Mr Charles Vernon; & yet inspite of his generous endeavours to excuse her, we know that she did, from the most selfish motives, take all possible pains to prevent his marrying Catherine.—

My Years & increasing Infirmities make me very desirous my dear Reginald, of seeing you settled in the world.—To the Fortune of your wife, the goodness of my own, will make me indifferent; but her family & character must be equally unexceptionable. When your choice is so fixed as that no objection can be made to either, I can promise you a ready & chearful consent; but it is my Duty to oppose a Match, which deep Art only could render probable, & must in the end make wretched.

It is possible that her behaviour may arise only from Vanity, or a wish of gaining the admiration of a Man whom she must imagine to be particularly prejudiced against her; but it is more likely that she should aim at something farther.—She is poor, & may naturally seek an alliance which must be advantageous to herself.—You know your own rights, and that it is out of my power to prevent your inheriting the family Estate. My Ability of distressing you during my Life, would be a species of revenge to which I should hardly stoop under any circumstances.—I honestly tell you my Sentiments & Intentions. I do not wish to work on your Fears, but on your Sense & Affection.—It would destroy every comfort of my Life, to know that you were married to Lady Susan Vernon. It would be the death of that honest Pride with which I have hitherto considered my son, I should blush to see him, to hear of him, to think of him.—

I may perhaps do no good, but that of releiving my own mind, by this Letter; but I felt it my Duty to tell you that your partiality for Lady Susan is no secret to your friends, & to warn you against her.—I should be glad to hear your reasons for disbeleiving Mr Smith's intelligence;—you had no doubt of it's authenticity a month ago.—

If you can give me your assurance of having no design beyond enjoying the conversation of a clever woman for a short period, & of yeilding admiration only to her Beauty & Abilities without being blinded by them to her faults, you will restore me to happiness; but if you cannot do this, explain to me at least what has occasioned so great an alteration in your opinion of her.

I am &c
Reg.^d De Courcy.

LETTER 13.

Lady De Courcy to Mrs Vernon—

Parklands

My dear Catherine,

Unluckily I was confined to my room when your last letter came, by a cold which affected my eyes so much as to prevent my reading it myself, so I could not refuse your Father when he offered to read it to me, by which means he became acquainted to my great vexation with all your fears about your Brother. I had intended to write to Reginald myself, as soon as my eyes would let me; to point out as well as I could the danger of an intimate acquaintance with so artful a woman as Lady Susan, to a young Man of his age & high expectations. I meant moreover to have reminded him of our being quite alone now, & very much in need of him to keep up our spirits these long winter evenings. Whether it would have done any good, can never be settled now; but I am excessively vexed that Sir Reginald should know anything of a matter which we foresaw would make him so uneasy.—He caught all your fears the moment he had read your Letter, & I am sure has not had the business out of his head since;—he wrote by the same post to Reginald, a long letter full of it all, & particularly asking an explanation of what he may have

[26]

heard from Lady Susan to contradict the late shocking reports. His answer came this morning, which I shall enclose to you, as I think you will like to see it; I wish it was more satisfactory, but it seems written with such a determination to think well of Lady Susan, that his assurances as to Marriage &c, do not set my heart at ease.—I say all I can however to satisfy your Father, & he is certainly less uneasy since Reginald's letter. How provoking it is my dear Catherine, that this unwelcome Guest of yours, should not only prevent our meeting this Christmas, but be the occasion of so much vexation & trouble.—Kiss the dear Children for me.—Your affec: Mother

C. De Courcy.—

LETTER 14.

Mr De Courcy to Sir Reginald—

Churchill

My dear Sir

I have this moment received your Letter, which has given me more astonishment than I ever felt before. I am to thank my Sister I suppose, for having represented me in such a light as to injure me in your opinion, & give you all this alarm.—I know not why she should chuse to make herself & her family uneasy by apprehending an Event, which no one but herself I can affirm, would ever have thought possible. To impute such a design to Lady Susan would be taking from her every claim to that excellent understanding which her bitterest Enemies have never denied her; & equally low must sink my pretensions to common sense, if I am suspected of matrimonial veiws in my behaviour to her.—Our difference of age must be an insuperable objection, & I entreat you my dear Sir to quiet your mind, & no longer harbour a suspicion which cannot be more injurious to your own peace, than to our Understandings.

I can have no veiw in remaining with Lady Susan than to enjoy for a short time (as you have yourself expressed it) the conversation of a Woman of high mental powers. If Mrs Vernon would allow something to my affection for herself & her husband in the length of my visit, she would do more justice to us all;—but my Sister is unhappily prejudiced beyond the hope of conviction against Lady Susan.—From an attachment to her husband which in itself does honour to both, she cannot forgive those endeavours at preventing their union, which have been attributed to selfishness in Lady Susan. But in this case, as well as in many others, the World has most grossly injured that Lady, by supposing the worst, where the motives of her conduct have been doubtful.—

Lady Susan had heard something so materially to the disadvantage of my Sister, as to persuade her that the happiness of Mr Vernon, to whom she was always much attached, would be absolutely destroyed by the Marriage. And this circumstance while it explains the true motive of Lady Susan's conduct, & removes all the blame which has been so lavished on her, may also convince us how little the general report of any one ought to be credited, since no character however upright, can escape the malevolence of slander. If my sister in the security of retirement, with as little opportunity as inclination to do Evil, could not avoid Censure, we must not rashly condemn those who living in the World & surrounded with temptation, should be accused of Errors which they are known to have the power of committing.—

I blame myself severely for having so easily beleived the scandalous tales invented by Charles Smith to the prejudice of Lady Susan, as I am now convinced how greatly they have traduced her. As to Mrs Manwaring's jealousy, it was totally his own invention; & his account of her attaching Miss Manwaring's Lover was scarcely better founded. Sir James Martin had been drawn-in by that young Lady to pay her some attention, and as he is a Man of fortune, it was easy to see that <u>her</u> veiws extended to Marriage.—It is well-known that Miss Manwaring is absolutely on the catch for a husband, & no one therefore can pity her, for losing by the superior attractions of another woman, the chance of being able to make a worthy Man completely miserable.—Lady Susan was far from intending such a conquest, & on finding how warmly Miss Manwaring resented her Lover's defection, determined, inspite of M.^r and Mrs Manwaring's most earnest entreaties, to leave the family.—I have reason to imagine that she did receive serious Proposals from Sir James, but her removing from Langford immediately on the discovery of his attachment, must acquit her on that article, with every Mind of common candour.—You will, I am sure my dear Sir, feel the truth of this reasoning, & will hereby learn to do justice to the character of a very injured woman.—

I know that Lady Susan in coming to Churchill was governed only by the most honourable & amiable intentions.—Her prudence & economy are exemplary, her regard for Mr Vernon equal even to <u>his</u> deserts, & her wish of obtaining my sister's good opinion merits a better return than it has received.—As a Mother she is unexceptionable. Her solid affection for her Child is shewn by placing her in hands, where her Education will be properly attended to; but because she has not the blind & weak partiality of most Mothers, she is accused of wanting Maternal Tenderness.—Every person of Sense however will know how to value & commend her well directed affection, & will join me in wishing that Frederica Vernon may prove more worthy than she has yet done, of her Mother's tender cares.

I have now my dear Sir, written my real sentiments of Lady Susan; you will know from this Letter, how highly I admire her Abilities, & esteem her Character; but if you are not equally convinced by my full & solemn assurance that your fears have been most idly created, you will deeply mortify & distress me.—I am &c
R De Courcy.—

LETTER 15.

Mrs Vernon to Lady De Courcy.

Churchill

My dear Mother
I return you Reginald's letter, & rejoice with all my heart that my Father is made easy by it. Tell him so, with my congratulations;—

but between ourselves, I must own it has only convinced me of my Brother's having no present intention of marrying Lady Susan— not that he is in no danger of doing so three months hence.—He gives a very plausible account of her behaviour at Langford, I wish it may be true, but his intelligence must come from herself, & I am less disposed to beleive it, than to lament the degree of intimacy subsisting between them, implied by the discussion of such a subject.

I am sorry to have incurred his displeasure, but can expect nothing better while he is so very eager in Lady Susan's justification.—He is very severe against me indeed, & yet I hope I have not been hasty in my judgement of her.—Poor Woman! tho' I have reasons enough for my dislike, I can not help pitying her at present as she is in real distress, & with too much cause.—She had this morning a letter from the Lady with whom she has placed her daughter, to request that Miss Vernon might be immediately removed, as she had been detected in an attempt to run away. Why, or whither she intended to go, does not appear; but as her situation seems to have been unexceptionable, it is a sad thing & of course highly afflicting to Lady Susan.—

Frederica must be as much as sixteen, & ought to know better, but from what her Mother insinuates I am afraid she is a perverse girl. She has been sadly neglected however, & her Mother ought to remember it.—

M.̱ Vernon set off for Town as soon as she had determined what should be done. He is if possible to prevail on Miss Summers to let Frederica continue with her, & if he cannot succeed, to bring her to Churchill for the present, till some other situation can be found for her.—Her Ladyship is comforting herself meanwhile by strolling along the Shrubbery with Reginald, calling forth all his tender feelings I suppose on this distressing occasion. She has been talking a great deal about it to me, she talks vastly well, I am afraid of being ungenerous or I should say she talks too well to feel so very deeply. But I will not look for Faults. She may be Reginald's Wife—Heaven forbid it!—but why should I be quicker sighted than any body else?—M.̱ Vernon declares that he never saw deeper distress than hers, on the receipt of the Letter—& is his Judgement inferior to mine?—

She was very unwilling that Frederica should be allowed to come to Churchill, & justly enough, as it seems a sort of reward to Behaviour deserving very differently. But it was impossible to take her any where else, & she is not to remain here long.—

"It will be absolutely necessary, said she, as you my dear sister must be sensible, to treat my daughter with some severity while she is here;—a most painful necessity, but I will <u>endeavour</u> to submit to it.—I am afraid I have been often too indulgent, but my poor Frederica's temper could never bear opposition well. You must support & encourage me—You must urge the necessity of reproof, if you see me too lenient."

All this sounds very reasonably.—Reginald is so incensed against the poor silly Girl!—Surely it is not to Lady Susan's credit that he should be so bitter against her daughter; his idea of her must be drawn from the Mother's description.—

Well, whatever may be his fate, we have the comfort of knowing that we have done our utmost to save him. We must commit the event to an Higher Power.—Yours Ever &c

Cath Vernon.

LETTER 16.

Lady Susan to Mrs Johnson

Churchill

Never my dearest Alicia, was I so provoked in my life as by a Letter this morning from Miss Summers. That horrid girl of mine has been trying to run away.—I had not a notion of her being such a little Devil before;—she seemed to have all the Vernon Milkiness; but on receiving the letter in which I declared my intentions about Sir James, she actually attempted to elope; at least, I cannot otherwise account for her doing it.—She meant I suppose to go to the Clarkes in Staffordshire, for she has no other acquaintance. But she <u>shall</u> be punished, she <u>shall</u> have him. I have sent Charles to Town to make matters up if he can, for I do not by any means want her here. If Miss Summers will not keep her, you must find me out another school, unless we can get her married immediately.—Miss S. writes word that she could not get the young Lady to assign any cause for her extraordinary conduct, which confirms me in my own private explanation of it.—

Frederica is too shy I think, & too much in awe of me, to tell tales; but if the mildness of her Uncle <u>should</u> get anything from her, I am not afraid. I trust I shall be able to make my story as good as her's.—If I am vain of any thing, it is of my eloquence. Consideration & Esteem as surely follow command of Language, as Admiration waits on Beauty. And here I have opportunity enough for the exercise of my Talent, as the cheif of my time is spent in Conversation. Reginald is never easy unless we are by ourselves, & when the weather is tolerable we pace the shrubbery for hours together.—I like him on the whole very well, he is clever & has a good deal to say, but he is sometimes impertinent & troublesome.—There is a sort of ridiculous delicacy about him which requires the fullest explanation of whatever he may have heard to my disadvantage, & is never satisfied till he thinks he has ascertained the beginning & end of everything.—

This is <u>one</u> sort of Love—but I confess it does not particularly recommend itself to me.—I infinitely prefer the tender & liberal spirit of Manwaring, which impressed with the deepest conviction of my merit, is satisfied that whatever I do must be right; & look with a degree of Contempt on the inquisitive & doubting Fancies of that Heart which seems always debating on the reasonableness of it's Emotions. Manwaring is indeed beyond compare superior to Reginald—superior in every thing but the power of being with me.—Poor fellow! he is quite distracted by Jealousy, which I am not sorry for, as I know no better support of Love.—He has been teizing me to allow of his coming into this country, & lodging somewhere near me <u>incog</u>—but I forbid every thing of the kind.—Those women are inexcusable who forget what is due to themselves & the opinion of the World.—

S. Vernon—

LETTER 17.

Mrs. Vernon to Lady De Courcy.

Churchill

My dear Mother

Mr. Vernon returned on Thursday night, bringing his neice with him. Lady Susan had received a line from him by that day's post informing her that Miss Summers had absolutely refused to allow of Miss Vernon's continuance in her Academy. We were therefore prepared for her arrival, & expected them impatiently the whole evening.—They came while we were at Tea, & I never saw any creature look so frightened in my life as Frederica when she entered the room.—

Lady Susan who had been shedding tears before & shewing great agitation at the idea of the meeting, received her with perfect self-command, & without betraying the least tenderness of spirit.—She hardly spoke to her, & on Frederica's bursting into tears as soon as we were seated, took her out of the room & did not return for some time; when she did, her eyes looked very red, and she was as much agitated as before.—We saw no more of her daughter.—

Poor Reginald was beyond measure concerned to see his fair friend in such distress, & watched her with so much tender solicitude that I, who occasionally caught her observing his countenance with exultation, was quite out of patience.—This pathetic representation lasted the whole evening, & so ostentatious & artful a display has entirely convinced me that she did in fact feel nothing.—

I am more angry with her than ever since I have seen her daughter.—The poor girl looks so unhappy that my heart aches for her.—Lady Susan is surely too severe, because Frederica does not seem to have the sort of temper to make severity necessary.—She looks perfectly timid, dejected & penitent.—

She is very pretty, tho' not so handsome as her Mother, nor at all like her. Her complexion is delicate, but neither so fair, nor so blooming as Lady Susan's—& she has quite the Vernon cast of countenance, the oval face & mild dark eyes, & there is peculiar sweetness in her look when she speaks either to her Uncle or me, for as we behave kindly to her, we have of course engaged her gratitude.—Her Mother has insinuated that her temper is untractable, but I never saw a face less indicative of any evil disposition than her's; & from what I now see of the behaviour of each to the other, the invariable severity of Lady Susan, & the silent dejection of Frederica, I am led to beleive as heretofore that the former has no real Love for her daughter & has never done her justice, or treated her affectionately.

I have not yet been able to have any conversation with my neice; she is shy, & I think I can see that some pains are taken to prevent her being much with me.—Nothing satisfactory transpires as to her reason for running away.—Her kind hearted Uncle you may be sure, was too fearful of distressing her, to ask many questions as they travelled.—I wish it had been possible for me to fetch her instead of him;—I think I should have discovered the truth in the course of a Thirty miles Journey.—

The small Pianoforté has been removed within these few days at Lady Susan's request, into her Dressing room, & Frederica spends great part of the day there;—<u>practising</u> it is called, but I seldom hear any noise when I pass that way.—What she does with herself there I do not know, there are plenty of books in the room, but it is not every girl who has been running wild the first fifteen years of her life, that can or will read.—Poor Creature! the prospect from her window is not very instructive, for that room overlooks the Lawn you know with the shrubbery on one side, where she may see her Mother walking for an hour together, in earnest conversation with Reginald.—A girl of Frederica's age must be childish indeed, if such things do not strike her.—Is it not inexcusable to give such an example to a daughter?—Yet Reginald still thinks Lady Susan the best of Mothers—still condemns Frederica as a worthless girl!—He is convinced that her attempt to run away, proceeded from no justifiable cause, & had no provocation. I am sure I cannot say that it <u>had</u>, but while Miss Summers declares that Miss Vernon shewed no sign of Obstinacy or Perverseness during her whole stay in Wigmore S.! till she was detected in this scheme, I cannot so readily credit what Lady Susan has made him and wants to make me beleive, that it was merely an impatience of restraint, and a desire of escaping from the tuition of Masters which brought on the plan of an elopement.—Oh! Reginald, how is your judgement enslaved!—He scarcely dares even allow her to be handsome, & when I speak of her beauty, replies only that her eyes have no Brilliancy.

Sometimes he is sure that she is deficient in Understanding, & at others that her temper only is in fault. In short when a person is always to deceive, it is impossible to be consistent. Lady Susan finds it necessary for her own justification that Frederica should be to blame, & probably has sometimes judged it expedient to accuse her of ill-nature & sometimes to lament her want of sense. Reginald is only repeating after her Ladyship.—

I am &c
Cath Vernon

LETTER 18.

From the same to the same.—

Churchill

My dear Madam

I am very glad to find that my description of Frederica Vernon has interested you, for I do beleive her truly deserving of our regard, & when I have communicated a notion that has recently struck me, your kind impression in her favour will I am sure be heightened. I cannot help fancying that she is growing partial to my brother, I so very often see her eyes fixed on his face with a remarkable expression of pensive admiration!—He is certainly very handsome—& yet more—there is an openness in his manner that must be highly prepossessing, & I am sure she feels it so.—Thoughtful & pensive in general her countenance always brightens with a smile when Reginald says anything amusing; & let the subject be ever so serious that he may be conversing on, I am much mistaken if a syllable of his uttering, escape her.—

I want to make <u>him</u> sensible of all this, for we know the power of gratitude on such a heart as his; & could Frederica's artless affection detach him from her Mother, we might bless the day which brought her to Churchill. I think my dear Madam, you would not disapprove of her as a Daughter. She is extremely young to be sure, has had a wretched Education and a dreadful example of Levity in her Mother; but yet I can pronounce her disposition to be excellent, & her natural abilities very good.—

Tho' totally without accomplishment, she is by no means so ignorant as one might expect to find her, being fond of books & spending the cheif of her time in reading. Her Mother leaves her more to herself now than she <u>did</u>, & I have her with me as much as possible, & have taken great pains to overcome her timidity. We are very good friends, & tho' she never opens her lips before her Mother, she talks enough when alone with me, to make it clear that if properly treated by Lady Susan she would always appear to much greater advantage. There cannot be a more gentle, affectionate heart, or more obliging manners, when acting without restraint. Her little Cousins are all very fond of her.—Y^{rs} affec:^{ly}

Cath Vernon

LETTER 19.

Lady Susan to Mrs Johnson

Churchill

You will be eager I know to hear something farther of Frederica, & perhaps may think me negligent for not writing before.—She arrived with her Uncle last Thursday fortnight, when of course I lost no time in demanding the reason of her behaviour, & soon found myself to have been perfectly right in attributing it to my own letter.—The purport of it frightened her so thoroughly that with a mixture of true girlish perverseness & folly, without considering that she could not escape from my authority by running away from Wigmore Street, she resolved on getting out of the house, &

[36]

proceeding directly by the stage to her friends the Clarkes, & had really got as far as the length of two streets in her journey, when she was fortunately miss'd, pursued, and overtaken.—

Such was the first distinguished exploit of Miss Frederica Susanna Vernon, & if we consider that it was atchieved at the tender age of sixteen we shall have room for the most flattering prognostics of her future renown.—I am excessively provoked however at the parade of propriety which prevented Miss Summers from keeping the girl; & it seems so extraordinary a peice of nicety, considering what are my daughter's family connections, that I can only suppose the Lady to be governed by the fear of never getting her money.—Be that as it may however, Frederica is returned on my hands, & having now nothing else to employ her, is busy in pursueing the plan of Romance begun at Langford.—She is actually falling in love with Reginald De Courcy.—To disobey her Mother by refusing an unexceptionable offer is not enough; her affections must likewise be given without her Mother's approbation.—I never saw a girl of her age, bid fairer to be the sport of Mankind. Her feelings are tolerably lively, & she is so charmingly artless in their display, as to afford the most reasonable hope of her being ridiculed & despised by every Man who sees her.—

Artlessness will never do in Love matters, & that girl is born a simpleton who has it either by nature or affectation.—I am not yet certain that Reginald sees what she is about; nor is it of much consequence;—she is now an object of indifference to him, she would be one of contempt were he to understand her Emotions.— Her beauty is much admired by the Vernons, but it has no effect on <u>him</u>. She is in high favour with her Aunt altogether—because she is so little like myself of course. She is exactly the companion for Mrs Vernon, who dearly loves to be first, & to have all the sense and all the wit of the Conversation to herself;—Frederica will never eclipse her.—When she first came, I was at some pains to prevent her seeing much of her Aunt, but I have since relaxed, as I beleive I may depend on her observing the rules I have laid down for their discourse.—

But do not imagine that with all this Lenity, I have for a moment given up my plan of her marriage;—No, I am unalterably fixed on that point, tho' I have not yet quite resolved on the manner of bringing it about.—I should not chuse to have the business brought forward here, & canvassed by the wise heads of M.^r and Mrs Vernon; & I cannot just now afford to go to Town.—Miss Frederica therefore must wait a little.—

Yours Ever
S. Vernon.—

LETTER 20.

Mrs Vernon to Lady De Courcy.

Churchill

We have a very unexpected Guest with us at present, my dear Mother.—He arrived yesterday.—I heard a carriage at the door as I was sitting with my Children while they dined, & supposing I should be wanted left the Nursery soon afterwards & was half way down stairs, when Frederica as pale as ashes came running up, & rushed by me into her own room.—I instantly followed, & asked her what was the matter.—"Oh! cried she, he is come, Sir James is come—& what am I to do?"—This was no explanation; I begged her to tell me what she meant. At that moment we were interrupted by a knock at the door;—it was Reginald, who came by Lady Susan's direction to call Frederica down.—"It is M.^r De Courcy, said she, colouring violently, Mama has sent for me, & I must go."—

We all three went down together, & I saw my Brother examining the terrified face of Frederica with surprise.—In the breakfast room we found Lady Susan & a young Man of genteel appearance, whom she introduced to me by the name of Sir James Martin, the very person, as you may remember, whom it was said she had been at pains to detach from Miss Manwaring.—But the conquest it seems was not designed for herself, or she has since transferred it to her daughter, for Sir James is now desperately in love with Frederica, & with full encouragement from Mama.—The poor girl however I am sure dislikes him; & tho' his person and address are very well, he appears both to M̲r̲ Vernon & me a very weak young Man.—

Frederica looked so shy, so confused, when we entered the room, that I felt for her exceedingly. Lady Susan behaved with great attention to her Visitor, & yet I thought I could perceive that she had no particular pleasure in seeing him.—Sir James talked a good deal, & made many civil excuses to me for the liberty he had taken in coming to Churchill, mixing more frequent laughter with his discourse than the subject required;—said many things over & over again, & told Lady Susan three times that he had seen M̲rs̲ Johnson a few Evenings before.—He now & then addressed Frederica, but more frequently her Mother.—The poor girl sat all this time without opening her lips;—her eyes cast down, & her colour varying every instant, while Reginald observed all that passed, in perfect silence.—

At length Lady Susan, weary I beleive of her situation, proposed walking, & we left the two Gentlemen together to put on our Pelisses.—*

As we went upstairs Lady Susan begged permission to attend me for a few moments in my Dressing room, as she was anxious to speak with me in private.—I led her thither accordingly, & as soon as the door was closed she said, "I was never more surprised in my life than by Sir James's arrival, & the suddenness of it requires some apology to You my dear Sister, tho' to me as a Mother, it is highly flattering.—He is so warmly attached to my daughter that he could exist no longer without seeing her.—Sir James is a young Man of an amiable disposition, & excellent character;—a little too much of the Rattle perhaps, but a year or two will rectify that, & he is in other respects so very eligible a Match for Frederica that I have always observed his attachment with the greatest pleasure, & am persuaded that you & my Brother will give the alliance your hearty approbation.—I have never before

---

* **Pelisse**: outerwear, a long cloak with armhole slits and a shoulder cape or hood, often made from a rich fabric.

mentioned the likelihood of it's taking place to any one, because I thought that while Frederica continued at school, it had better not be known to exist;—but now, as I am convinced that Frederica is too old ever to submit to school confinement, & have therefore begun to consider her union with Sir James as not very distant, I had intended within a few days to acquaint yourself & Mr Vernon with the whole business.—I am sure my dear Sister, you will excuse my remaining silent on it so long, & agree with me that such circumstances, while they continue from any cause in suspense, cannot be too cautiously concealed.—When you have the happiness of bestowing your sweet little Catherine some years hence on a Man, who in connection & character is alike unexceptionable, you will know what I feel now;—tho' Thank Heaven! you cannot have all my reasons for rejoicing in such an Event.—Catherine will be amply provided for, & not like my Frederica endebted to a fortunate Establishment for the comforts of Life."—

She concluded by demanding my congratulations.—I gave them somewhat awkwardly I beleive;—for in fact, the sudden disclosure of so important a matter took from me the power of speaking with any clearness.—She thanked me however most affectionately for my kind concern in the welfare of herself & her daughter, & then said,

"I am not apt to deal in professions, my dear Mrs Vernon, & I never had the convenient talent of affecting sensations foreign to my heart; & therefore I trust you will beleive me when I declare that much as I had heard in your praise before I knew you, I had no idea that I should ever love you as I now do;—and I must farther say that your friendship towards me is more particularly gratifying, because I have reason to beleive that some attempts were made to prejudice you against me.—I only wish that They—whoever they are—to whom I am endebted for such kind intentions, could see the terms on which we now are together, & understand the real affection we feel for each other!—But I will not detain you any longer.—God bless you, for your goodness to me & my girl, & continue to you all your present happiness."

What can one say of such a woman, my dear Mother?—such earnestness, such solemnity of expression!—And yet I cannot help suspecting the truth of everything she said.—

As for Reginald, I beleive he does not know what to make of the matter.—When Sir James first came, he appeared all astonishment & perplexity. The folly of the young Man, & the confusion of Frederica entirely engrossed him; & tho' a little private discourse with Lady Susan has since had it's effect, he is still hurt I am sure at her allowing of such a Man's attentions to her daughter.—

Sir James invited himself with great composure to remain here a few days;—hoped we would not think it odd, was aware of it's being very impertinent, but he took the liberty of a relation, & concluded by wishing with a laugh, that he might be really one soon.—Even Lady Susan seemed a little disconcerted by this forwardness;—in her heart I am persuaded, she sincerely wishes him gone.—

But something must be done for this poor Girl, if her feelings are such as both her Uncle & I beleive them to be. She must not be sacrificed to Policy or Ambition, she must not be even left to suffer from the dread of it.—The Girl, whose heart can distinguish Reginald De Courcy, deserves, however he may slight her, a better fate than to be Sir James Martin's wife.—As soon as I can get her alone, I will discover the real Truth, but she seems to wish to avoid me.—I hope this does not proceed from any thing wrong, & that I shall not find out I have thought too well of her.—Her behaviour before Sir James certainly speaks the greatest consciousness & Embarrassment; but I see nothing in it more like Encouragement.—

Adeiu my dear Madam,

Y^{rs} &c Cath Vernon.—

LETTER 21.

Miss Vernon to M^r De Courcy—

Sir,

I hope you will excuse this liberty, I am forced upon it by the greatest distress, or I should be ashamed to trouble you.—I am very miserable about Sir James Martin, & have no other way in the world of helping myself but by writing to you, for I am forbidden ever speaking to my Uncle or Aunt on the subject; & this being the case, I am afraid my applying to you will appear no better than equivocation, & as if I attended only to the letter & not the spirit of Mama's commands, but if <u>you</u> do not take my part, & persuade her to break it off, I shall be half-distracted, for I can not bear him.—No human Being but <u>you</u> could have any chance of prevailing with her.—If you will therefore have the unspeakable great kindness of taking my part with her, & persuading her to send Sir James away, I shall be more obliged to you than it is possible for me to express.—I always disliked him from the first, it is not a sudden fancy I assure you Sir, I always thought him silly & impertinent & disagreable, & now he is grown worse than ever.—I would rather work for my bread than marry him.—I do not know how to apologise enough for this Letter, I know it is taking so great a liberty, I am aware how dreadfully angry it will make Mama, but I must run the risk.—I am Sir, Your most Hum[ble]. Serv[t].

F. S. V.—

LETTER 22.

Lady Susan to M[rs]. Johnson

Churchill

This is insufferable!—My dearest friend, I was never so enraged before, & must releive myself by writing to you, who I know will enter into all my feelings.—Who should come on Tuesday but Sir James Martin?—Guess my astonishment & vexation—for as you well know, I never wished him to be seen at Churchill. What a pity that you should not have known his intentions!—Not content with coming, he actually invited himself to remain here a few days. I could have poisoned him;—I made the best of it however, & told my story with great success to M[rs]. Vernon who, whatever might be her real sentiments, said nothing in opposition to mine. I made a point also of Frederica's behaving civilly to Sir James, & gave her to understand that I was absolutely determined on her marrying him.—She said something of her misery, but that was all.—I have for some time been more particularly resolved on the Match, from seeing the rapid increase of her affection for Reginald, & from not feeling perfectly secure that a knowledge of <u>that</u> affection might not in the end awaken a return.—Contemptible as a regard founded only on compassion, must make them both, in my eyes, I felt by no means assured that such might not be the consequence.—It is true that Reginald had not in any degree grown cool towards me;—but yet he had lately mentioned Frederica spontaneously & unnecessarily, & once had said something in praise of her person.—

<u>He</u> was all astonishment at the appearance of my visitor; & at first observed Sir James with an attention which I was pleased to see not unmixed with jealousy;—but unluckily it was impossible for me really to torment him, as Sir James tho' extremely gallant to me, very soon made the whole party understand that his heart was devoted to my daughter.—

I had no great difficulty in convincing De Courcy when we were alone, that I was perfectly justified, all things considered, in desiring the match; & the whole business seemed most comfortably arranged.—They could none of them help perceiving that Sir James was no Solomon, but I had positively forbidden Frederica's complaining to Charles Vernon or his wife, & they had therefore no pretence for Interference, tho' my impertinent Sister I beleive wanted only opportunity for doing so.—

Everything however was going on calmly & quietly; & tho' I counted the hours of Sir James's stay, my mind was entirely satisfied with the posture of affairs.—Guess then what I must feel at the sudden disturbance of all my schemes, & that too from a quarter, whence I had least reason to apprehend it.—Reginald came this morning into my Dressing room, with a very unusual solemnity of countenance, & after some preface informed me in so many words, that he wished to reason with me on the Impropriety & Unkindness of allowing Sir James Martin to address my Daughter, contrary to <u>her</u> inclination.—I was all amazement.—When I found that he was not to be laughed out of his design, I calmly required an explanation, & begged to know by what he was impelled & by whom commissioned to reprimand me.

He then told me, mixing in his speech a few insolent compliments & ill timed expressions of Tenderness to which I listened with perfect indifference, that my daughter had acquainted him with some circumstances concerning herself, Sir James, & me, which gave him great uneasiness.—

In short, I found that she had in the first place actually written to him, to request his interference, & that on receiving her Letter he had conversed with her on the subject of it, in order to understand the particulars & assure himself of her real wishes!—

I have not a doubt but that the girl took this opportunity of making down right Love to him; I am convinced of it, from the manner in which he spoke of her. Much good, may such Love do him!—I shall ever despise the Man who can be gratified by the Passion, which he never wished to inspire, nor solicited the avowal of.—I shall always detest them both.—He can have no true regard for me, or he would not have listened to her;—And she, with her little rebellious heart & indelicate feelings to throw herself into the protection of a young Man with whom she had scarcely ever exchanged two words before. I am equally confounded at <u>her</u> Impudence and <u>his</u> Credulity.—How dared he beleive what she told him in my disfavour!—Ought he not to have felt assured that I must have unanswerable Motives for all that I had done!—Where was his reliance on my Sense or Goodness then; where the resentment which true Love would have dictated against the person defaming me, that person too, a Chit, a Child, without Talent or Education, whom he had been always taught to despise?—

I was calm for some time, but the greatest degree of Forbearance may be overcome; & I hope I was afterwards sufficiently keen.—He endeavoured, long endeavoured to soften my resentment, but that woman is a fool indeed who while insulted by accusation, can be worked on by compliments.—At length he left me as deeply provoked as myself, & he shewed his anger <u>more</u>.—I was quite cool, but he gave way to the most violent indignation.—I may therefore expect it will the sooner subside; & perhaps his may be vanished for ever, while mine will be found still fresh & implacable.

He is now shut up in his apartment, whither I heard him go, on leaving mine.—How unpleasant, one would think, must his reflections be!—But some people's feelings are incomprehensible.—I have not yet tranquillized myself enough to see Frederica. <u>She</u> shall not soon forget the occurrences of this day.—She shall find that she has poured forth her tender Tale of Love in vain, & exposed herself forever to the contempt of the whole world, & the severest Resentment of her injured Mother.—Y^{rs} affec:^{ly}

S. Vernon

LETTER 23.

M^{rs}. Vernon to Lady De Courcy

Churchill

Let me congratulate you, my dearest Mother. The affair which has given us so much anxiety is drawing to a happy conclusion. Our prospect is most delightful;—and since matters have now taken so favourable a turn, I am quite sorry that I ever imparted my apprehensions to you; for the pleasure of learning that the Danger is over, is perhaps dearly purchased by all that you have previously suffered.—

I am so much agitated by Delight that I can scarcely hold a pen, but am determined to send you a few lines by James, that you may have some explanation of what must so greatly astonish you, as that Reginald should be returning to Parklands.—

I was sitting about half an hour ago with Sir James in the Breakfast parlour, when my Brother called me out of the room.—I instantly saw that something was the matter;—his complexion was raised, & he spoke with great emotion.—You know his eager manner, my dear Madam, when his mind is interested.—

"Catherine, said he, I am going home today. I am sorry to leave you, but I must go.—It is a great while since I have seen my Father

& Mother.—I am going to send James forward with my Hunters immediately, if you have any Letter therefore he can take it.—I shall not be at home myself till Wednesday or Thursday, as I shall go through London, where I have business.—But before I leave you, he continued, speaking in a lower voice & with still greater energy, I must warn you of one thing.—Do not let Frederica Vernon be made unhappy by that Martin.—He wants to marry her—her Mother promotes the Match—but <u>she</u> cannot endure the idea of it.—Be assured that I speak from the fullest conviction of the Truth of what I say.—I <u>know</u> that Frederica is made wretched by Sir James' continuing here.—She is a sweet girl, & deserves a better fate.—Send him away immediately. <u>He</u> is only a fool—but what her Mother can mean, Heaven only knows!—Good bye, he added shaking my hand with earnestness—I do not know when you will see me again. But remember what I tell you of Frederica;— you <u>must</u> make it your business to see justice done her.—She is an amiable girl, and has a very superior Mind to what we have ever given her credit for.—"

He then left me & ran upstairs.—I would not try to stop him, for I knew what his feelings must be; the nature of mine as I listened to him, I need not attempt to describe.—For a minute or two I remained in the same spot, overpowered by wonder—of a most agreable sort indeed; yet it required some consideration to be tranquilly happy.—

In about ten minutes after my return to the parlour, Lady Susan entered the room.—I concluded of course that she & Reginald had been quarrelling, & looked with anxious curiosity for a confirmation of my beleif in her face.—Mistress of Deceit however she appeared perfectly unconcerned, & after chatting on indifferent subjects for a short time, said to me,

"I find from Wilson that we are going to lose M.̲ De Courcy.—Is it true that he leaves Churchill this morning?"—

I replied that it was.—

"He told us nothing of all this last night, said she laughing, or even this morning at Breakfast. But perhaps he did not know it himself.—Young Men are often hasty in their resolutions—& not more sudden in forming, than unsteady in keeping them.—I should not be surprised if he were to change his mind at last, & not go."—

She soon afterwards left the room.—I trust however my dear Mother, that we have no reason to fear an alteration of his present plan; things have gone too far.—They must have quarrelled, & about Frederica too.—Her calmness astonishes me.—What delight will be yours in seeing him again, in seeing him still worthy your Esteem, still capable of forming your Happiness!

When I next write, I shall be able I hope to tell you that Sir James is gone, Lady Susan vanquished, & Frederica at peace.—We have much to do, but it shall be done.—I am all impatience to know how this astonishing change was effected.—I finish as I began, with the warmest congratulations.—Y^{rs} Ever,

Cath Vernon.

LETTER 24.

From the same to the same.

Churchill

Little did I imagine my dear Mother, when I sent off my last letter, that the delightful perturbation of spirits I was then in, would undergo so speedy, so melancholy a reverse!—I never can sufficiently regret that I wrote to you at all.—Yet who could have foreseen what has happened? My dear Mother, every hope which but two hours ago made me so happy, is vanished. The quarrel between Lady Susan & Reginald is made up, & we are all as we were before. One point only is gained; Sir James Martin is dismissed.—What are we now to look forward to?—I am indeed disappointed. Reginald was all but gone; his horse was ordered, & almost brought to the door!—Who would not have felt safe?—

For half an hour I was in momentary expectation of his departure.—After I had sent off my Letter to you, I went to Mr Vernon & sat with him in his room, talking over the whole matter.—I then determined to look for Frederica, whom I had not seen since breakfast.—I met her on the stairs & saw that she was crying.

"My dear Aunt, said she, he is going, M.^r De Courcy is going, & it is all my fault. I am afraid you will be angry, but indeed I had no idea it would end so."—

"My Love, replied I, do not think it necessary to apologize to me on that account.—I shall feel myself under an obligation to any one who is the means of sending my brother home;—because, (recollecting myself) I know my Father wants very much to see him. But what is it that you have done to occasion all this?"—

She blushed deeply as she answered, "I was so unhappy about Sir James that I could not help—I have done something very wrong I know—but you have not an idea of the misery I have been in, & Mama had ordered me never to speak to you or my Uncle about it,—and"—

"You therefore spoke to my Brother, to engage his interference";—said I, wishing to save her the explanation.—

"No—but I wrote to him.—I did indeed.—I got up this morning before it was light—I was two hours about it—& when my Letter was done, I thought I never should have courage to give it.—After breakfast however, as I was going to my own room I met him in the passage, & then as I knew that every thing must depend on that moment, I forced myself to give it.—He was so good as to take it immediately;—I dared not look at him—& ran away directly.—I was in such a fright that I could hardly breathe.—My dear Aunt, you do not know how miserable I have been."

"Frederica, said I, you ought to have told me all your distresses.— You would have found in me a friend always ready to assist you.—Do you think that your Uncle & I should not have espoused your cause as warmly as my Brother?"—

"Indeed I did not doubt your goodness, said she colouring again, but I thought that M.^r De Courcy could do anything with my Mother;—but I was mistaken;—they have had a dreadful quarrel about it, & he is going.—Mama will never forgive me, & I shall be worse off than ever."—

"No, you shall not, replied I.—In such a point as this, your Mother's prohibition ought not to have prevented your speaking to me on the subject. She has no right to make you unhappy, & she shall <u>not</u> do it.—Your applying however to Reginald can be productive only of Good to all parties. I beleive it is best as it is.—Depend upon it that you shall not be made unhappy any longer."

At that moment, how great was my astonishment at seeing Reginald come out of Lady Susan's Dressing room. My heart misgave me instantly. His confusion on seeing me was very evident.—Frederica immediately disappeared.

"Are you going?—said I. You will find M.ʳ Vernon in his own room."—

"No Catherine, replied he.—I am <u>not</u> going.—Will you let me speak to you a moment?"

We went into my room. "I find, continued he, his confusion increasing as he spoke, that I have been acting with my usual foolish Impetuosity.—I have entirely misunderstood Lady Susan, & was on the point of leaving the house under a false impression of her conduct.—There has been some very great mistake—we have been all mistaken I fancy.—Frederica does not know her Mother—Lady Susan means nothing but her Good—but Frederica will not make a friend of her.—Lady Susan therefore does not always know what will make her daughter happy.—Besides <u>I</u> could have no right to interfere—Miss Vernon was mistaken in applying to me.—In short Catherine, every thing has gone wrong—but it is now all happily settled.—Lady Susan I beleive wishes to speak to you about it, if you are at leisure."—

"Certainly;" replied I, deeply sighing at the recital of so lame a story.—I made no remarks however, for words would have been vain. Reginald was glad to get away, & I went to Lady Susan; curious indeed to hear her account of it.—

"Did not I tell you, said she with a smile, that your Brother would not leave us after all?"

"You did indeed, replied I very gravely, but I flattered myself that you would be mistaken."

"I should not have hazarded such an opinion, returned she, if it had not at that moment occurred to me, that his resolution of going might be occasioned by a Conversation in which we had been this morning engaged, & which had ended very much to his Dissatisfaction from our not rightly understanding each other's meaning.—This idea struck me at the moment, & I instantly determined that an accidental dispute in which I might probably be as much to blame as himself, should not deprive you of your Brother.—If you remember, I left the room almost immediately.—I was resolved to lose no time in clearing up these mistakes as far as I could.—The case was this.—Frederica had set herself violently against marrying Sir James"—

—"And can your Ladyship wonder that she should? cried I with some warmth.—Frederica has an excellent Understanding, & Sir James has none."

"I am at least very far from regretting it, my dear Sister, said she; on the contrary, I am grateful for so favourable a sign of my Daughter's sense. Sir James is certainly under par—(his boyish manners make him appear the worse)—& had Frederica possessed the penetration, the abilities, which I could have wished in my daughter, or had I even known her to possess so much as she does, I should not have been anxious for the match."

"It is odd that you alone should be ignorant of your Daughter's sense."

"Frederica never does justice to herself;—her manners are shy & childish.—She is besides afraid of me; she scarcely loves me.—During her poor Father's life she was a spoilt child; the severity which it has since been necessary for me to shew, has entirely alienated her affection;—neither has she any of that Brilliancy of Intellect, that Genius, or vigour of Mind which will force itself forward."

"Say rather that she has been unfortunate in her Education."

"Heaven knows my dearest M^{rs}. Vernon, how fully I am aware of <u>that</u>; but I would wish to forget every circumstance that might throw blame on the memory of one, whose name is sacred with me."

Here she pretended to cry.—I was out of patience with her.— "But what, said I, was your Ladyship going to tell me about your disagreement with my Brother?"—

"It originated in an action of my Daughter's, which equally marks her want of Judgement, & the unfortunate Dread of me I have been mentioning.—She wrote to M.ʳ De Courcy."—

"I know she did.—You had forbidden her speaking to M.ʳ Vernon or to me on the cause of her distress:—what could she do therefore but apply to my Brother?"

"Good God!—she exclaimed, what an opinion must you have of me!—Can you possibly suppose that I was aware of her unhappiness? that it was my object to make my own child miserable, & that I had forbidden her speaking to you on the subject, from a fear of your interrupting the Diabolical scheme?—Do you think me destitute of every honest, every natural feeling?—Am I capable of consigning <u>her</u> to everlasting Misery, whose welfare it is my first Earthly Duty to promote?"—

"The idea is horrible.—What then was your intention when you insisted on her silence?"—

"Of what use my dear Sister, could be any application to you, however the affair might stand? Why should I subject you to entreaties, which I refused to attend to myself?—Neither for your sake, for hers, nor for my own, could such a thing be desireable.—Where my own resolution was taken, I could not wish for the interference, however friendly, of another person.—I was mistaken, it is true, but I beleived myself to be right."—

"But what was this mistake, to which your Ladyship so often alludes? From whence arose so astonishing a misapprehension of your Daughter's feelings?—Did not you know that she disliked Sir James?—"

"I knew that he was not absolutely the Man whom she would have chosen.—But I was persuaded that her objections to him did not arise from any perception of his Deficiency.—You must not question me however my dear Sister, too minutely on this point—continued she, taking me affectionately by the hand.—I honestly own that there is something to conceal.—Frederica makes me very unhappy.—Her applying to M.ʳ De Courcy hurt me particularly."

"What is it that you mean to infer said I, by this appearance of mystery?—If you think your daughter at all attached to Reginald, her objecting to Sir James could not less deserve to be attended to,

[*51*]

than if the cause of her objecting had been a consciousness of his folly.—And why should your Ladyship at any rate quarrel with my brother for an interference which you must know, it was not in his nature to refuse, when urged in such a manner?"

"His disposition you know is warm, & he came to expostulate with me, his compassion all alive for this ill-used Girl, this Heroine in distress!—We misunderstood each other. He beleived me more to blame than I really was; I considered his interference as less excusable than I now find it. I have a real regard for him, & was beyond expression mortified to find it as I thought so ill bestowed. We were both warm, & of course both to blame.—His resolution of leaving Churchill is consistent with his general eagerness;—when I understood his intention however, & at the same time began to think that we had perhaps been equally mistaken in each other's meaning, I resolved to have an explanation before it were too late.—For any Member of your Family I must always feel a degree of affection, & I own it would have sensibly hurt me, if my acquaintance with M.^r De Courcy had ended so gloomily. I have now only to say farther, that as I am convinced of Frederica's having a reasonable dislike to Sir James, I shall instantly inform him that he must give up all hope of her.—I reproach myself for having ever, tho' so innocently, made her unhappy on that score.—She shall have all the retribution in my power to make;—if she value her own happiness as much as I do, if she judge wisely & command herself as she ought, she may now be easy.—Excuse me, my dearest Sister, for thus trespassing on your time, but I owed it to my own Character; & after this explanation I trust I am in no danger of sinking in your opinion."

I could have said "Not much indeed";—but I left her almost in silence.—It was the greatest stretch of Forbearance I could practise. I could not have stopped myself, had I begun.—Her assurance, her Deceit—but I will not allow myself to dwell on them;—they will strike you sufficiently. My heart sickens within me.—

As soon as I was tolerably composed, I returned to the Parlour. Sir James's carriage was at the door, & he, merry as usual, soon afterwards took his leave.—How easily does her Ladyship encourage, or dismiss a Lover!—

In spite of this release, Frederica still looks unhappy, still fearful perhaps of her Mother's anger, & tho' dreading my Brother's departure jealous, it may be, of his staying.—I see how closely she observes him & Lady Susan.—Poor Girl, I have now no hope for her. There is not a chance of her affection being returned.—He thinks very differently of her, from what he used to do, he does her some justice, but his reconciliation with her Mother precludes every dearer hope.—

Prepare my dear Madam, for the worst.—The probability of their marrying is surely heightened. He is more securely her's than ever.—When that wretched Event takes place, Frederica must belong wholly to us.—

I am thankful that my last Letter will precede this by so little, as every moment that you can be saved from feeling a Joy which leads only to disappointment is of consequence.—

Y^{rs} Ever, Cath Vernon.

LETTER 25.

Lady Susan to Mrs Johnson

Churchill

I call on you dear Alicia, for congratulations. I am again myself;—gay & triumphant.—When I wrote to you the other day, I was in truth in high irritation, & with ample cause.—Nay, I know not whether I ought to be quite tranquil now, for I have had more trouble in restoring peace than I ever intended to submit to.—This Reginald has a proud spirit of his own!—a spirit too, resulting from a fancied sense of superior Integrity which is peculiarly insolent.—I shall not easily forgive him I assure you. He was actually on the point of leaving Churchill!—I had scarcely concluded my last, when Wilson brought me word of it.—I found therefore that something must be done, for I did not chuse to have my character at the mercy of a Man whose passions were so violent & resentful.—It would have been trifling with my reputation, to allow of his departing with such an impression in my disfavour;—in this light, condescension was necessary.—

I sent Wilson to say that I desired to speak with him before he went.—He came immediately. The angry emotions which had marked every feature when we last parted, were partially subdued. He seemed astonished at the summons, & looked as if half wishing & half fearing to be softened by what I might say.—

If my Countenance expressed what I aimed at, it was composed & dignified—& yet with a degree of pensiveness which might convince him that I was not quite happy.—

"I beg your pardon Sir, for the liberty I have taken in sending to you, said I; but as I have just learnt your intention of leaving this place to day, I feel it my duty to entreat that you will not on my account shorten your visit here, even an hour.—I am perfectly aware that after what has passed between us, it would ill suit the feelings of either to remain longer in the same house.—

So very great, so total a change from the intimacy of Friendship, must render any future intercourse the severest punishment;—& your resolution of quitting Churchill is undoubtedly in unison with our situation & with those lively feelings which I know you to possess.—But at the same time, it is not for me to suffer such a sacrifice, as it must be, to leave Relations to whom you are so much attached & are so dear. My remaining here cannot give that pleasure to M.^r & Mrs Vernon which your society must;—& my visit has already perhaps been too long. My removal therefore, which must at any rate take place soon, may with perfect convenience be hastened;—& I make it my particular request that I may not in any way be instrumental in separating a family so affectionately attached to each other.—Where I go, is of no consequence to anyone; of very little to myself; but you are of importance to all your connections."

Here I concluded, & I hope you will be satisfied with my speech.— It's effect on Reginald justifies some portion of vanity, for it was no less favourable than instantaneous.—Oh! how delightful it was, to watch the variations of his Countenance while I spoke, to see the struggle between returning Tenderness & the remains of Displeasure.—There is something agreable in feelings so easily worked on. Not that I envy him their possession, nor would for the world have such myself, but they are very convenient when one wishes to influence the passions of another. And yet this Reginald, whom a very few words from me softened at once into the utmost submission, & rendered more tractable, more attached, more devoted than ever, would have left me in the first angry swelling of his proud heart, without deigning to seek an explanation!—

Humbled as he now is, I cannot forgive him such an instance of Pride; & am doubtful whether I ought not to punish him, by dismissing him at once after this our reconciliation, or by marrying & teizing him for ever.—But these measures are each too violent to be adopted without some deliberation. At present my Thoughts are fluctuating between various schemes.—I have many things to compass.—I must punish Frederica, & pretty severely too, for her application to Reginald;—I must punish him for receiving it so favourably, & for the rest of his conduct. I must torment my Sister-in-law for the insolent triumph of her Look & Manner since Sir James has been dismissed—for in reconciling Reginald to me, I was not able to save that ill-fated young Man;—& I must make myself amends for the humiliations to which I have stooped within these few days.—To effect all this I have various plans.—I have also an idea of being soon in Town, & whatever may be my determination as to the rest, I shall probably put <u>that</u> project in execution—for London will be always the fairest field of action, however my veiws may be directed, & at any rate, I shall there be rewarded by your society & a little Dissipation for a ten weeks penance at Churchill.—

I beleive I owe it to my own Character, to complete the match between my daughter & Sir James, after having so long intended it.—Let me know your opinion on this point.—Flexibility of Mind, a Disposition easily biassed by others, is an attribute which you know I am not very desirous of obtaining;—nor has Frederica any claim to the indulgence of her whims, at the expence of her Mother's inclination.—Her idle Love for Reginald too;—it is surely my duty to discourage such romantic nonsense.—All things considered therefore, it seems encumbent on me to take her to Town, & marry her immediately to Sir James.

When my own will is effected, contrary to his, I shall have some credit in being on good terms with Reginald, which at present in fact I have not, for tho' he is still in my power, I have given up the very article by which our Quarrel was produced, & at best, the honour of victory is doubtful.—

Send me your opinion on all these matters, my dear Alicia, & let me know whether you can get Lodgings to suit me within a short distance of you.—Y.^r most attached

S. Vernon.

LETTER 26.

Mrs Johnson to Lady Susan.

Edward S.^t—

I am gratified by your reference, & this is my advice; that you come to Town yourself without loss of time, but that you leave Frederica behind. It would surely be much more to the purpose to get yourself well established by marrying M.^r De Courcy, than to irritate him & the rest of his family, by making her marry Sir James.—You should think more of yourself, & less of your Daughter.—She is not of a disposition to do you credit in the World, & seems precisely in her proper place, at Churchill with the Vernons;—but <u>You</u> are fitted for Society, & it is shameful to have you exiled from it.—Leave Frederica therefore to punish herself for the plague she has given you, by indulging that romantic tender-heartedness which will always ensure her misery enough; & come yourself to Town, as soon as you can.—

I have another reason for urging this.—Manwaring came to Town last week, & has contrived, inspite of Mr Johnson, to make opportunities of seeing me.—He is absolutely miserable about you, & jealous to such a degree of De Courcy, that it would be highly unadvisable for them to meet at present; & yet if you do not allow him to see you here, I cannot answer for his not committing some great imprudence—such as going to Churchill for instance, which would be dreadful.—Besides, if you take my advice, & resolve to marry De Courcy, it will be indispensably necessary for you to get Manwaring out of the way, & you only can have influence enough to send him back to his wife.—

I have still another motive for your coming. M̃ʳ Johnson leaves London next Tuesday. He is going for his health to Bath, where if the waters are favourable to his constitution & my wishes, he will be laid up with the Gout many weeks.—During his absence we shall be able to chuse our own society, & have true enjoyment.—I would ask you to Edward S!̃ but that he once forced from me a kind of promise never to invite you to my house. Nothing but my being in the utmost distress for Money, could have extorted it from me.—I can get you however a very nice Drawing room-apartment in Upper Seymour S!̃, & we may be always together, there or here, for I consider my promise to M̃ʳ Johnson as comprehending only (at least in his absence) your not sleeping in the House.—

Poor Manwaring gives me such histories of his wife's jealousy!—Silly woman, to expect constancy from so charming a Man!—But she was always silly; intolerably so, in marrying him at all. She, the Heiress of a large Fortune, he without a shilling!—<u>One</u> Title I know she might have had, besides Baronets.—Her folly in forming the connection was so great, that tho' M̃ʳ Johnson was her Guardian & I do not in general share his feelings, I never can forgive her.—

Adeiu. Yours, <u>Alicia</u>.—

LETTER 27.

M?ˢ Vernon to Lady De Courcy.

Churchill

This Letter my dear Mother, will be brought you by Reginald. His long visit is about to be concluded at last, but I fear the separation takes place too late to do us any good.—<u>She</u> is going to Town, to see her particular friend, M?ˢ Johnson. It was at first her intention that Frederica should accompany her for the benefit of Masters, but we over-ruled her there. Frederica was wretched in the idea of going, &

I could not bear to have her at the mercy of her Mother. Not all the Masters in London could compensate for the ruin of her comfort. I should have feared too for her health, & for every thing in short but her Principles; <u>there</u> I beleive she is not to be injured, even by her Mother, or all her Mother's friends;—but with those friends (a very bad set I doubt not) she must have mixed, or have been left in total solitude, & I can hardly tell which would have been worse for her.—If she is with her Mother moreover, she must alas! in all probability, be with Reginald—and that would be the greatest evil of all.—

Here, we shall in time be at peace.—Our regular employments, our Books & conversation, with Exercise, the Children, & every domestic pleasure in my power to procure her, will, I trust, gradually overcome this youthful attachment. I should not have a doubt of it, were she slighted for any other woman in the world, than her own Mother.—

How long Lady Susan will be in Town, or whether she returns here again, I know not.—I could not be cordial in my invitation; but if she chuses to come, no want of cordiality on my part will keep her away.—

I could not help asking Reginald if he intended being in Town this winter, as soon as I found that her Ladyship's steps would be bent thither; & tho' he professed himself quite undetermined, there was a something in his Look & voice as he spoke, which contradicted his words.—I have done with Lamentation.—I look upon the Event as so far decided, that I resign myself to it in despair. If he leaves you soon for London, every thing will be concluded.—Yours affec:ly

Cath Vernon.

LETTER 28.

M:rs Johnson to Lady Susan

Edward St—

My dearest Friend,

I write in the greatest distress; the most unfortunate event has just taken place. M:r Johnson has hit on the most effectual manner of plaguing us all.—He had heard I imagine by some means or other, that you were soon to be in London, & immediately contrived to have such an attack of the Gout, as must at least delay his journey to Bath, if not wholly prevent it.—I am persuaded the Gout is brought on, or kept off at pleasure;—it was the same, when I wanted to join the Hamiltons to the Lakes; & three years ago when I had a fancy for Bath, nothing could induce him to have a gouty symptom.

I have received yours, & have engaged the Lodgings in consequence.—I am pleased to find that my Letter had so much effect on you, & that De Courcy is certainly your own.—Let me hear from you as soon as you arrive, & in particular tell me what you mean to do with Manwaring.—It is impossible to say when I shall be able to see you. My confinement must be great. It is such an abominable trick, to be ill here, instead of at Bath, that I can scarcely command myself at all.—At Bath, his old Aunts would have nursed him, but here it all falls upon me—& he bears pain with such patience that I have not the common excuse for losing my temper.

Y^{rs} Ever, <u>Alicia.</u>

LETTER 29.

Lady Susan to Mrs Johnson

Upper Seymour S^t

My dear Alicia

There needed not this last fit of the Gout to make me detest Mr Johnson; but now the extent of my aversion is not to be estimated.—To have you confined, a Nurse, in his apartment!—My dear Alicia, of what a mistake were you guilty in marrying a Man of his age!—just old enough to be formal, ungovernable & to have the Gout—too old to be agreable, & too young to die.

I arrived last night about five, & had scarcely swallowed my dinner when Manwaring made his appearance.—I will not dissemble what real pleasure his sight afforded me, nor how strongly I felt the contrast between his person & manners, & those of Reginald, to the infinite disadvantage of the latter.—For an hour or two, I was even stagger'd in my resolution of marrying him—& tho' this was too idle & nonsensical an idea to remain long on my mind, I do not feel very eager for the conclusion of my marriage, or look forward with much impatience to the time when Reginald according to our agreement is to be in Town.—I shall probably put off his arrival, under some pretence or other. He must not come till Manwaring is gone.

I am still doubtful at times, as to Marriage.—If the old Man would die, I might not hesitate; but a state of dependance on the caprice of Sir Reginald, will not suit the freedom of my spirit;—and if I resolve to wait for that event, I shall have excuse enough at present, in having been scarcely ten months a Widow.

I have not given Manwaring any hint of my intention—or allowed him to consider my acquaintance with Reginald as more than the commonest flirtation;—& he is tolerably appeased.—Adeiu till we meet.—I am enchanted with my Lodgings. Y^{rs}. Ever,
S. Vernon.—

LETTER 30.

Lady Susan to M^r De Courcy.—

Upper Seymour S^t.

I have received your Letter; & tho' I do not attempt to conceal that I am gratified by your impatience for the hour of meeting, I yet feel myself under the necessity of delaying that hour beyond the time originally fixed.—Do not think me unkind for such an exercise of my power, or accuse me of Instability, without first hearing my reasons.—In the course of my journey from Churchill, I had ample leisure for reflection on the present state of our affairs, & every reveiw has served to convince me that they require a delicacy & cautiousness of conduct, to which we have hitherto been too little attentive.—We have been hurried on by our feelings to a degree of Precipitance which ill accords with the claims of our Friends, or the opinion of the world.—We have been unguarded in forming this hasty Engagement; but we must not complete the imprudence by ratifying it, while there is so much reason to fear the Connection would be opposed by those Friends on whom you depend.

It is not for us to blame any expectation on your Father's side of your marrying to advantage; where possessions are so extensive as those of your Family, the wish of increasing them, if not strictly reasonable, is too common to excite surprise or resentment.—He has a right to require a woman of fortune in his daughter in law; & I am sometimes quarreling with myself for suffering you to form a connection so imprudent.—But the influence of reason is often acknowledged too late by those who feel like me.—

I have now been but a few months a widow; & however little endebted to my Husband's memory for any happiness derived from him during an Union of some years, I cannot forget that the indelicacy of so early a second marriage, must subject me to the censure of the World, & incur what would be still more insupportable, the displeasure of Mr Vernon.—I might perhaps harden myself in time against the injustice of general reproach; but the loss of <u>his</u> valued Esteem, I am as you well know, ill fitted to endure;—and when to this, may be added the consciousness of having injured you with your Family, how am I to support myself.—With feelings so poignant as mine, the conviction of having divided the son from his Parents, would make me, even with <u>you</u>, the most miserable of Beings.—

It will surely therefore be advisable to delay our Union, to delay it till appearances are more promising, till affairs have taken a more favourable turn.—To assist us in such a resolution, I feel that absence will be necessary. We must not meet.—Cruel as this sentence may appear, the necessity of pronouncing it, which can alone reconcile it to myself, will be evident to you when you have considered our situation in the light in which I have found myself imperiously obliged to place it.—You may be, you must be well assured that nothing but the strongest conviction of Duty, could induce me to wound my own feelings by urging a lengthened separation; & of Insensibility to yours, you will hardly suspect me.—Again therefore I say that we ought not, we must not yet meet.—By a removal for some Months from each other, we shall tranquillize the sisterly fears of M^{rs}. Vernon, who, accustomed herself to the enjoyment of riches, considers Fortune as necessary every where, and whose sensibilities are not of a nature to comprehend ours.—

Let me hear from you soon, very soon. Tell me that you submit to my Arguments, & do not reproach me for using such.—I cannot bear reproaches. My spirits are not so high as to need being repressed.—I must endeavour to seek amusement abroad, & fortunately many of my Friends are in Town—among them, the Manwarings.—You know how sincerely I regard both Husband & Wife.—I am ever, Faithfully Yours

S. Vernon—

LETTER 31.

Lady Susan to M^{rs}. Johnson

Upper Seymour S^t

My dear Friend,

That tormenting creature Reginald is here. My Letter which was intended to keep him longer in the Country, has hastened him to Town. Much as I wish him away however, I cannot help being pleased with such a proof of attachment. He is devoted to me, heart & soul.—He will carry this note himself, which is to serve as an Introduction to you, with whom he longs to be acquainted. Allow him to spend the Evening with you, that I may be in no danger of his returning here.—I have told him that I am not quite well, & must be alone—& should he call again there might be confusion, for it is impossible to be sure of servants.—Keep him therefore I entreat you in Edward S^t—You will not find him a heavy companion, & I allow you to flirt with him as much as you like. At the same time do not forget my real interest;—say all that you can to convince him that I shall be quite wretched if he remain here;—you know my reasons—Propriety & so forth.—I would urge them more myself, but that I am impatient to be rid of him, as Manwaring comes within half an hour.

Adeiu. S V.—

LETTER 32.

M^{rs}. *Johnson to Lady Susan*—

Edward S^t

My dear Creature,

I am in agonies, & know not what to do, nor what <u>you</u> can do.—M^r. De Courcy arrived, just when he should not. M^{rs}. Manwaring had that instant entered the House, & forced herself into her Guardian's presence, tho' I did not know a syllable of it till afterwards, for I was out when both she & Reginald came, or I would have sent him away at all events; but <u>she</u> was shut up with M^r. Johnson, while <u>he</u> waited in the Drawing room for me.—

She arrived yesterday in pursuit of her Husband;—but perhaps you know this already from himself.—She came to this house to entreat my Husband's interference, & before I could be aware of it, everything that you could wish to be concealed, was known to him; & unluckily she had wormed out of Manwaring's servant that he had visited you every day since your being in Town, & had just watched him to your door herself!—What could I do?—Facts are such horrid things!—All is by this time known to De Courcy, who is now alone with M^r. Johnson.—Do not accuse me;—indeed, it was impossible to prevent it.—M^r. Johnson has for some time suspected De Courcy of intending to marry you, & would speak with him alone, as soon as he knew him to be in the House.—

That detestable M^{rs}. Manwaring, who for your comfort, has fretted herself thinner & uglier than ever, is still here, & they have been all closeted together. What can be done?—If Manwaring is now with you, he had better be gone.—At any rate I hope he will plague his wife more than ever.—With anxious wishes, Y^{rs}. faithfully

<u>Alicia</u>.

LETTER 33.

Lady Susan to M^rs. Johnson.

Upper Seymour S^t

This Eclaircissement is rather provoking.—How unlucky that you should have been from home!—I thought myself sure of you at 7.—I am undismayed however. Do not torment yourself with fears on my account.—Depend upon it, I can make my own story good with Reginald. Manwaring is just gone; he brought me the news of his wife's arrival. Silly Woman! what does she expect by such manouvres?—yet, I wish she had staid quietly at Langford.—

Reginald will be a little enraged at first, but by Tomorrow's Dinner, every thing will be well again.—Adeiu. <u>S V</u>.

LETTER 34.

M^r De Courcy to Lady Susan.

Hotel

I write only to bid you Farewell.—The spell is removed. I see you as you are.—Since we parted yesterday, I have received from indisputable authority, such an history of you, as must bring the most mortifying conviction of the Imposition I have been under, & the absolute necessity of an immediate & eternal separation from you.—You cannot doubt to what I allude;—Langford—Langford—that word will be sufficient.—I received <u>my</u> information in Mr Johnson's house, from Mrs Manwaring herself.—

You know how I have loved you, you can intimately judge of my present feelings; but I am not so weak as to find indulgence in describing them to a woman who will glory in having excited their anguish, but whose affection they have never been able to gain.

R De Courcy.

LETTER 35.

Lady Susan to M^r De Courcy.

Upper Seymour S^t

I will not attempt to describe my astonishment on reading the note, this moment received from you. I am bewilder'd in my endeavours to form some rational conjecture of what Mrs Manwaring can have told you, to occasion so extraordinary a change in your sentiments.—Have I not explained everything to you with respect to myself which could bear a doubtful meaning, & which the illnature of the world had interpreted to my Discredit?—What can you <u>now</u> have heard to stagger your Esteem for me?—Have I ever had a concealment from you?—Reginald, you agitate me beyond expression.—I cannot suppose that the old story of Mrs Manwaring's jealousy can be revived again, or at least, be <u>listened</u> to again.—Come to me immediately, & explain what is at present absolutely incomprehensible.—Beleive me, the single word of <u>Langford</u> is not of such potent intelligence, as to supersede the necessity of more.—If we <u>are</u> to part, it will at least be handsome to take your personal Leave.—But I have little heart to jest; in truth, I am serious enough—for to be sunk, tho' but an hour, in your opinion, is an humiliation to which I know not how to submit. I shall count every moment till your arrival.

<u>S. V.</u>

LETTER 36.

M^r De Courcy to Lady Susan

Hotel

Why would you write to me?—Why do you require particulars?—But since it must be so, I am obliged to declare that all the accounts of your misconduct during the life & since the death of

M.r Vernon which had reached me in common with the World in general, & gained my entire beleif before I saw you, but which you by the exertion of your perverted Abilities had made me resolve to disallow, have been unanswerably proved to me.—Nay, more, I am assured that a Connection, of which I had never before entertained a thought, has for some time existed, & still continues to exist between you and the Man, whose family you robbed of it's Peace, in return for the hospitality with which you were received into it!—That you have corresponded with him ever since your leaving Langford—not with his wife—but with him—& that he now visits you every day.—Can you, dare you deny it?—And all this at the time when I was an encouraged, an accepted Lover!—From what have I not escaped!—I have only to be grateful.—Far from me be all Complaint, & every sigh of regret. My own Folly had endangered me, my Preservation I owe to the kindness, the Integrity of another.—But the unfortunate M.rs Manwaring, whose agonies while she related the past, seem'd to threaten her reason—how is <u>she</u> to be consoled?

After such a discovery as this, you will scarcely affect farther wonder at my meaning in bidding you Adeiu.—My Understanding is at length restored, & teaches me no less to abhor the Artifices which had subdued me, than to despise myself for the weakness, on which their strength was founded.—

R De Courcy.—

LETTER 37

Lady Susan to M.r De Courcy

Upper Seymour S.t

I am satisfied—& will trouble you no more when these few Lines are dismissed.—The Engagement which you were eager to form a fortnight ago, is no longer compatible with your veiws, & I rejoice to find that the prudent advice of your Parents has not been given in vain.—Your restoration to Peace will, I doubt not, speedily follow this act of filial Obedience, & I flatter myself with the hope of surviving <u>my</u> share in this disappointment.

<u>S V.</u>

LETTER 38.

M^{rs}. Johnson to Lady Susan

Edward S^t

I am greived, tho' I cannot be astonished at your rupture with M^r. De Courcy;—he has just informed M^r. Johnson of it by letter. He leaves London he says to day.—Be assured that I partake in all your feelings, & do not be angry if I say that our intercourse even by letter must soon be given up.—It makes me miserable—but M^r. Johnson vows that if I persist in the connection, he will settle in the country for the rest of his life—& you know it is impossible to submit to such an extremity while any other alternative remains.—

You have heard of course that the Manwarings are to part; I am afraid M^{rs}. M. will come home to us again. But she is still so fond of her Husband & frets so much about him that perhaps she may not live long.—

Miss Manwaring is just come to Town to be with her Aunt, & they say, that she declares she will have Sir James Martin before she leaves London again.—If I were you, I would certainly get him myself.—I had almost forgot to give you my opinion of De Courcy, I am really delighted with him, he is full as handsome I think as Manwaring, & with such an open, good humoured Countenance that one cannot help loving him at first sight.—M^r. Johnson & he are the greatest friends in the World. Adeiu, my dearest Susan.—I wish matters did not go so perversely. That unlucky visit to Langford!—But I dare say you did all for the best, & there is no defying Destiny.—

Y^r. sincerely attached
<u>Alicia.</u>

LETTER 39.

Lady Susan to M͞*ʳˢ Johnson*

Upper Seymour S͞ᵗ

My dear Alicia

I yeild to the necessity which parts us. Under such circumstances you could not act otherwise. Our friendship cannot be impaired by it; & in happier times, when your situation is as independant as mine, it will unite us again in the same Intimacy as ever.—For this, I shall impatiently wait; & meanwhile can safely assure you that I never was more at ease, or better satisfied with myself & every thing about me, than at the present hour.—Your Husband I abhor—Reginald I despise—& I am secure of never seeing either again. Have I not reason to rejoice?—Manwaring is more devoted to me than ever; & were he at liberty, I doubt if I could resist even Matrimony offered by <u>him</u>. This Event, if his wife live with you, it may be in your power to hasten. The violence of her feelings, which must wear her out, may be easily kept in irritation.—I rely on your friendship for this.—I am now satisfied that I never could have brought myself to marry Reginald; & am equally determined that Frederica never <u>shall</u>. Tomorrow I shall fetch her from Churchill, & let Maria Manwaring tremble for the consequence. Frederica shall be Sir James's wife before she quits my house. <u>She</u> may whimper & the Vernons may storm;—I regard them not. I am tired of submitting my will to the Caprices of others—of resigning my own Judgement in deference to those, to whom I owe no Duty, & for whom I feel no respect.—I have given up too much—have been too easily worked on; but Frederica shall now find the difference.—Adeiu, dearest of Friends. May the next Gouty Attack be more favourable—& may you always regard me as unalterably Yours

S. Vernon.—

LETTER 40.

Lady De Courcy to M:^s Vernon

Parklands

My dear Catherine

I have charming news for you, & if I had not sent off my Letter this morning, you might have been spared the vexation of knowing of Reginald's being gone to Town, for he is returned, Reginald is returned, not to ask our consent to his marrying Lady Susan, but to tell us that they are parted forever!—He has been only an hour in the House, & I have not been able to learn particulars, for he is so very low, that I have not the heart to ask questions; but I hope we shall soon know all.—This is the most joyful hour he has ever given us, since the day of his birth. Nothing is wanting but to have you here, & it is our particular wish & entreaty that you would come to us as soon as you can. You have owed us a visit many long weeks.—I hope nothing will make it inconvenient to M:^r Vernon, & pray bring all my Grand Children, & your dear Neice is included of course; I long to see her.—It has been a sad heavy winter hitherto, without Reginald, & seeing nobody from Churchill; I never found the season so dreary before, but this happy meeting will make us young again.—Frederica runs much in my thoughts, & when Reginald has recovered his usual good spirits, (as I trust he soon will) we will try to rob him of his heart once more, & I am full of hopes of seeing their hands joined at no great distance.

Y:^r affec: Mother
C. De Courcy.

LETTER 41.

M:̣ Vernon to Lady De Courcy.

Churchill

My dear Madam

Your Letter has surprised me beyond measure. Can it be true that they are really separated—& for ever?—I should be overjoyed if I dared depend on it, but after all that I have seen, how can one be secure?—And Reginald really with you!—My surprise is the greater, because on wednesday, the very day of his coming to Parklands, we had a most unexpected & unwelcome visit from Lady Susan, looking all chearfulness & good humour, & seeming more as if she were to marry him when she got back to Town, than as if parted from him for ever.—She staid nearly two hours, was as affectionate & agreable as ever, & not a syllable, not a hint was dropped of any Disagreement or Coolness between them. I asked her whether she had seen my Brother since his arrival in Town—not as you may suppose with any doubt of the fact—but merely to see how she looked.—She immediately answered without any embarrassment that he had been kind enough to call on her on Monday, but she beleived he had already returned home—which I was very far from crediting.—

Your kind invitation is accepted by us with pleasure, & on Thursday next, we & our little ones will be with you.—Pray Heaven! Reginald may not be in Town again by that time!—

I wish we could bring dear Frederica too, but I am sorry to add that her Mother's errand hither was to fetch her away; & miserable as it made the poor Girl, it was impossible to detain her. I was thoroughly unwilling to let her go, & so was her Uncle; & all that could be urged, we <u>did</u> urge. But Lady Susan declared that as she was now about to fix herself in Town for several months she could not be easy if her Daughter were not with her, for Masters, &c.—Her Manner, to be sure, was very kind & proper—& M:̣

Vernon beleives that Frederica will now be treated with affection. I wish I could think so too!—

The poor girl's heart was almost broke at taking leave of us. I charged her to write to me very often, & to remember that if she were in any distress, we should be always her friends.—I took care to see her alone, that I might say all this, & I hope made her a little more comfortable.—But I shall not be easy till I can go to Town & judge of her situation myself.—

I wish there were a better prospect than now appears, of the Match, which the conclusion of your Letter declares your expectation of.—At present it is not very likely.—

Y^{rs} &c
Cath Vernon.

CONCLUSION

This Correspondence, by a meeting between some of the Parties & a separation between the others, could not, to the great detriment of the Post office Revenue, be continued longer.—Very little assistance to the State could be derived from the Epistolary Intercourse of Mrs Vernon & her Neice, for the former soon perceived by the stile of Frederica's Letters, that they were written under her Mother's inspection, & therefore deferring all particular enquiry till she could make it personally in Town, ceased writing minutely or often.—

Having learnt enough in the meanwhile from her openhearted Brother, of what had passed between him & Lady Susan to sink the latter lower than ever in her opinion, she was proportionably more anxious to get Frederica removed from such a Mother, & placed under her own care; & tho' with little hope of success, was resolved to leave nothing unattempted that might offer a chance of obtaining her sister in law's consent to it.—Her anxiety on the subject made her press for an early visit to London; & Mr Vernon who, as it must have already appeared, lived only to do whatever he was desired, soon found some accomodating Business to call him thither.—With a heart full of the Matter, M^rs. Vernon waited on Lady Susan, shortly after her arrival in Town; & was met with such an easy & chearful affection as made her almost turn from her with horror.—No remembrance of Reginald, no consciousness of Guilt, gave one look of embarrassment.—She was in excellent spirits, & seemed eager to shew at once, by every possible attention to her Brother & Sister, her sense of their kindness, & her pleasure in their society.—

Frederica was no more altered than Lady Susan;—the same restrained Manners, the same timid Look in the presence of her Mother as heretofore, assured her Aunt of her Situation's being uncomfortable, & confirmed her in the plan of altering it.—No unkindness however on the part of Lady Susan appeared. Persecution on the subject of Sir James was entirely at an end—his name merely mentioned to say that he was not in London; and in all her conversation she was solicitous only for the welfare & improvement of her Daughter, acknowledging in terms of grateful delight that Frederica was now growing every day more & more what a Parent could desire.—

M^rs. Vernon surprised & incredulous, knew not what to suspect, & without any change in her own veiws, only feared greater difficulty in accomplishing them. The first hope of any thing better was derived from Lady Susan's asking her whether she thought Frederica looked quite as well as she had done at Churchill, as she must confess herself to have sometimes an anxious doubt of London's perfectly agreeing with her.—

M^rs. Vernon encouraging the doubt, directly proposed her Neice's returning with them into the country. Lady Susan was unable to express her sense of such kindness; yet knew not from a variety of reasons how to part with her Daughter; & as, tho' her own plans were not yet wholly fixed, she trusted it would ere long be in her power to take Frederica into the country herself, concluded by declining entirely to profit by such unexampled attention.—M^rs. Vernon however persevered in the offer of it; & tho' Lady Susan continued to resist, her resistance in the course of a few days seemed somewhat less formidable.

The lucky alarm of an Influenza, decided what might not have been decided quite so soon.—Lady Susan's maternal fears were then too much awakened for her to think of any thing but Frederica's removal from the risk of infection. Above all Disorders in the World, she most dreaded the Influenza for her daughter's constitution. Frederica returned to Churchill with her Uncle & Aunt, & three weeks afterwards Lady Susan announced her being married to Sir James Martin.—

Mrs. Vernon was then convinced of what she had only suspected before, that she might have spared herself all the trouble of urging a removal, which Lady Susan had doubtless resolved on from the first.—Frederica's visit was nominally for six weeks;—but her Mother, tho' inviting her to return in one or two affectionate Letters, was very ready to oblige the whole Party by consenting to a prolongation of her stay, & in the course of two months ceased to write of her absence, & in the course of two more, to write to her at all.

Frederica was therefore fixed in the family of her Uncle & Aunt, till such time as Reginald De Courcy could be talked, flattered & finessed into an affection for her—which, allowing leisure for the conquest of his attachment to her Mother, for his abjuring all future attachments & detesting the Sex, might be reasonably looked for in the course of a Twelvemonth. Three Months might have done it in general, but Reginald's feelings were no less lasting than lively.—

Whether Lady Susan was, or was not happy in her second Choice—I do not see how it can ever be ascertained—for who would take her assurance of it, on either side of the question?—The World must judge from Probability.—She had nothing against her, but her Husband & her Conscience.

Sir James may seem to have drawn an harder Lot than mere Folly merited.—I leave him therefore to all the Pity that any body can give him. For myself, I confess that I can pity only Miss Manwaring, who coming to Town & putting herself to an expence in Cloathes, which impoverished her for two years, on purpose to secure him, was defrauded of her due by a Woman ten years older than herself.

FINIS.

NOTES TO 'LADY SUSAN'

EDUCATION

Girls in the upper ranks were often educated at home, and conduct manuals of the time criticised mothers leaving girls to the care of inadequate **governesses** or uneducated **servants**. Some girls were sent away to school, either for educational and social benefits or because unwanted at home.

Girls' **private schools** were usually small, run and owned by a head teacher, like Mrs Goddard's modest establishment for middle-class girls in *Emma*. If fashionable, a school curriculum would stress ornamental **accomplishments** such as dancing, drawing, playing on the 'pianoforte', singing, embroidering, deportment and French, all useful for attracting a husband in the genteel market, less so for being a wife and mother after marriage. It was important that upper-class girls not be given too much instruction in subjects like science and the classical languages or they might become **Bluestockings**, consequently less marriageable.

Board and education near and in London would cost between 16 and 35 guineas a year, but one of the elite London schools could cost 100 guineas or more; there would also be an entrance fee. A superior kind of school might call itself an **Academy**.

LETTERS

Letters were sent without envelopes, sheets of paper being folded, sealed and addressed. If secrecy were required, the address would be to a third person. **Members of Parliament** could **frank** their own letters, that is send them with a signature rather than paying postage; they could extend this privilege to friends and family. Otherwise, the cost was paid by the recipient. Until 1801, this was one penny for a single sheet sent within London; outside it was threepence for a single sheet travelling up to fifteen miles, with higher rates for more sheets and longer distances. The postal service was operated privately, but fees had to be paid to the state. To avoid costs, letters were often sent through travelling friends or servants.

Letter-writing was regarded as an elegant accomplishment of leisured women, keeping families in touch with each other and spreading news and gossip. Correspondence between an unrelated man and woman was unusual without a formal engagement. Marianne and Willoughby correspond improperly in *Sense and Sensibility* and Catherine and Henry Tilney with more propriety at the end of *Northanger Abbey*.

MARRIAGE

When considered to be 'out' in her late teens, a girl might receive marriage proposals through her family; these would include details of financial settlements. An 'absolute engagement' was a firm commitment to marriage which could be broken only at the cost of public scandal and loss of good reputation. Further down the social scale from the characters in 'Lady Susan', Edward Ferrars in *Sense and Sensibility* is lucky to escape from his secret but definite engagement with Lucy Steele when she decides to move her attentions to his wealthier brother.

Divorce required an Act of Parliament and was available only to the wealthy. Even if not at fault, a woman would suffer more than the man in any formal separation or divorce: her social position would be compromised and, since her property or income would usually have been transferred by law to her husband, she would be reliant upon her family for maintenance. See the situations of Eliza Brandon in *Sense and Sensibility* and Maria Rushworth in *Mansfield Park*.

A **widow** of the upper classes was supposed to spend a full year in deep or full mourning, wearing black and living quietly. In the next year, she would be in half or second mourning; this allowed a more relaxed dress code and some public activities. Men's mourning protocols were supposedly similar but commonly less strict and might include simply the wearing of a black crape band on the arm or round the hat.

MONEY

Family estates and fortunes passed down generations through eldest sons or the next closest male relative, often through an **entail**, a legally binding agreement intended to keep the estate intact. With an entail, a father could not disinherit his eldest son but, while he lived, he could withhold the son's allowance. If not entailed, an estate might be sold, but the need to sell suggested financial mismanagement by the holder. Selling to a younger son kept an estate within the family.

If he did not inherit an estate from another relative, younger sons often had to take up a professional **occupation** in the Church, the army, the law or banking.

PLACES

Fictional names include Langford and Churchill, but most place names in 'Lady Susan' are real. **Staffordshire** is a county in the English Midlands and **Sussex** and **Kent** counties on the south coast. The 'Lakes' refers to the **Lake District** in the North West, a popular tourist destination in the late eighteenth and early nineteenth centuries as interest grew in sublime and picturesque locations and William Gilpin's *Tours* explained to the public where to travel and what to appreciate.

The addresses in **London** (referred to as **the Town**) are in the newly built streets on Portman Estate land north of Oxford Street. **Wigmore Street**, parallel with Oxford Street, contained houses for the gentry, as well as some commercial businesses; **Edward Street** was the former name of the part of Wigmore Street between Marylebone Lane and Duke Street. **Upper Seymour Street** ran westwards from **Portman Square**, which is given as a fashionable address in 'Lesley Castle' in *Childhood Writings*.

The elegant city of **Bath** was a favoured resort for the sick who came to drink and bathe in its medicinal waters. The natural mineral water from the springs were seen as particularly effective for gout. Bath was also a fashionable place for the healthy and leisured. The city of Bath is the location of much of the action in *Northanger Abbey* and *Persuasion*.

A **drawing-room apartment** was a suite of rooms, sometimes quite extensive, including a reception room for visitors.

SOCIAL CUSTOMS

For men and women of the aristocracy and gentry, life often consisted of a round of social **visits** to friends and relatives; see the beginning of *Pride and Prejudice* where Mrs Bennet urges her husband formally to visit Netherfield, so that later visits of the two families can follow. Among the middling ranks in the country, **dinner**, the main meal of the day, was usually eaten between 3 and 5 p.m., but among the highest ranks in London or the country it would be far later. Where dinner was early, **tea** was often drunk several hours afterwards but, when dinner was late, tea could be drunk following the meal.

It was customary to stay with people for long periods, especially in the country, and uncommon to refuse to host a relative; it was, however, impolite to expect to stay with someone one did not know or to whom one was not related.

The upper orders would travel between estates and to London in their own **coaches**, often using hired **post-horses** for speed. The less affluent might rely on the **stagecoach**, a form of public transport between major towns and between these towns and different parts of London. Respectable ladies would not usually travel alone. By sending his guest home unchaperoned, General Tilney in *Northanger Abbey* is offering a calculated insult to young Catherine Morland. See also Austen's poem 'Oh Mr Best' in this volume (p. 237).

The main London **social season** stretched from after Christmas to spring, coinciding with the sitting of Parliament and ending when warm weather encouraged landowners to return to their country estates. It was regarded as virtuous for a wife to be contented with a country existence, busying herself with the

household and local community and not hankering after the social distractions of London.

Men relished the country mainly for the expensive pursuit of **hunting**, which required special 'hunters' and grooms and hunting dogs; when a stay was prolonged a man could send for his own hunters. In *Mansfield Park* the possession of hunters underlines Henry Crawford's wealth, but Willoughby's possession in *Sense and Sensibility* suggests he is living beyond his means.

Open weather was mild weather free from frost and fog, just right for hunting.

THE WATSONS

PREFACE TO 'THE WATSONS'

'THE WATSONS' is the first novel Austen began after drafting early versions of *Northanger Abbey, Sense and Sensibility* and *Pride and Prejudice* in the 1790s. The fragment shares the psychological and social realism of the published novels but differs from them in its powerful study of the life of those ranking below the gentry: the claustrophobic lower middle class. Some of the fragment's details of social embarrassment and family discomfiture found their way into later works, especially *Emma* and *Mansfield Park*, but no later novel shares the special bleak atmosphere of 'The Watsons'.

Through the two main characters introduced so far, Emma and Elizabeth Watson, the work presents (relative) poverty, social discomfort, reduced gentility and the meanness involved in simultaneously retrenching and keeping up appearances. The sisters splash along dirty lanes in a 'chair' pulled by an old mare, eat supper by the fire on trays and help with the spring and autumn 'great wash'. The struggle for status of those who live in the shadow of the upper ranks impinges on all aspects of life including dress, gestures and food. Some characters manoeuvre to enter a room accompanied by those ranked above them, while others hesitate to speak in the presence of their betters.

Osborne Castle, seat of Lord Osborne, would clearly have featured prominently in the completed story of 'The Watsons' but, in the fragment, we see only the houses of the middle class: an elevated townhouse entered up stone steps; a pretentious dwelling on the edge of town with a shrubbery and driveway; and the cramped Watson rectory with only a paved footpath from its gate. The heroine, Emma Watson, has been genteelly raised by a rich aunt but, on the aunt's marriage, she is thrown back on her poorer family 'without a sixpence', to quote her lawyer brother. In the circumstances she cannot avoid feeling some shame at the shabbiness of her home – and even more at the vulgarity of her siblings and sister-in-law.

An intriguing central character, Emma Watson is outspoken in the mode of Elizabeth Bennet in *Pride and Prejudice*, but primmer and without the latter's flirtatious wit, though she is given one striking response: 'Female economy will do a great deal my Lord, but it cannot turn a small income into a large one.' Although she seems unlikely to think being mistress of Osborne Castle 'something', she does echo Elizabeth Bennet when contriving to improve the manners of its ungentlemanly owner.

More than any of Austen's mature works, the fragment follows the teenage 'Catharine, or the Bower' in illustrating the urgency of women's need for marriage. Refined young Emma thinks it beneath her to pursue a man, believing poverty not the greatest evil for 'a woman of education and feeling'. With more experience of work outside the home, the pragmatic Elizabeth, nearing thirty, thinks that spinsterhood could be pleasing with money but without it marriage is a better prospect than teaching in a school or family. In this distaste, she echoes the feminist writer Mary Wollstonecraft in *Thoughts on the Education of Daughters* (1787), who describes the distress experienced by genteel girls forced to work as teachers in vulgar surroundings.

All Austen's comic novels end in marriage. We may think we see where Emma is tending, but what would the happy conclusion be for the older Elizabeth, who has lost her first love? And, whatever sexual rivalry was intended, it promises to include an unusual player in the world of Austen books: a 'very handsome' dowager nearly fifty years old.

THE WATSONS

THE FIRST WINTER assembly in the town of D. in Surry was to be held on Tuesday October the 13th, and it was generally expected to be a very good one; a long list of country families was confidently run over as sure of attending, and sanguine hopes were entertained that the Osbornes themselves would be there.— The Edwards's invitation to the Watsons followed of course. The Edwardses were people of fortune who lived in the town and kept their coach; the Watsons inhabited a village about three miles distant, were poor and had no close carriage; and ever since there had been balls in the place, the former were accustomed to invite the latter to dress, dine and sleep at their house, on every monthly return throughout the winter.—On the present occasion, as only two of Mr. Watson's children were at home, and one was always necessary as companion to himself, for he was sickly and had lost his wife, one only could profit by the kindness of their friends; Miss Emma Watson, who was very recently returned to her family from the care of an aunt who had brought her up, was to make her first public appearance in the neighbourhood;—and her eldest sister, whose delight in a ball was not lessened by a ten years enjoyment, had some merit in cheerfully undertaking to drive her and all her finery in the old chair to D. on the important morning.—

As they splashed along the dirty lane Miss Watson thus instructed and cautioned her inexperienced sister.—

"I dare say it will be a very good ball, and among so many officers, you will hardly want partners. You will find Mrs. Edwards's maid very willing to help you, and I would advise you to ask Mary Edwards's opinion if you are at all at a loss for she has a very good taste.—If Mr. Edwards does not lose his money at cards, you will stay as late as you can wish for; if he does, he will hurry you home perhaps—but you are sure of some comfortable soup.—I hope you will be in good looks—. I should not be surprised if you were to be thought one of the prettiest girls in the room, there is a great deal in novelty. Perhaps Tom Musgrave may take notice of you—but I would advise you by all means not to give him any encouragement. He generally pays attention to every new girl, but he is a great flirt and never means anything serious."

"I think I have heard you speak of him before," said Emma. "Who is he?"

"A young man of very good fortune, quite independent, and remarkably agreeable, an universal favourite wherever he goes. Most of the girls hereabouts are in love with him, or have been. I believe I am the only one among them that have escaped with a whole heart, and yet I was the first he paid attention to, when he came into this country,* six years ago; and very great attention indeed did he pay me. Some people say that he has never seemed to like any girl so well since, though he is always behaving in a particular way to one or another."—

"And how came *your* heart to be the only cold one?—" said Emma smiling.

"There was a reason for that—" replied Miss Watson, changing colour.—"I have not been very well used Emma among them, I hope you will have better luck."—

"Dear sister, I beg your pardon, if I have unthinkingly given you pain."—

"When first we knew Tom Musgrave," continued Miss Watson without seeming to hear her, "I was very much attached to a young man of the name of Purvis, a particular friend of Robert's, who used to be with us a great deal. Every body thought it would have been a match."

A sigh accompanied these words, which Emma respected in silence—; but her sister, after a short pause, went on—

---

* **Country**: county.

"You will naturally ask why it did not take place, and why he is married to another woman, while I am still single.—But you must ask him—not me—you must ask Penelope.—Yes Emma, Penelope was at the bottom of it all.—She thinks everything fair for a husband; I trusted her, she set him against me, with a view of gaining him herself, and it ended in his discontinuing his visits and soon after marrying somebody else.—Penelope makes light of her conduct, but I think such treachery very bad. It has been the ruin of my happiness. I shall never love any man as I loved Purvis. I do not think Tom Musgrave should be named with him in the same day.—"

"You quite shock me by what you say of Penelope—" said Emma. "Could a sister do such a thing?—Rivalry, treachery between sisters!—I shall be afraid of being acquainted with her—but I hope it was not so. Appearances were against her"—

"You do not know Penelope.—There is nothing she would not do to get married—she would as good as tell you so herself.—Do not trust her with any secrets of your own, take warning by me, do not trust her; she has her good qualities, but she has no faith, no honour, no scruples, if she can promote her own advantage.—I wish with all my heart she was well married. I declare I had rather have her well-married than myself."—

"Than yourself!—Yes I can suppose so. A heart, wounded like yours, can have little inclination for matrimony."—

"Not much indeed—but you know we must marry.—I could do very well single for my own part—A little company, and a pleasant ball now and then, would be enough for me, if one could be young for ever, but my father cannot provide for us, and it is very bad to grow old and be poor and laughed at.—I have lost Purvis, it is true, but very few people marry their first loves. I should not refuse a man because he was not Purvis—. Not that I can ever quite forgive Penelope.—" Emma shook her head in acquiescence.—

"Penelope however has had her troubles—" continued Miss Watson.—"She was sadly disappointed in Tom Musgrave, who afterwards transferred his attentions from me to her, and whom she was very fond of;—but he never means anything serious, and when he had trifled with her long enough, he began to slight her for Margaret, and poor Penelope was very wretched—. And since then, she has been trying to make some match at Chichester; she won't tell us with whom, but I believe it is a rich old Dr. Harding, uncle to the friend she goes to see;—and she has taken a vast deal of trouble about him and given up a great deal of time to no purpose as yet.—When she went away the other day, she said it should be the last time.—I suppose you did not know what her particular business was at Chichester—nor guess at the object that could take her away from Stanton just as you were coming home after so many years absence."—

"No indeed, I had not the smallest suspicion of it. I considered her engagement to Mrs. Shaw just at that time as very unfortunate for me. I had hoped to find all my sisters at home; to be able to make an immediate friend of each."—

"I suspect the Doctor to have had an attack of the asthma,—and that she was hurried away on that account—the Shaws are quite on her side.—At least I believe so—but she tells me nothing. She professes to keep her own counsel; she says, and truly enough, that 'Too many cooks spoil the broth'."—

"I am sorry for her anxieties," said Emma,—"but I do not like her plans or her opinions. I shall be afraid of her.—She must have too masculine and bold a temper.—To be so bent on marriage—to pursue a man merely for the sake of situation—is a sort of thing that shocks me; I cannot understand it. Poverty is a great evil, but to a woman of education and feeling it ought not, it cannot be the greatest.—I would rather be teacher at a school (and I can think of nothing worse) than marry a man I did not like.—"

"I would rather do any thing than be teacher at a school—" said her sister. "*I* have been at school, Emma, and know what a life they lead; *you* never have.—I should not like marrying a disagreeable man any more than yourself,—but I do not think there *are* many very disagreeable men;—I think I could like any good-humoured man with a comfortable income.—I suppose my aunt brought you up to be rather refined."

"Indeed I do not know.—My conduct must tell you how I have been brought up. I am no judge of it myself. I cannot compare my aunt's method with any other person's, because I know no other."—

"But I can see in a great many things that you are very refined. I have observed it ever since you came home, and I am afraid it will not be for your happiness. Penelope will laugh at you very much."

"*That* will not be for my happiness I am sure.—If my opinions are wrong, I must correct them—if they are above my situation, I must endeavour to conceal them.—But I doubt whether ridicule—Has Penelope much wit?"—

"Yes—she has great spirits, and never cares what she says."—

"Margaret is more gentle I imagine?"—

"Yes—especially in company; she is all gentleness and mildness when anybody is by.—But she is a little fretful and perverse among ourselves.—Poor creature!—she is possessed with the notion of Tom Musgrave's being more seriously in love with her, than he ever was with any body else, and is always expecting him to come to the point. This is the second time within this twelvemonth that she has gone to spend a month with Robert and Jane on purpose to egg him on, by her absence—but I am sure she is mistaken, and that he will no more follow her to Croydon now than he did last March.—He will never marry unless he can marry somebody very great; Miss Osborne perhaps, or something in that style.—"

"Your account of this Tom Musgrave, Elizabeth, gives me very little inclination for his acquaintance."

"You are afraid of him, I do not wonder at you."—

"No indeed—I dislike and despise him."—

"Dislike and despise Tom Musgrave! No, *that* you never can. I defy you not to be delighted with him if he takes notice of you.—I hope he will dance with you—and I dare say he will, unless the Osbornes come with a large party, and then he will not speak to any body else.—"

"He seems to have most engaging manners!"—said Emma.—"Well, we shall see how irresistible Mr. Tom Musgrave and I find each other.—I suppose I shall know him as soon as I enter the ball-room;—he *must* carry some of his charms in his face."—

"You will not find him in the ball-room I can tell you. You will go early that Mrs. Edwards may get a good place by the fire, and he never comes till late; and if the Osbornes are coming, he will wait in the passage, and come in with them.—I should like to look in upon you, Emma. If it was but a good day with my father, I would wrap myself up, and James should drive me over, as soon as I had made tea for him, and I should be with you by the time the dancing began."

"What! would you come late at night in this chair?"—

"To be sure I would.—There, I said you were very refined;—and *that*'s an instance of it.—"

Emma for a moment made no answer—at last she said—"I wish, Elizabeth, you had not made a point of my going to this ball, I wish you were going instead of me. Your pleasure would be greater than mine. I am a stranger here, and know nobody but the Edwardses—my enjoyment therefore must be very doubtful. Yours among all your acquaintance would be certain.—It is not too late to change. Very little apology could be requisite to the Edwardses, who must be more glad of your company than of mine, and I should most readily return to my father; and should not be at all afraid to drive this quiet old creature home. Your clothes I would undertake to find means of sending to you."—

"My dearest Emma," cried Elizabeth warmly—"do you think I would do such a thing?—Not for the universe—but I shall never forget your good nature in proposing it. You must have a sweet temper indeed!—I never met with any thing like it!—And would you really give up the ball, that I might be able to go to it!—Believe me Emma, I am not so selfish as that comes to. No, though I am nine years older than you are, I would not be the means of keeping you from being seen.—You are very pretty, and it would be very hard that you should not have as fair a chance as we have all had, to make your fortune.—No Emma, whoever stays at home this winter, it shan't be you. I am sure I should never have forgiven the person who kept me from a ball at nineteen."

Emma expressed her gratitude, and for a few minutes they jogged on in silence.—Elizabeth first spoke.—

"You will take notice who Mary Edwards dances with."—

"I will remember her partners if I can—but you know they will be all strangers to me."

"Only observe whether she dances with Captain Hunter, more than once; I have my fears in that quarter. Not that her father or mother like officers, but if she does, you know, it is all over with poor Sam.—And I have promised to write him word who she dances with."

"Is Sam attached to Miss Edwards?"—

"Did not you know *that*?"—

"How should I know it?—How should I know in Shropshire, what is passing of that nature in Surry?—It is not likely that circumstances of such delicacy should make any part of the scanty communication which passed between you and me for the last fourteen years."

"I wonder I never mentioned it when I wrote. Since you have been at home, I have been so busy with my poor father and our great wash that I have had no leisure to tell you anything—but indeed I concluded you knew it all.—He has been very much in love with her these two years, and it is a great disappointment to him that he cannot always get away to our balls—but Mr. Curtis won't often spare him, and just now it is a sickly time at Guilford—"

"Do you suppose Miss Edwards inclined to like him—?"

"I am afraid not: you know she is an only child, and will have at least ten thousand pounds."—

"But still she may like our brother."

"Oh! no—. The Edwardses look much higher. Her father and mother would never consent to it. Sam is only a surgeon you know.— Sometimes I think she does like him. But Mary Edwards is rather prim and reserved; I do not always know what she would be at."—

"Unless Sam feels on sure grounds with the lady herself, it seems a pity to me that he should be encouraged to think of her at all."—

"A young man must think of somebody," said Elizabeth—"and why should not he be as lucky as Robert, who has got a good wife and six thousand pounds?"

"We must not all expect to be individually lucky," replied Emma. "The luck of one member of a family is luck to all.—"

"Mine is all to come I am sure—" said Elizabeth, giving another sigh to the remembrance of Purvis.—"I have been unlucky enough, and I cannot say much for you, as my aunt married again so foolishly.—Well—you will have a good ball I dare say. The next turning will bring us to the turnpike. You may see the church tower over the hedge, and the White Hart is close by it.—I shall long to know what you think of Tom Musgrave."

Such were the last audible sounds of Miss Watson's voice, before they passed through the turnpike gate and entered on the pitching of the town—the jumbling and noise of which made farther conversation most thoroughly undesirable.—The old mare trotted heavily on, wanting no direction of the reins to take the right turning, and making only one blunder, in proposing to stop at the milliners, before she drew up towards Mr. Edwards's door.—Mr. Edwards lived in the best house in the street, and the best in the place, if Mr. Tomlinson the banker might be indulged in calling his newly erected house at the end of the town, with a shrubbery and sweep, in the country.—Mr. Edwards's house was higher than most of its neighbours, with windows on each side the door, the windows guarded by posts and chain, the door approached by a flight of stone steps.—

"Here we are—" said Elizabeth, as the carriage ceased moving—"safely arrived;—and by the market clock, we have been only five and thirty minutes coming—which *I* think is doing pretty well, though it would be nothing for Penelope.—Is not it a nice town?—The Edwardses have a noble house, you see, and they live quite in stile. The door will be opened by a man in livery with a powdered head, I can tell you."

Emma had seen the Edwardses only one morning at Stanton, they were therefore all but strangers to her, and though her spirits were by no means insensible to the expected joys of the evening, she felt a little uncomfortable in the thought of all that was to precede them. Her conversation with Elizabeth too, giving her some very unpleasant feelings with respect to her own family, had made her more open to disagreeable impressions from any other cause, and increased her sense of the awkwardness of rushing into intimacy on so slight an acquaintance.—

There was nothing in the manners of Mrs. or Miss Edwards to give immediate change to these ideas;—the mother, though a very friendly woman, had a reserved air, and a great deal of formal civility—and the daughter, a genteel looking girl of twenty two, with her hair in papers, seemed very naturally to have caught something of the stile of the mother who had brought her up.—Emma was soon left to know what they could be, by Elizabeth's being obliged to hurry away—and some very, very languid remarks on the probable brilliancy of the ball, were all that broke at intervals a silence of half an hour before they were joined by the master of the house.—Mr. Edwards had a much easier and more communicative air than the ladies of the family; he was fresh from the street, and he came ready to tell whatever might interest.—After a cordial reception of Emma, he turned to his daughter with "Well Mary, I bring you good news.—The Osbornes will certainly be at the ball to night.—Horses for two carriages are ordered from the White Hart, to be at Osborne Castle by nine."—

"I am glad of it—" observed Mrs. Edwards, "because their coming gives a credit to our assemblies. The Osbornes being known to have been at the first ball, will dispose a great many people to attend the second.—It is more than they deserve, for in fact they add nothing to the pleasure of the evening, they come so late, and go so early;—but great people have always their charm."—

Mr. Edwards proceeded to relate every other little article of news which his morning's lounge had supplied him with, and they chatted with greater briskness, till Mrs. Edwards's moment for dressing arrived, and the young ladies were carefully recommended to lose no time.—Emma was shewn to a very comfortable apartment, and as soon as Mrs. Edwards's civilities could leave her to herself, the happy occupation, the first bliss of a ball began.—

The girls, dressing in some measure together, grew unavoidably better acquainted; Emma found in Miss Edwards the shew of good sense, a modest unpretending mind, and a great wish of obliging—

and when they returned to the parlour where Mrs. Edwards was sitting respectably attired in one of the two satin gowns which went through the winter, and a new cap from the milliners, they entered it with much easier feelings and more natural smiles than they had taken away.—

Their dress was now to be examined; Mrs. Edwards acknowledged herself too old-fashioned to approve of every modern extravagance however sanctioned—and though complacently viewing her daughter's good looks, would give but a qualified admiration; and Mr. Edwards, not less satisfied with Mary, paid some compliments of good humoured gallantry to Emma at her expence.— The discussion led to more intimate remarks, and Miss Edwards gently asked Emma if she were not often reckoned very like her youngest brother.—Emma thought she could perceive a faint blush accompany the question, and there seemed something still more suspicious in the manner in which Mr. Edwards took up the subject.

"—You are paying Miss Emma no great compliment I think Mary," said he hastily—. "Mr. Sam Watson is a very good sort of young man, and I dare say a very clever surgeon, but his complexion has been rather too much exposed to all weathers, to make a likeness to him very flattering."

Mary apologized in some confusion. "She had not thought a strong likeness at all incompatible with very different degrees of beauty.—There might be resemblance in countenance; and the complexion, and even the features be very unlike."—

"I know nothing of my brother's beauty," said Emma, "for I have not seen him since he was seven years old—but my father reckons us alike."

"Mr. Watson!—" cried Mr. Edwards. "Well, you astonish me.— There is not the least likeness in the world; your brother's eyes are grey, yours are brown, he has a long face, and a wide mouth.—My dear, do *you* perceive the least resemblance?"—

"Not the least.—Miss Emma Watson puts me very much in mind of her eldest sister, and sometimes I see a look of Miss Penelope— and once or twice there has been a glance of Mr. Robert—but I cannot perceive any likeness to Mr. Samuel."

"I see the likeness between her and Miss Watson," replied Mr. Edwards, "very strongly—but I am not sensible of the others.—I do not much think she is like any of the family *but* Miss Watson; but I am very sure there is no resemblance between her and Sam."—

This matter was settled, and they went to dinner.—

"Your father, Miss Emma, is one of my oldest friends—" said Mr. Edwards, as he helped her to wine, when they were drawn round the fire to enjoy their desert.—"We must drink to his better health.—It is a great concern to me I assure you that he should be such an invalid.—I know nobody who likes a game of cards in a social way, better than he does;—and very few people that play a fairer rubber.—It is a thousand pities that he should be so deprived of the pleasure. For now we have a quiet little whist club that meets three times a week at the White Hart, and, if he could but have his health, how much he would enjoy it."

"I dare say he would Sir—and I wish with all my heart he were equal to it."

"Your club would be better fitted for an invalid," said Mrs. Edwards, "if you did not keep it up so late."—

This was an old grievance.—

"So late, my dear, what are you talking of?" cried the husband with sturdy pleasantry—. "We are always at home before midnight. They would laugh at Osborne Castle to hear you call *that* late; they are but just rising from dinner at midnight."—

"That is nothing to the purpose—" retorted the lady calmly. "The Osbornes are to be no rule for us. You had better meet every night, and break up two hours sooner."

So far, the subject was very often carried;—but Mr. and Mrs. Edwards were so wise as never to pass that point; and Mr. Edwards now turned to something else.—He had lived long enough in the idleness of a town to become a little of a gossip, and having some curiosity to know more of the circumstances of his young guest than had yet reached him, he began with,

"I think, Miss Emma, I remember your aunt very well about thirty years ago; I am pretty sure I danced with her in the old rooms at Bath, the year before I married—. She was a very fine woman then—but like other people I suppose she is grown somewhat older since that time.—I hope she is likely to be happy in her second choice."

"I hope so, I believe so, Sir—" said Emma in some agitation.—

"Mr. Turner had not been dead a great while I think?"

"About two years Sir."

"I forget what her name is now?"—

"O'Brien."

"Irish! Ah! I remember—and she is gone to settle in Ireland.—I do not wonder that you should not wish to go with her into *that* country Miss Emma—; but it must be a great deprivation to her, poor lady!—After bringing you up like a child of her own."—

"I was not so ungrateful Sir," said Emma warmly, "as to wish to be any where but with her.—It did not suit them, it did not suit Captain O'Brien that I should be of the party.—"

"Captain!—" repeated Mrs. Edwards. "The gentleman is in the army then?"

"Yes Ma'am."—

"Aye—there is nothing like your officers for captivating the ladies, young or old.—There is no resisting a cockade my dear."—

"I hope there is,"—said Mrs. Edwards gravely, with a quick glance at her daughter;—and Emma had just recovered from her own perturbation in time to see a blush on Miss Edwards's cheek, and in remembering what Elizabeth had said of Captain Hunter, to wonder and waver between his influence and her brother's.—

"Elderly ladies should be careful how they make a second choice," observed Mr. Edwards.—

"Carefulness—discretion—should not be confined to elderly ladies, or to a second choice," added his wife. "It is quite as necessary to young ladies in their first."—

"Rather more so, my dear—" replied he, "because young ladies are likely to feel the effects of it longer. When an old lady plays the fool, it is not in the course of nature that she should suffer from it many years." Emma drew her hand across her eyes—and Mrs. Edwards, on perceiving it, changed the subject to one of less anxiety to all.—

With nothing to do but to expect the hour of setting off, the afternoon was long to the two young ladies; and though Miss Edwards was rather discomposed at the very early hour which her mother always fixed for going, that early hour itself was watched for with some eagerness.—The entrance of the tea things at seven o'clock was some relief—and luckily Mr. and Mrs. Edwards always drank a dish extraordinary, and ate an additional muffin when they were going to sit up late, which lengthened the ceremony almost to the wished for moment. At a little before eight, the Tomlinsons' carriage was heard to go by, which was the constant signal for Mrs. Edwards to order hers to the door; and in a very few minutes, the party were transported from the quiet warmth of a snug parlour, to the bustle, noise and draughts of air of the broad entrance-passage of an inn.—

Mrs. Edwards, carefully guarding her own dress, while she attended with yet greater solicitude to the proper security of her young charges' shoulders and throats, led the way up the wide staircase, while no sound of a ball but the first scrape of one violin blessed the ears of her followers, and Miss Edwards, on hazarding the anxious enquiry of whether there were many people come yet, was told by the waiter, as she knew she should, that "Mr. Tomlinson's family were in the room."

In passing along a short gallery to the assembly-room, brilliant in lights before them, they were accosted by a young man in a morning dress and boots, who was standing in the doorway of a bed chamber, apparently on purpose to see them go by.—

"Ah! Mrs. Edwards—how do you do?—How do you do Miss Edwards?—" he cried, with an easy air.—"You are determined to be in good time I see, as usual.—The candles are but this moment lit—"

"I like to get a good seat by the fire you know, Mr. Musgrave," replied Mrs. Edwards.

"I am this moment going to dress," said he—"I am waiting for my stupid fellow.—We shall have a famous ball. The Osbornes are certainly coming; you may depend upon *that* for I was with Lord Osborne this morning.—"

The party passed on—Mrs. Edwards's satin gown swept along the clean floor of the ball-room, to the fireplace at the upper end, where one party only were formally seated, while three or four officers were lounging together, passing in and out from the adjoining card-room.—A very stiff meeting between these near neighbours ensued—and as soon as they were all duly placed again, Emma, in the low whisper which became the solemn scene, said to Miss Edwards, "The gentleman we passed in the passage was Mr. Musgrave, then.—He is reckoned remarkably agreeable I understand.—"

Miss Edwards answered hesitatingly—"Yes—he is very much liked by many people.—But *we* are not very intimate."—

"He is rich, is not he?"—

"He has about eight or nine hundred pounds a year I believe.—He came into possession of it when he was very young, and my father and mother think it has given him rather an unsettled turn.—He is no favourite with them."—

The cold and empty appearance of the room and the demure air of the small cluster of females at one end of it began soon to give way; the inspiriting sound of other carriages was heard, and continual accessions of portly chaperons, and strings of smartly-dressed girls were received, with now and then a fresh gentleman straggler, who if not enough in love to station himself near any fair creature seemed glad to escape into the card-room.—Among the increasing numbers of military men, one now made his way to Miss Edwards, with an air of empressément,* which decidedly said to her companion "I am Captain Hunter"—and Emma, who could not but watch her at such a moment, saw her looking rather distressed, but by no means displeased, and heard an engagement formed for the two first dances, which made her think her brother Sam's a hopeless case.—

Emma in the mean while was not unobserved, or unadmired herself.—A new face, and a very pretty one, could not be slighted—her name was whispered from one party to another, and no sooner had

---

* **Empressément**: an animated display of cordiality, the use of the French term suggesting some self-regard.

the signal been given, by the orchestra's striking up a favourite air, which seemed to call the young men to their duty, and people the centre of the room, than she found herself engaged to dance with a brother officer, introduced by Captain Hunter.—Emma Watson was not more than of the middle height—well made and plump, with an air of healthy vigour.—Her skin was very brown, but clear, smooth and glowing—; which with a lively eye, a sweet smile, and an open countenance, gave beauty to attract, and expression to make that beauty improve on acquaintance.—Having no reason to be dissatisfied with her partner, the evening began very pleasantly to her; and her feelings perfectly coincided with the re-iterated observation of others, that it was an excellent ball.—

The two first dances were not quite over, when the returning sound of carriages after a long interruption called general notice, and "the Osbornes are coming, the Osbornes are coming"—was repeated round the room.—After some minutes of extraordinary bustle without, and watchful curiosity within, the important party, preceded by the attentive master of the inn to open a door which was never shut, made their appearance. They consisted of Lady Osborne, her son Lord Osborne, her daughter Miss Osborne; Miss Carr, her daughter's friend, Mr. Howard, formerly tutor to Lord Osborne, now clergyman of the parish in which the castle stood, Mrs. Blake, a widow-sister who lived with him, her son, a fine boy of ten years old, and Mr. Tom Musgrave; who, probably imprisoned within his own room, had been listening in bitter impatience to the sound of the music, for the last half hour. In their progress up the room, they paused almost immediately behind Emma, to receive the compliments of some acquaintance, and she heard Lady Osborne observe that they had made a point of coming early for the gratification of Mrs. Blake's little boy, who was uncommonly fond of dancing.—Emma looked at them all as they passed—but chiefly and with most interest on Tom Musgrave, who was certainly a genteel, good looking young man.—Of the females, Lady Osborne had by much the finest person;—though nearly fifty, she was very handsome, and had all the dignity of rank.—

Lord Osborne was a very fine young man; but there was an air of coldness, of carelessness, even of awkwardness about him, which seemed to speak him out of his element in a ball room. He came in fact only because it was judged expedient for him to please the Borough—he was not fond of women's company, and he never danced.—Mr. Howard was an agreeable-looking man, a little more than thirty.—

At the conclusion of the two dances, Emma found herself, she knew not how, seated amongst the Osborne set; and she was immediately struck with the fine countenance and animated gestures of the little boy, as he was standing before his mother, wondering when they should begin.—

"You will not be surprised at Charles's impatience," said Mrs. Blake, a lively pleasant-looking little woman of five or six and thirty, to a lady who was standing near her, "when you know what a partner he is to have. Miss Osborne has been so very kind as to promise to dance the two first dances with him."—

"Oh! yes—we have been engaged this week," cried the boy, "and we are to dance down every couple."—

On the other side of Emma, Miss Osborne, Miss Carr, and a party of young men were standing engaged in very lively consultation—and soon afterwards she saw the smartest officer of the set walking off to the orchestra to order the dance, while Miss Osborne, passing before her, to her little expecting partner hastily said—"Charles, I beg your pardon for not keeping my engagement, but I am going to dance these two dances with Colonel Beresford. I know you will excuse me, and I will certainly dance with you after tea." And without staying for an answer, she turned again to Miss Carr, and in another minute was led by Colonel Beresford to begin the set.

If the poor little boy's face had in its happiness been interesting to Emma, it was infinitely more so under this sudden reverse;— he stood the picture of disappointment, with crimsoned cheeks, quivering lips, and eyes bent on the floor. His mother, stifling her own mortification, tried to soothe his, with the prospect of Miss Osborne's second promise; but though he contrived to utter with an effort of boyish bravery "Oh! I do not mind it"—it was very evident by the unceasing agitation of his features that he minded it as much as ever.—

Emma did not think, or reflect;—she felt and acted—.

"I shall be very happy to dance with you Sir, if you like it," said she, holding out her hand with the most unaffected good humour.—

The boy in one moment restored to all his first delight looked joyfully at his mother; and stepping forward with an honest and simple "Thank you Ma'am" was instantly ready to attend his new acquaintance.—The thankfulness of Mrs. Blake was more diffuse;—with a look, most expressive of unexpected pleasure and lively gratitude, she turned to her neighbour with repeated and fervent acknowledgements of so great and condescending a kindness to her boy.—Emma with perfect truth could assure her that she could not be giving greater pleasure than she felt herself—and Charles being provided with his gloves and charged to keep them on, they joined the set which was now rapidly forming, with nearly equal complacency.—

It was a partnership which could not be noticed without surprise. It gained her a broad stare from Miss Osborne and Miss Carr as they passed her in the dance. "Upon my word Charles you are in luck, (said the former as she turned him) you have got a better partner than me"—to which the happy Charles answered "Yes."—Tom Musgrave, who was dancing with Miss Carr, gave her many inquisitive glances; and after a time Lord Osborne himself came and under pretence of talking to Charles, stood to look at his partner.—Though rather distressed by such observation, Emma could not repent what she had done, so happy had it made both the boy and his mother; the latter of whom was continually making opportunities of addressing her with the warmest civility.—

Her little partner she found, though bent chiefly on dancing, was not unwilling to speak, when her questions or remarks gave him anything to say; and she learnt, by a sort of inevitable enquiry, that "he had two brothers and a sister, that they and their mama all lived with his uncle at Wickstead, that his uncle taught him Latin, that he was very fond of riding, and had a horse of his own given him by Lord Osborne; and that he had been out once already with Lord Osborne's hounds."—

At the end of these dances Emma found they were to drink tea;—Miss Edwards gave her a caution to be at hand, in a manner which convinced her of Mrs. Edwards's holding it very important to have them both close to her when she moved into the tea room; and Emma was accordingly on the alert to gain her proper station. It was always the pleasure of the company to have a little bustle and crowd when they thus adjourned for refreshment.—The tea room was a small room within the card room, and in passing through the latter, where the passage was straitened by tables, Mrs. Edwards and her party were for a few moments hemmed in. It happened close by Lady Osborne's cassino table; Mr. Howard who belonged to it spoke to his nephew; and Emma on perceiving herself the object of attention both to Lady Osborne and him, had just turned away her eyes in time, to avoid seeming to hear her young companion delightedly whisper aloud—"Oh! Uncle, do look at my partner. She is so pretty!"

As they were immediately in motion again however, Charles was hurried off without being able to receive his uncle's suffrage.—On entering the tea room, in which two long tables were prepared, Lord Osborne was to be seen quite alone at the end of one, as if retreating as far as he could from the ball, to enjoy his own thoughts, and gape without restraint.—Charles instantly pointed him out to Emma—

"There's Lord Osborne—let you and I go and sit by him."—

"No, no," said Emma laughing, "you must sit with my friends."

Charles was now free enough to hazard a few questions in his turn. "What o'clock was it?—"

"Eleven."—

"Eleven!—And I am not at all sleepy. Mama said I should be asleep before ten.—Do you think Miss Osborne will keep her word with me, when tea is over?"

"Oh! yes.—I suppose so"—though she felt that she had no better reason to give than that Miss Osborne had *not* kept it before.—

"When shall you come to Osborne Castle?"—

"Never, probably.—I am not acquainted with the family."

"But you may come to Wickstead and see Mama, and she can take you to the Castle.—There is a monstrous curious stuffed fox there, and a badger—any body would think they were alive. It is a pity you should not see them."—

On rising from tea, there was again a scramble for the pleasure of being first out of the room, which happened to be increased by one or two of the card parties having just broken up and the players being disposed to move exactly the different way. Among these was Mr. Howard—his sister leaning on his arm—and no sooner were they within reach of Emma, than Mrs. Blake, calling her notice by a friendly touch, said

"Your goodness to Charles, my dear Miss Watson, brings all his family upon you. Give me leave to introduce my brother—Mr. Howard."

Emma curtsied, the gentleman bowed—made a hasty request for the honour of her hand in the two next dances, to which as hasty an affirmative was given, and they were immediately impelled in opposite directions.—Emma was very well pleased with the circumstance;— there was a quietly cheerful, gentlemanlike air in Mr. Howard which suited her—and in a few minutes afterwards, the value of her engagement increased when as she was sitting in the card room somewhat screened by a door, she heard Lord Osborne, who was lounging on a vacant table near her, call Tom Musgrave towards him and say,

"Why do not you dance with that beautiful Emma Watson?—I want you to dance with her—and I will come and stand by you."—

"I was determining on it this very moment my Lord; I'll be introduced and dance with her directly.—"

"Aye do—and if you find she does not want much talking to, you may introduce me by and bye."—

"Very well my Lord—. If she is like her sisters, she will only want to be listened to.—I will go this moment. I shall find her in the tea room. That stiff old Mrs. Edwards has never done tea."—

Away he went—Lord Osborne after him—and Emma lost no time in hurrying from her corner, exactly the other way, forgetting in her haste that she left Mrs. Edwards behind.—

"We had quite lost you—" said Mrs. Edwards—who followed her with Mary, in less than five minutes.—"If you prefer this room to the other, there is no reason why you should not be here, but we had better all be together."

Emma was saved the trouble of apologizing, by their being joined at the moment by Tom Musgrave, who, requesting Mrs. Edwards aloud to do him the honour of presenting him to Miss Emma Watson, left that good lady without any choice in the business, but that of testifying by the coldness of her manner that she did it unwillingly. The honour of dancing with her, was solicited without loss of time—and Emma, however she might like to be thought a beautiful girl by lord or commoner, was so little disposed to favour Tom Musgrave himself, that she had considerable satisfaction in avowing her prior engagement.—He was evidently surprised and discomposed.—The stile of her last partner had probably led him to believe her not overpowered with applications.—

"My little friend Charles Blake," he cried, "must not expect to engross you the whole evening. We can never suffer this—it is against the rules of the assembly—and I am sure it will never be patronised by our good friend here Mrs. Edwards; she is by much too nice a judge of decorum to give her license to such a dangerous particularity."—

"I am not going to dance with Master Blake Sir."

The gentleman, a little disconcerted, could only hope he might be more fortunate another time—and seeming unwilling to leave her—though his friend Lord Osborne was waiting in the doorway for the result, as Emma with some amusement perceived—he began to make civil enquiries after her family.—

"How comes it, that we have not the pleasure of seeing your sisters here this evening?—Our assemblies have been used to be so well treated by them, that we do not know how to take this neglect."—

"My eldest sister is the only one at home—and she could not leave my father—"

"Miss Watson the only one at home!—You astonish me!—It seems but the day before yesterday that I saw them all three in this town. But I am afraid I have been a very sad neighbour of late. I hear dreadful complaints of my negligence wherever I go,—and I confess it is a shameful length of time since I was at Stanton.—But I shall *now* endeavour to make myself amends for the past."—

Emma's calm curtsey in reply must have struck him as very unlike the encouraging warmth he had been used to receive from her sisters, and gave him probably the novel sensation of doubting his own influence, and of wishing for more attention than she bestowed.—

The dancing now recommenced; Miss Carr being impatient to *call*, everybody was required to stand up—and Tom Musgrave's curiosity was appeased, on seeing Mr. Howard come forward and claim Emma's hand—"That will do as well for *me*"—was Lord Osborne's remark, when his friend carried him the news—and he was continually at Howard's elbow during the two dances.— The frequency of his appearance there, was the only unpleasant part of her engagement, the only objection she could make to Mr. Howard.—In himself, she thought him as agreeable as he looked; though chatting on the commonest topics he had a sensible, unaffected way of expressing himself, which made them all worth hearing, and she only regretted that he had not been able to make his pupil's manners as unexceptionable as his own.—The two dances seemed very short, and she had her partner's authority for considering them so.—At their conclusion the Osbornes and their train were all on the move.

"We are off at last," said his Lordship to Tom—"How much longer do *you* stay in this heavenly place?—till sunrise?"—

"No, faith! my Lord, I have had quite enough of it I assure you—I shall not shew myself here again when I have had the honour of attending Lady Osborne to her carriage. I shall retreat in as much secrecy as possible to the most remote corner of the house, where I shall order a barrel of oysters, and be famously snug."

"Let us see you soon at the Castle; and bring me word how she looks by daylight."—

Emma and Mrs. Blake parted as old acquaintance, and Charles shook her by the hand and wished her "good bye" at least a dozen times. From Miss Osborne and Miss Carr she received something like a jerking curtsey as they passed her; even Lady Osborne gave her a look of complacency—and his Lordship actually came back after the others were out of the room, to "beg her pardon", and look in the window seat behind her for the gloves which were visibly compressed in his hand.—

As Tom Musgrave was seen no more, we may suppose his plan to have succeeded, and imagine him mortifying with his barrel of oysters, in dreary solitude—or gladly assisting the landlady in her bar to make fresh negus for the happy dancers above.

Emma could not help missing the party, by whom she had been, though in some respects unpleasantly, distinguished, and the two dances which followed and concluded the ball were rather flat, in comparison with the others.—Mr. Edwards having played with good luck, they were some of the last in the room—

"Here we are, back again I declare—" said Emma sorrowfully, as she walked into the dining room, where the table was prepared, and the neat upper maid was lighting the candles—"My dear Miss Edwards—how soon it is at an end!—I wish it could all come over again!—"

A great deal of kind pleasure was expressed in her having enjoyed the evening so much—and Mr. Edwards was as warm as herself, in praise of the fullness, brilliancy and spirit of the meeting; though as he had been fixed the whole time at the same table in the same room, with only one change of chairs, it might have seemed a matter scarcely perceived.—But he had won four rubbers out of five, and everything went well. His daughter felt the advantage of this gratified state of mind, in the course of the remarks and retrospections which now ensued, over the welcome soup.—

"How came you not to dance with either of the Mr. Tomlinsons, Mary?—" said her mother.

"I was always engaged when they asked me."

[*104*]

"I thought you were to have stood up with Mr. James, the two last dances; Mrs. Tomlinson told me he was gone to ask you—and I had heard you say two minutes before that you were *not* engaged.—"

"Yes—but—there was a mistake—I had misunderstood—I did not know I was engaged—I thought it had been for the two dances after, if we staid so long—but Captain Hunter assured me it was for those very two.—"—

"So, you ended with Captain Hunter Mary, did you?" said her father. "And who did you begin with?"

"Captain Hunter" was repeated, in a very humble tone.—

"Hum!—That is being constant however. But who else did you dance with?"

"Mr. Norton, and Mr. Styles."

"And who are they?"

"Mr. Norton is a cousin of Captain Hunter's."—

"And who is Mr. Styles?"

"One of his particular friends."—

"All in the same regiment," added Mrs. Edwards.—"Mary was surrounded by red coats the whole evening. I should have been better pleased to see her dancing with some of our old neighbours I confess.—"

"Yes, yes, we must not neglect our old neighbours—. But if these soldiers are quicker than other people in a ball room, what are young ladies to do?"

"I think there is no occasion for their engaging themselves so many dances beforehand, Mr. Edwards."—

"No—perhaps not—but I remember my dear when you and I did the same."—

Mrs. Edwards said no more, and Mary breathed again.—A great deal of good-humoured pleasantry followed—and Emma went to bed in charming spirits, her head full of Osbornes, Blakes and Howards.—

The next morning brought a great many visitors. It was the way of the place always to call on Mrs. Edwards on the morning after a ball, and this neighbourly inclination was increased in the present instance by a general spirit of curiosity on Emma's account, as everybody wanted to look again at the girl who had been admired the night before by Lord Osborne—.

Many were the eyes, and various the degrees of approbation with which she was examined. Some saw no fault, and some no beauty—. With some her brown skin was the annihilation of every grace, and others could never be persuaded that she were half so handsome as Elizabeth Watson had been ten years ago.—

The morning passed quietly away in discussing the merits of the ball with all this succession of company—and Emma was at once astonished by finding it two o'clock, and considering that she had heard nothing of her father's chair. After this discovery she had walked twice to the window to examine the street, and was on the point of asking leave to ring the bell and make enquiries, when the light sound of a carriage driving up to the door set her heart at ease. She stepped again to the window—but instead of the convenient though very un-smart family equipage perceived a neat curricle.—Mr. Musgrave was shortly afterwards announced;—and Mrs. Edwards put on her very stiffest look at the sound.—Not at all dismayed however by her chilling air, he paid his compliments to each of the ladies with no unbecoming ease, and continuing to address Emma, presented her a note, which he had "the honour of bringing from her sister; but to which he must observe that a verbal postscript from himself would be requisite."—

The note, which Emma was beginning to read rather *before* Mrs. Edwards had entreated her to use no ceremony, contained a few lines from Elizabeth importing that their father in consequence of being unusually well had taken the sudden resolution of attending the visitation that day, and that as his road lay quite wide from R. it was impossible for her to come home till the following morning, unless the Edwardses would send her, which was hardly to be expected, or she could meet with any chance conveyance, or did not mind walking so far.—She had scarcely run her eye through the whole, before she found herself obliged to listen to Tom Musgrave's farther account.

"I received that note from the fair hands of Miss Watson only ten minutes ago," said he—"I met her in the village of Stanton, whither my good stars prompted me to turn my horses' heads—she was at that moment in quest of a person to employ on the errand, and I was fortunate enough to convince her that she could not find a more willing or speedy messenger than myself—. Remember, I say nothing of my disinterestedness.—My reward is to be the indulgence of conveying you to Stanton in my curricle.—Though they are not written down, I bring your sister's orders for the same.—"

Emma felt distressed; she did not like the proposal—she did not wish to be on terms of intimacy with the proposer—and yet fearful of encroaching on the Edwardses, as well as wishing to go home herself, she was at a loss how entirely to decline what he offered—. Mrs. Edwards continued silent, either not understanding the case, or waiting to see how the young lady's inclination lay. Emma thanked him—but professed herself very unwilling to give him so much trouble. "The trouble was of course, honour, pleasure, delight. What had he or his horses to do?"—Still she hesitated. "She believed she must beg leave to decline his assistance—She was rather afraid of the sort of carriage—. The distance was not beyond a walk.—"—

Mrs. Edwards was silent no longer. She enquired into the particulars—and then said, "We shall be extremely happy, Miss Emma, if you can give us the pleasure of your company till tomorrow—but if you can not conveniently do so, our carriage is quite at your service, and Mary will be pleased with the opportunity of seeing your sister."—

This was precisely what Emma had longed for, and she accepted the offer most thankfully; acknowledging that as Elizabeth was entirely alone, it was her wish to return home to dinner.—The plan was warmly opposed by their visitor.

"I cannot suffer it indeed. I must not be deprived of the happiness of escorting you. I assure you there is not a possibility of fear with my horses. You might guide them yourself. *Your sisters* all know how quiet they are; they have none of them the smallest scruple in trusting themselves with me, even on a race-course.—Believe me—" added he lowering his voice—"*You* are quite safe, the danger is only *mine*."—Emma was not more disposed to oblige him for all this.—"And as to Mrs. Edwards's carriage being used the day after a ball, it is a thing quite out of rule I assure you—never heard of before—the old coachman will look as black as his horses—. Won't he Miss Edwards?"—No notice was taken. The ladies were silently firm, and the gentleman found himself obliged to submit.—

"What a famous ball we had last night!—" he cried, after a short pause. "How long did you keep it up, after the Osbornes and I went away?"—

"We had two dances more."—

"It is making it too much of a fatigue I think, to stay so late.—I suppose your set was not a very full one."—

"Yes, quite as full as ever, except the Osbornes. There seemed no vacancy anywhere—and everybody danced with uncommon spirit to the very last."—Emma said this—though against her conscience.—

"Indeed! perhaps I might have looked in upon you again, if I had been aware of as much;—for I am rather fond of dancing than not.—Miss Osborne is a charming girl, is not she?"

"I do not think her handsome," replied Emma, to whom all this was chiefly addressed.

"Perhaps she is not critically handsome, but her manners are delightful. And Fanny Carr is a most interesting little creature. You can imagine nothing more *naive* or *piquante*; and what do you think of *Lord Osborne*, Miss Watson?"

"That he would be handsome, even though he were *not* a Lord—and perhaps—better bred; more desirous of pleasing, and shewing himself pleased in a right place.—"

"Upon my word, you are severe upon my friend!—I assure you Lord Osborne is a very good fellow."—

"I do not dispute his virtues—but I do not like his careless air."—

"If it were not a breach of confidence," replied Tom with an important look, "perhaps I might be able to win a more favourable opinion of poor Osborne.—"

Emma gave him no encouragement, and he was obliged to keep his friend's secret.—He was also obliged to put an end to his visit—for Mrs. Edwards having ordered her carriage, there was no time to be lost on Emma's side in preparing for it.—Miss Edwards accompanied her home, but as it was dinner hour at Stanton, staid with them only a few minutes.—

"Now my dear Emma," said Miss Watson, as soon as they were alone, "you must talk to me all the rest of the day, without stopping, or I shall not be satisfied. But first of all Nanny shall bring in the dinner. Poor thing!—You will not dine as you did yesterday, for we have nothing but some fried beef.—How nice Mary Edwards looks in her new pelisse!—And now tell me how you like them all, and what I am to say to Sam. I have begun my letter, Jack Stokes is to call for it tomorrow, for his uncle is going within a mile of Guilford the next day.—"

Nanny brought in the dinner.—

"We will wait upon ourselves," continued Elizabeth, "and then we shall lose no time.—And so, you would not come home with Tom Musgrave?"—

"No. You had said so much against him that I could not wish either for the obligation, or the intimacy which the use of his carriage must have created—. I should not even have liked the appearance of it."—

"You did very right; though I wonder at your forbearance, and I do not think I could have done it myself.—He seemed so eager to fetch you, that I could not say no, though it rather went against me to be throwing you together, so well as I knew his tricks;—but I did long to see you, and it was a clever way of getting you home; besides—it won't do to be too nice.—Nobody could have thought of the Edwardses letting you have their coach,—after the horses being out so late.—But what am I to say to Sam?"—

"If you are guided by me, you will not encourage him to think of Miss Edwards.—The father is decidedly against him, the mother shews him no favour, and I doubt his having any interest with Mary. She danced twice with Captain Hunter, and I think shews him in general as much encouragement as is consistent with her disposition, and the circumstances she is placed in.—She once mentioned Sam, and certainly with a little confusion—but that was perhaps merely owing to the consciousness of his liking her, which may very probably have come to her knowledge."—

"Oh! dear! yes—she has heard enough of that from us all. Poor Sam!—He is out of luck as well as other people.—For the life of me, Emma, I cannot help feeling for those that are crossed in love.—Well—now begin, and give me an account of every thing as it happened.—"

Emma obeyed her—and Elizabeth listened with very little interruption till she heard of Mr. Howard as a partner.—

"Dance with Mr. Howard—Good heavens! You don't say so!—Why—he is quite one of the great and grand ones.—Did not you find him very high?—"

"His manners are of a kind to give *me* much more ease and confidence than Tom Musgrave's."

"Well—go on. I should have been frightened out of my wits, to have had anything to do with the Osbornes' set."—Emma concluded her narration.—"And so, you really did not dance with Tom Musgrave at all?—But you must have liked him, you must have been struck with him altogether."—

"I do *not* like him, Elizabeth—. I allow his person and air to be good—and that his manners to a certain point—his address rather—is pleasing.—But I see nothing else to admire in him.—On the contrary, he seems very vain, very conceited, absurdly anxious for distinction, and absolutely contemptible in some of the measures he takes for becoming so.—There is a ridiculousness about him that entertains me—but his company gives me no other agreeable emotion."

"My dearest Emma!—You are like nobody else in the world.—It is well Margaret is not by.—You do not offend *me*, though I hardly know how to believe you. But Margaret would never forgive such words."

"I wish Margaret could have heard him profess his ignorance of her being out of the country;—he declared it seemed only two days since he had seen her.—"

"Aye—that is just like him. And yet this is the man, she *will* fancy so desperately in love with her.—He is no favourite of mine, as you well know, Emma;—but you must think him agreeable. Can you lay your hand on your heart, and say you do not?"—

"Indeed I can. Both hands; and spread to their widest extent.—"

"I should like to know the man you *do* think agreeable."

"His name is Howard."

"Howard! Dear me. I cannot think of *him*, but as playing cards with Lady Osborne, and looking proud.—I must own however that it *is* a relief to me, to find you can speak as you do, of Tom Musgrave; my heart did misgive me that you would like him too well. You talked so stoutly beforehand, that I was sadly afraid your brag would be punished.—I only hope it will last;—and that he will not come on to pay you much attention; it is a hard thing for a woman to stand against the flattering ways of a man, when he is bent upon pleasing her.—"

As their quietly-sociable little meal concluded, Miss Watson could not help observing how comfortably it had passed.

"It is so delightful to me," said she, "to have things going on in peace and good humour. Nobody can tell how much I hate quarrelling. Now, though we have had nothing but fried beef, how good it has all seemed.—I wish everybody were as easily satisfied as you—but poor Margaret is very snappish, and Penelope owns she had rather have quarrelling going on, than nothing at all."—

Mr. Watson returned in the evening, not the worse for the exertion of the day, and consequently pleased with what he had done, and glad to talk of it, over his own fireside.—Emma had not foreseen any interest to herself in the occurrences of a visitation—but when she heard Mr. Howard spoken of as the preacher, and as having given them an excellent sermon, she could not help listening with a quicker ear.—

"I do not know when I have heard a discourse more to my mind—" continued Mr. Watson—"or one better delivered.—He reads extremely well, with great propriety and in a very impressive manner; and at the same time without any theatrical grimace or violence.—I own, I do not like much action in the pulpit—I do not like the studied air and artificial inflexions of voice, which your very popular and most admired preachers generally have.—A simple delivery is much better calculated to inspire devotion, and shews a much better taste.—Mr. Howard read like a scholar and a gentleman."—

"And what had you for dinner Sir?" said his eldest daughter.—

He related the dishes and told what he had ate himself. "Upon the whole," he added, "I have had a very comfortable day; my old friends were quite surprised to see me amongst them—and I must say that everybody paid me great attention, and seemed to feel for me as an invalid.—They would make me sit near the fire, and as the partridges were pretty high, Dr. Richards would have them sent away to the other end of the table, that they might not offend Mr. Watson—which I thought very kind of him.—But what pleased me as much as anything was Mr. Howard's attention.—There is a pretty steep flight of steps up to the room we dine in—which do not quite agree with my gouty foot—and Mr. Howard walked by me from the bottom to the top, and would make me take his arm.—It struck me as very becoming in so young a man, but I am sure I had no claim to expect it; for I never saw him before in my life.—By the bye, he enquired after one of my daughters, but I do not know which. I suppose you know among yourselves."—

On the third day after the ball, as Nanny, at five minutes before three, was beginning to bustle into the parlour with the tray and the knife-case, she was suddenly called to the front door, by the sound of as smart a rap as the end of a riding-whip could give—and though charged by Miss Watson to let nobody in, returned in half a minute, with a look of awkward dismay, to hold the parlour door open for Lord Osborne and Tom Musgrave.—The surprise of the young ladies may be imagined. No visitors would have been welcome at such a moment; but such visitors as these—such a one as Lord Osborne at least, a nobleman and a stranger, was really distressing.—He looked a little embarrassed himself,—as, on being introduced by his easy, voluble friend, he muttered something of doing himself the honour of waiting on Mr. Watson.—

Though Emma could not but take the compliment of the visit to herself, she was very far from enjoying it. She felt all the inconsistency of such an acquaintance with the very humble stile in which they were obliged to live; and having in her aunt's family been used to many of the elegancies of life, was fully sensible of all that must be open to the ridicule of richer people in her present home.—Of the pain of such feelings, Elizabeth knew very little;—her simpler mind, or juster reason, saved her from such mortification—and though shrinking under a general sense of inferiority, she felt no particular shame.—Mr. Watson, as the gentlemen had already heard from Nanny, was not well enough to be down stairs.—With much concern they took their seats—Lord Osborne near Emma, and the convenient Mr. Musgrave in high spirits at his own importance, on the other side of the fireplace with Elizabeth.—*He* was at no loss for words;—but when Lord Osborne had hoped that Emma had not caught cold at the ball, he had nothing more to say for some time, and could only gratify his eye by occasional glances at his fair neighbour.—Emma was not inclined to give herself much trouble for his entertainment—and after hard labour of mind, he produced the remark of its being a very fine day, and followed it up with the question of, "Have you been walking this morning?"

"No, my Lord. We thought it too dirty."

"You should wear half-boots."—

After another pause, "Nothing sets off a neat ancle more than a half-boot; nankin galoshed with black looks very well.—Do not you like half-boots?"

"Yes—but unless they are so stout as to injure their beauty, they are not fit for country walking.—"

"Ladies should ride in dirty weather.—Do you ride?"

"No my Lord."

"I wonder every lady does not.—A woman never looks better than on horseback.—"

"But every woman may not have the inclination, or the means."

"If they knew how much it became them, they would all have the inclination—and I fancy Miss Watson—when once they had the inclination, the means would soon follow."—

"Your Lordship thinks we always have our own way.—*That* is a point on which ladies and gentlemen have long disagreed.—But without pretending to decide it, I may say that there are some circumstances which even *women* cannot controul.—Female economy will do a great deal my Lord, but it cannot turn a small income into a large one."—

Lord Osborne was silenced. Her manner had been neither sententious nor sarcastic, but there was a something in its mild seriousness, as well as in the words themselves, which made his Lordship think;—and when he addressed her again, it was with a degree of considerate propriety, totally unlike the half-awkward, half-fearless stile of his former remarks.—It was a new thing with him to wish to please a woman; it was the first time that he had ever felt what was due to a woman, in Emma's situation.—But as he wanted neither sense nor a good disposition, he did not feel it without effect.—

"You have not been long in this country I understand," said he in the tone of a gentleman. "I hope you are pleased with it."—

He was rewarded by a gracious answer, and a more liberal full view of her face than she had yet bestowed. Unused to exert himself, and happy in contemplating her, he then sat in silence for some minutes longer, while Tom Musgrave was chattering to Elizabeth, till they were interrupted by Nanny's approach, who half opening the door and putting in her head, said, "Please Ma'am, master wants to know why he be'nt to have his dinner."—

The gentlemen, who had hitherto disregarded every symptom, however positive, of the nearness of that meal, now jumped up with apologies, while Elizabeth called briskly after Nanny "to tell Betty to take up the fowls."—

"I am sorry it happens so—" she added, turning good humouredly towards Musgrave—"but you know what early hours we keep.—"

Tom had nothing to say for himself, he knew it very well, and such honest simplicity, such shameless truth rather bewildered him.—Lord Osborne's parting compliments took some time, his inclination for speech seeming to increase with the shortness of the term for indulgence.—He recommended exercise in defiance of dirt—spoke again in praise of half-boots—begged that his sister might be allowed to send Emma the name of her shoemaker—and concluded with saying,

"My hounds will be hunting this country next week—I believe they will throw off at Stanton Wood on Wednesday—at nine o'clock.—I mention this, in hopes of your being drawn out to see what's going on.—If the morning's tolerable, pray do us the honour of giving us your good wishes in person."

The sisters looked on each other with astonishment, when their visitors had withdrawn.

"Here's an unaccountable honour!" cried Elizabeth at last. "Who would have thought of Lord Osborne's coming to Stanton.—He is very handsome;—but Tom Musgrave looks, all to nothing, the smartest and most fashionable man of the two. I am glad he did not say anything to me; I would not have had to talk to such a great man for the world. Tom was very agreeable, was not he?—But did you hear him ask where Miss Penelope and Miss Margaret were, when he first came in?—It put me out of patience.—I am glad Nanny had not laid the cloth however, it would have looked so awkward;—just the tray did not signify.—"

To say that Emma was not flattered by Lord Osborne's visit, would be to assert a very unlikely thing, and describe a very odd young lady; but the gratification was by no means unalloyed; his coming was a sort of notice which might please her vanity, but did not suit her pride, and she would rather have known that he wished the visit without presuming to make it, than have seen him at Stanton.—Among other unsatisfactory feelings it once occurred to her to wonder why Mr. Howard had not taken the same privilege of coming, and accompanied his Lordship—but she was willing to suppose that he had either known nothing about it, or had declined any share in a measure which carried quite as much impertinence in its form as good breeding.—

Mr. Watson was very far from being delighted, when he heard what had passed;—a little peevish under immediate pain, and ill-disposed to be pleased, he only replied—"Phoo! phoo!—what occasion could there be for Lord Osborne's coming. I have lived here fourteen years without being noticed by any of the family. It is some foolery of that idle fellow Tom Musgrave. I cannot return the visit.—I would not if I could." And when Tom Musgrave was met with again, he was commissioned with a message of excuse to Osborne Castle, on the too-sufficient plea of Mr. Watson's infirm state of health.—

A week or ten days rolled quietly away after this visit, before any new bustle arose to interrupt, even for half a day, the tranquil and affectionate intercourse of the two sisters, whose mutual regard was increasing with the intimate knowledge of each other which such intercourse produced.—The first circumstance to break in on this serenity was the receipt of a letter from Croydon to announce the speedy return of Margaret, and a visit of two or three days from Mr. and Mrs. Robert Watson, who undertook to bring her home and wished to see their sister Emma.—It was an expectation to fill the thoughts of the sisters at Stanton, and to busy the hours of one of them at least—for as Jane had been a woman of fortune, the preparations for her entertainment were considerable, and as Elizabeth had at all times more good will than method in her guidance of the house, she could make no change without a bustle.—An absence of fourteen years had made all her brothers and sisters strangers to Emma, but in her expectation of Margaret there was more than the awkwardness of such an alienation; she had heard things which made her dread her return; and the day which brought the party to Stanton seemed to her the probable conclusion of almost all that had been comfortable in the house.—

Robert Watson was an attorney at Croydon, in a good way of business; very well satisfied with himself for the same, and for having married the only daughter of the attorney to whom he had been clerk, with a fortune of six thousand pounds.—Mrs. Robert was not less pleased with herself for having had that six thousand pounds, and for being now in possession of a very smart house in Croydon, where she gave genteel parties, and wore fine clothes.—In her person there was nothing remarkable; her manners were pert and conceited.—

Margaret was not without beauty; she had a slight, pretty figure, and rather wanted countenance* than good features;—but the sharp and anxious expression of her face made her beauty in general little felt.—On meeting her long-absent sister, as on every occasion of shew, her manner was all affection and her voice all gentleness; continual smiles and a very slow articulation being her constant resource when determined on pleasing.—

She was now so "delighted to see dear, dear Emma" that she could hardly speak a word in a minute.—"I am sure we shall be great friends—" she observed, with much sentiment, as they were sitting together.—

Emma scarcely knew how to answer such a proposition—and the manner in which it was spoken, she could not attempt to equal. Mrs. Robert Watson eyed her with much familiar curiosity and triumphant compassion;—the loss of the aunt's fortune was uppermost in her mind, at the moment of meeting;—and she could not but feel how much better it was to be the daughter of a gentleman of property in Croydon, than the niece of an old woman who threw herself away on an Irish captain.—Robert was carelessly kind, as became a prosperous man and a brother; more intent on settling with the post-boy, inveighing against the exorbitant advance in posting, and pondering over a doubtful halfcrown, than on welcoming a sister, who was no longer likely to have any property for him to get the direction of.—

"Your road through the village is infamous, Elizabeth," said he; "worse than ever it was. By heaven! I would endite it if I lived near you. Who is surveyor now?"—

There was a little niece at Croydon, to be fondly enquired after by the kind-hearted Elizabeth, who regretted very much her not being of the party.—

"You are very good—" replied her mother—"and I assure you it went very hard with Augusta to have us come away without her. I was forced to say we were only going to church and promise to come back for her directly.—But you know it would not do, to bring

---

* **Countenance**: an appropriate demeanour, including facial expression.

her without her maid, and I am as particular as ever in having her properly attended to."

"Sweet little darling!—" cried Margaret.—"It quite broke my heart to leave her.—"

"Then why was you in such a hurry to run away from her?" cried Mrs. Robert.—"You are a sad shabby girl.—I have been quarrelling with you all the way we came, have not I?—Such a visit as this, I never heard of!—You know how glad we are to have any of you with us—if it be for months together.—And I am sorry, (with a witty smile) we have not been able to make Croydon agreeable this Autumn."—

"My dearest Jane—do not overpower me with your raillery.—You know what inducements I had to bring me home.—Spare me, I entreat you—I am no match for your arch sallies."—

"Well, I only beg you will not set your neighbours against the place.—Perhaps Emma may be tempted to go back with us, and stay till Christmas, if you don't put in your word."—Emma was greatly obliged. "I assure you we have very good society at Croydon.—I do not much attend the balls, they are rather too mixed,—but our parties are very select and good.—I had seven tables last week in my drawing room.—Are you fond of the country? How do you like Stanton?"—

"Very much"—replied Emma, who thought a comprehensive answer most to the purpose.—She saw that her sister in law despised her immediately.—Mrs. Robert Watson was indeed wondering what sort of a home Emma could possibly have been used to in Shropshire, and setting it down as certain that the aunt could never have had six thousand pounds.—

"How charming Emma is!—" whispered Margaret to Mrs. Robert in her most languishing tone.—

Emma was quite distressed by such behaviour;—and she did not like it better when she heard Margaret five minutes afterwards say to Elizabeth in a sharp quick accent, totally unlike the first—

"Have you heard from Penelope since she went to Chichester?—I had a letter the other day.—I don't find she is likely to make anything of it. I fancy she'll come back 'Miss Penelope' as she went.—"—

Such, she feared would be Margaret's common voice, when the novelty of her own appearance were over; the tone of artificial sensibility was not recommended by the idea.—The ladies were invited upstairs to prepare for dinner.

"I hope you will find things tolerably comfortable Jane"—said Elizabeth as she opened the door of the spare bedchamber.—

"My good creature," replied Jane, "use no ceremony with me, I intreat you. I am one of those who always take things as they find them. I hope I can put up with a small apartment for two or three nights, without making a piece of work. I always wish to be treated quite 'en famille' when I come to see you—and now I do hope you have not been getting a great dinner for us.—Remember we never eat suppers."—

"I suppose," said Margaret rather quickly to Emma, "you and I are to be together; Elizabeth always takes care to have a room to herself."—

"No—Elizabeth gives me half hers."—

"Oh!—(in a softened voice, and rather mortified to find that she was not ill used) I am sorry I am not to have the pleasure of your company—especially as it makes me nervous to be much alone."—

Emma was the first of the females in the parlour again; on entering it she found her brother alone.—

"So Emma," said he, "you are quite the stranger at home. It must seem odd enough to you to be here.—A pretty piece of work your aunt Turner has made of it!—By heaven! a woman should never be trusted with money. I always said she ought to have settled something on you, as soon as her husband died."

"But that would have been trusting *me* with money," replied Emma, "and *I* am a woman too.—"

"It might have been secured to your future use, without your having any power over it now.—What a blow it must have been upon you!—To find yourself, instead of heiress of eight or nine thousand pounds, sent back a weight upon your family, without a sixpence.—I hope the old woman will smart for it."

"Do not speak disrespectfully of her—she was very good to me; and if she has made an imprudent choice, she will suffer more from it herself, than *I* can possibly do."

"I do not mean to distress you, but you know every body must think her an old fool.—I thought Turner had been reckoned an extraordinary sensible, clever man.—How the devil came he to make such a will?"—

"My uncle's sense is not at all impeached, in my opinion, by his attachment to my aunt. She had been an excellent wife to him. The most liberal and enlightened minds are always the most confiding.—The event has been unfortunate, but my uncle's memory is if possible endeared to me by such a proof of tender respect for my aunt."—

"That's odd sort of talking!—He might have provided decently for his widow, without leaving every thing that he had to dispose of, or any part of it, at her mercy.—"

"My aunt may have erred—" said Emma warmly—"she *has* erred—but my uncle's conduct was faultless. I was her own niece, and he left to herself the power and the pleasure of providing for me."—

"But unluckily she has left the pleasure of providing for you, to your father, and without the power.—That's the long and the short of the business. After keeping you at a distance from your family for such a length of time as must do away all natural affection among us and breeding you up (I suppose) in a superior stile, you are returned upon their hands without a sixpence."

"You know," replied Emma struggling with her tears, "my uncle's melancholy state of health.—He was a greater invalid than my father. He could not leave home."

"I do not mean to make you cry—" said Robert rather softened—and after a short silence, by way of changing the subject, he added—"I am just come from my father's room, he seems very indifferent. It will be a sad break-up when he dies. Pity, you can none of you get married!—You must come to Croydon as well as the rest, and see what you can do there.—I believe if Margaret had had a thousand or fifteen hundred pounds, there was a young man who would have thought of her."

Emma was glad when they were joined by the others; it was better to look at her sister in law's finery, than listen to Robert, who had equally irritated and grieved her.—Mrs. Robert, exactly as smart as she had been at her own party, came in with apologies for her dress—

"I would not make you wait," said she, "so I put on the first thing I met with.—I am afraid I am a sad figure.—My dear Mr. Watson—(to her husband) you have not put any fresh powder in your hair."—

"No—I do not intend it.—I think there is powder enough in my hair for my wife and sisters."—

"Indeed you ought to make some alteration in your dress before dinner when you are out visiting, though you do not at home."

"Nonsense.—"

"It is very odd you should not like to do what other gentlemen do. Mr. Marshall and Mr. Hemmings change their dress every day of their lives before dinner. And what was the use of my putting up your last new coat, if you are never to wear it."—

"Do be satisfied with being fine yourself, and leave your husband alone."—

To put an end to this altercation, and soften the evident vexation of her sister in law, Emma, (though in no spirits to make such nonsense easy) began to admire her gown.—It produced immediate complacency.—

"Do you like it?—" said she.—"I am very happy.—It has been excessively admired;—but sometimes I think the pattern too large.—I shall wear one tomorrow that I think you will prefer to this.—Have you seen the one I gave Margaret?"—

Dinner came, and except when Mrs. Robert looked at her husband's head, she continued gay and flippant, chiding Elizabeth for the profusion on the table, and absolutely protesting against the entrance of the roast turkey—which formed the only exception to "You see your dinner".—

"I do beg and entreat that no turkey may be seen to day. I am really frightened out of my wits with the number of dishes we have already. Let us have no turkey I beseech you."—

"My dear," replied Elizabeth, "the turkey is roasted, and it may just as well come in, as stay in the kitchen. Besides, if it is cut, I am in hopes my father may be tempted to eat a bit, for it is rather a favourite dish."

"You may have it in my dear, but I assure you *I* shan't touch it."—

Mr. Watson had not been well enough to join the party at dinner, but was prevailed on to come down and drink tea with them.—

"I wish we may be able to have a game of cards tonight," said Elizabeth to Mrs. Robert after seeing her father comfortably seated in his arm chair.—

"Not on my account my dear, I beg. You know I am no card player. I think a snug chat infinitely better. I always say cards are very well sometimes, to break a formal circle, but one never wants them among friends."

"I was thinking of its being something to amuse my father," answered Elizabeth—"if it was not disagreeable to you. He says his head won't bear whist—but perhaps if we make a round game he may be tempted to sit down with us."—

"By all means my dear creature. I am quite at your service. Only do not oblige me to chuse the game, that's all. *Speculation* is the only round game at Croydon now, but I can play any thing.—When there is only one or two of you at home, you must be quite at a loss to amuse him—why do not you get him to play at cribbage?—Margaret and I have played at cribbage, most nights that we have not been engaged."—

A sound like a distant carriage was at this moment caught; every body listened, it became more decided; it certainly drew nearer.—It was an unusual sound in Stanton at any time of the day, for the village was on no very public road, and contained no gentleman's family but the rector's.—The wheels rapidly approached;—in two minutes the general expectation was answered; they stopped beyond a doubt at the garden gate of the parsonage. "Who could it be?—it was certainly a postchaise.—Penelope was the only creature to be thought of. She might perhaps have met with some unexpected opportunity of returning."—A pause of suspense ensued.—Steps were distinguished, first along the paved footway which led under the windows of the house to the front door, and then within the passage. They were the steps of a man. It could not be Penelope. It must be Samuel.—The door opened, and displayed Tom Musgrave in the wrap of a traveller.—He had been in London and was now on his way home, and he had come half a mile out of his road merely to call for ten minutes at Stanton. He loved to take people by surprise, with sudden visits at extraordinary seasons; and in the present instance had had the additional motive of being able to tell the Miss Watsons, whom he depended on finding sitting quietly employed after tea, that he was going home to an eight o'clock dinner.—

As it happened however, he did not give more surprise than he received, when instead of being shewn into the usual little sitting room, the door of the best parlour a foot larger each way than the other was thrown open, and he beheld a circle of smart people whom he could not immediately recognise arranged with all the honours of visiting round the fire, and Miss Watson sitting at the best pembroke table, with the best tea things before her. He stood a few seconds, in silent amazement.—

"Musgrave!"—ejaculated Margaret in a tender voice.—

He recollected himself, and came forward, delighted to find such a circle of friends, and blessing his good fortune for the unlooked-for indulgence.—He shook hands with Robert, bowed and smiled to the ladies, and did everything very prettily; but as to any particularity of address or emotion towards Margaret, Emma, who closely observed him, perceived nothing that did not justify Elizabeth's opinions though Margaret's modest smiles imported that she meant to take the visit to herself.—

He was persuaded without much difficulty to throw off his great coat, and drink tea with them. "For whether he dined at eight or nine, as he observed, was a matter of very little consequence"—and without seeming to seek, he did not turn away from the chair close to Margaret which she was assiduous in providing him.—She had thus secured him from her sisters—but it was not immediately in her power to preserve him from her brother's claims, for as he came avowedly from London, and had left it only four hours ago, the last current report as to public news, and the general opinion of the day must be understood, before Robert could let his attention be yielded to the less national, and important demands of the women.—At last however he was at liberty to hear Margaret's soft address, as she spoke her fears of his having had a most terrible, cold, dark, dreadful journey.—

"Indeed you should not have set out so late.—"

"I could not be earlier," he replied. "I was detained chatting at the Bedford, by a friend.—All hours are alike to me.—How long have you been in the country Miss Margaret?"—

"We came only this morning.—My kind brother and sister brought me home this very morning.—'Tis singular is not it?"

"You were gone a great while, were not you? a fortnight I suppose?"—

"*You* may call a fortnight a great while Mr. Musgrave," said Mrs. Robert smartly—"but *we* think a month very little. I assure you we bring her home at the end of a month, much against our will."

"A month! have you really been gone a month! 'tis amazing how time flies.—"

"You may imagine," said Margaret in a sort of whisper, "what are my sensations in finding myself once more at Stanton. You know what a sad visitor I make.—And I was so excessively impatient to see Emma;—I dreaded the meeting, and at the same time longed for it.—Do not you comprehend the sort of feeling?"—

"Not at all," cried he aloud. "I could never dread a meeting with Miss Emma Watson,—or any of her sisters." It was lucky that he added that finish.—

"Were you speaking to me?—" said Emma, who had caught her own name.—

"Not absolutely—" he answered—"but I was thinking of you,—as many at a greater distance are probably doing at this moment.— Fine open weather Miss Emma!—Charming season for hunting."

"Emma is delightful, is not she?—" whispered Margaret. "I have found her more than answer my warmest hopes.—Did you ever see any thing more perfectly beautiful?—I think even *you* must be a convert to a brown complexion."—

He hesitated; Margaret was fair herself, and he did not particularly want to compliment her; but Miss Osborne and Miss Carr were likewise fair, and his devotion to them carried the day.

"Your sister's complexion," said he at last, "is as fine as a dark complexion can be, but I still profess my preference of a white skin. You have seen Miss Osborne?—She is my model for a truly feminine complexion, and she is very fair."—

"Is she fairer than me?"—

Tom made no reply.—

"Upon my honour ladies," said he, giving a glance over his own person, "I am highly endebted to your condescension for admitting me, in such dishabille, into your drawing room. I really did not consider how unfit I was to be here, or I hope I should have kept my distance. Lady Osborne would tell me that I were growing as careless as her son, if she saw me in this condition."—

The ladies were not wanting in civil returns; and Robert Watson, stealing a view of his own head in an opposite glass, said with equal civility,

"You cannot be more in dishabille than myself.—We got here so late, that I had not time even to put a little fresh powder in my hair."—

Emma could not help entering into what she supposed her sister in law's feelings at that moment.—

When the tea things were removed, Tom began to talk of his carriage—but the old card table being set out, and the fish and counters with a tolerably clean pack brought forward from the beaufit by Miss Watson, the general voice was so urgent with him to join their party, that he agreed to allow himself another quarter of an hour. Even Emma was pleased that he would stay, for she was beginning to feel that a family party might be the worst of all parties; and the others were delighted.—

"What's your game?"—cried he, as they stood round the table.—

"Speculation I believe," said Elizabeth.—"My sister recommends it, and I fancy we all like it. I know *you* do, Tom."—

"It is the only round game played at Croydon now," said Mrs. Robert—"we never think of any other. I am glad it is a favourite with you."—

"Oh! me!" cried Tom. "Whatever you decide on, will be a favourite with *me*.—I have had some pleasant hours at Speculation in my time—but I have not been in the way of it now for a long while.—Vingt-un is the game at Osborne Castle; I have played nothing but Vingt-un of late. You would be astonished to hear the noise we make there.—The fine old, lofty drawing-room rings again. Lady Osborne sometimes declares she cannot hear herself speak.—Lord Osborne enjoys it famously and he makes the best dealer without exception that I ever beheld—such quickness and spirit! he lets nobody dream over their cards.—I wish you could see him overdraw himself on both his own cards—it is worth any thing in the world!"—

"Dear me!—" cried Margaret, "why should not we play at Vingt-un?—I think it is a much better game than Speculation. I cannot say I am very fond of Speculation." Mrs. Robert offered not another word in support of the game.—She was quite vanquished, and the fashions of Osborne Castle carried it over the fashions of Croydon.—

"Do you see much of the Parsonage-family at the Castle, Mr. Musgrave?—" said Emma, as they were taking their seats.—

"Oh! yes—they are almost always there. Mrs. Blake is a nice little good-humoured woman, she and I are sworn friends; and Howard's a very gentlemanlike good sort of fellow!—You are not forgotten I assure you by any of the party. I fancy you must have a little cheek-glowing now and then Miss Emma. Were not you rather warm last Saturday about nine or ten o'clock in the evening—? I will tell you how it was.—I see you are dying to know.—Says Howard to Lord Osborne—"—

At this interesting moment he was called on by the others, to regulate the game and determine some disputable point; and his attention was so totally engaged in the business and afterwards by the course of the game as never to revert to what he had been saying before;—and Emma, though suffering a good deal from curiosity, dared not remind him.—

He proved a very useful addition at their table; without him, it would have been a party of such very near relations as could have felt little interest, and perhaps maintained little complaisance, but his presence gave variety and secured good manners.—He was in fact excellently qualified to shine at a round game; and few situations made him appear to greater advantage. He played with spirit, and had a great deal to say, and though with no wit himself, could sometimes make use of the wit of an absent friend; and had a lively way of retailing a commonplace, or saying a mere nothing, that had great effect at a card table. The ways, and good jokes, of Osborne Castle were now added to his ordinary means of entertainment; he repeated the smart sayings of one lady, detailed the oversights of another, and indulged them even with a copy of Lord Osborne's stile of overdrawing himself on both cards.—

The clock struck nine, while he was thus agreeably occupied; and when Nanny came in with her master's basin of gruel, he had the pleasure of observing to Mr. Watson that he should leave him at supper, while he went home to dinner himself.—The carriage was ordered to the door—and no entreaties for his staying longer could now avail,—for he well knew, that if he staid he must sit down to supper in less than ten minutes—which to a man whose heart had been long fixed on calling his next meal a dinner, was quite insupportable.—

On finding him determined to go, Margaret began to wink and nod at Elizabeth to ask him to dinner for the following day; and Elizabeth at last not able to resist hints, which her own hospitable, social temper more than half seconded, gave the invitation. "Would he give Robert the meeting, they should be very happy."

"With the greatest pleasure"—was his first reply. In a moment afterwards—"That is if I can possibly get here in time—but I shoot with Lord Osborne, and therefore must not engage.—You will not think of me unless you see me."—And so, he departed, delighted with the uncertainty in which he had left it.—

Margaret, in the joy of her heart under circumstances which she chose to consider as peculiarly propitious, would willingly have made a confidante of Emma when they were alone for a short time the next morning; and had proceeded so far as to say—"The young man who was here last night my dear Emma and returns to day, is more interesting to me, than perhaps you may be aware—" but Emma, pretending to understand nothing extraordinary in the words, made some very inapplicable reply, and jumping up, ran away from a subject which was odious to her feelings.—

As Margaret would not allow a doubt to be repeated of Musgrave's coming to dinner, preparations were made for his entertainment much exceeding what had been deemed necessary the day before;—and taking the office of superintendance entirely from her sister, she was half the morning in the kitchen herself directing and scolding.—After a great deal of indifferent cooking and anxious suspense, however, they were obliged to sit down without their guest.—Tom Musgrave never came, and Margaret was at no pains to conceal her vexation under the disappointment, or repress the peevishness of her temper—.

The peace of the party for the remainder of that day, and the whole of the next, which comprised the length of Robert and Jane's visit, was continually invaded by her fretful displeasure, and querulous attacks.—Elizabeth was the usual object of both. Margaret had just respect enough for her brother and sister's opinion, to behave properly by *them*, but Elizabeth and the maids could never do any thing right—and Emma, whom she seemed no longer to think about, found the continuance of the gentle voice beyond her calculation short. Eager to be as little among them as possible, Emma was delighted with the alternative of sitting above, with her father, and warmly entreated to be his constant companion each evening—and as Elizabeth loved company of any kind too well, not to prefer being below, at all risks, as she had rather talk of Croydon to Jane, with every interruption of Margaret's perverseness, than sit with only her father, who frequently could not endure talking at all, the affair was so settled, as soon as she could be persuaded to believe it no sacrifice on her sister's part.—To Emma, the exchange was most acceptable, and delightful. Her father, if ill, required little more than gentleness and silence; and, being a man of sense and education, was, if able to converse, a welcome companion.—In *his* chamber, Emma was at peace from the dreadful mortifications of unequal society, and family discord—from the immediate endurance of hardhearted prosperity, low-minded conceit, and wrong-headed folly, engrafted on an untoward disposition.—She still suffered from them in the contemplation of their existence; in memory and in prospect, but for the moment, she ceased to be tortured by their effects.—She was at leisure, she could read and think,—though her situation was hardly such as to make reflection very soothing. The evils arising from the loss of her uncle were neither trifling, nor likely to lessen; and when thought had been freely indulged, in contrasting the past and the present, the employment of mind, the dissipation of unpleasant ideas which only reading could produce, made her thankfully turn to a book.—

The change in her home society and stile of life in consequence of the death of one friend and the imprudence of another had indeed been striking.—From being the first object of hope and solicitude to an uncle who had formed her mind with the care of a parent, and of tenderness to an aunt whose amiable temper had delighted to give her every indulgence, from being the life and spirit of a house, where all had been comfort and elegance, and the expected heiress of an easy independence, she was become of importance to no one, a burden on those, whose affection she could not expect, an addition in an house, already overstocked, surrounded by inferior minds with little chance of domestic comfort, and as little hope of future support.—It was well for her that she was naturally cheerful;—for the change had been such as might have plunged weak spirits in despondence.—

She was very much pressed by Robert and Jane to return with them to Croydon, and had some difficulty in getting a refusal accepted; as they thought too highly of their own kindness and situation to suppose the offer could appear in a less advantageous light to anybody else.—Elizabeth gave them her interest, though evidently against her own, in privately urging Emma to go—

"You do not know what you refuse Emma—" said she—"nor what you have to bear at home.—I would advise you by all means to accept the invitation; there is always something lively going on at Croydon. You will be in company almost every day, and Robert and Jane will be very kind to you.—As for me, I shall be no worse off without you, than I have been used to be; but poor Margaret's disagreeable ways are new to *you*, and they would vex you more than you think for, if you stay at home.—"

Emma was of course un-influenced, except to greater esteem for Elizabeth, by such representations—and the visitors departed without her.—

NOTES TO 'THE WATSONS'

ASSEMBLIES

During the autumn and winter months, most provincial towns held monthly evening assemblies at local inns or special assembly rooms, usually at full moon for ease of travelling. Designed to allow genteel young people to meet for dancing and socialising, assemblies were funded by subscriptions from patrons and attendees. As well as a dance hall, **assembly rooms** might include a **tearoom**, card room and places for changing. It was important for the prestige of an assembly that people from the higher or richer families attend; hence the enthusiasm at the Meryton assembly at the arrival of the party from Netherfield described in *Pride and Prejudice*. At a **private ball**, substantial fare would be served during an interval, but at a public assembly there would be only light refreshments such as **negus**, a drink or soup made of fortified wine and boiling water, usually flavoured with a combination of lemon, spices, sugar and calves-foot jelly.

For dancing it was considered desirable to have several **partners**; the first two dances would usually be prearranged with the same person but more than that would suggest some favouring. The power of choice was the gentleman's, of refusal the lady's, but could be politely given only if the lady had a prior engagement. This rule irks young Catherine Morland in *Northanger Abbey* when she finds herself addressed by undesirable John Thorpe instead of the interesting Henry Tilney.

For some **country dances**, the participants would stand in long lines of couples and, during the dance, move gradually down the set. To **dance down every couple** was to dance right down the set without pausing to rest, while to **call the dance** was to select the tune and figure of the dance and then lead at the top of the set. The privilege of calling moved down the ladies present according to rank. A gentleman dancing with a lady immediately before the interval would join her party of friends and relatives. When dancing, both men and women wore **gloves**, usually white. While the young people danced, their **chaperones** might converse by the fireside or play cards.

CARRIAGES

Keeping a carriage or coach was a mark of wealth and status. It required an annual income of at least £800–1,000, since it assumed a vehicle, horses, a groom and stabling. Substantial **family carriages** were 'close', with seats covered by a wooden structure; a coachman would sit upfront on a box seat. Open carriages such as the **gig** (a two-wheeled, one-horse light carriage) and more expensive **curricle** (a light two-wheeled carriage drawn by two horses) exposed passengers to the weather but were the usual vehicles for fashionable young men driving themselves.

Turnpike roads were kept up by private trusts which charged tolls used for the upkeep of the roads. These were usually in fairly good order. Local roads were the responsibility of the parish through which they passed and were often in a poorer condition. The **pitching** was a road surface of cobblestones.

DRESS

Women of the gentry and middle class dressed to keep up the family appearance. For a ball or important social visit, they would spend much time on preparing clothes and hair. Putting **hair in papers** was twisting hair round pieces of soft paper, usually overnight, so as to appear the next day as fashionable curls.

The new wardrobe for winter of the middle-class Mrs Edwards includes two **gowns** of **satin**, a luxurious silk fabric suited to the high-waisted fashion of the period, and a new **cap**, possibly quite a substantial headdress fastened with a pin and suitable for a mature woman. The **pelisse** was an outer garment, a long cloak with armhole slits and a shoulder cape or hood, often made from a rich fabric. **Half boots** for walking were fashionable but not practical on any difficult surface or muddy path; they reached above the ankle, were fastened by front laces and could be made of **nankin** or nankeen, pale yellow cotton originally from Nanking, China. Emma wears half boots for walking with Harriet in *Emma*. A **galosh** was a piece of leather round the lower part of the boot above the sole.

By 1800 **powder** for the hair (scented flour or starch) was going out of fashion for gentlemen (except for some professional men such as lawyers), but it remained a mark of status to have a liveried servant with a powdered head. In 1795 the government taxed hair powder to help pay for the expensive French Wars.

FOOD

Various types of food indicated different degrees of wealth. For a dinner with guests the dishes were usually set out together on the table so that people might choose what they wanted, but the Watsons' expensive **turkey** appears to have been served separately. A mark of their relative poverty is that the sisters dine on **fried beef**, presumably a leftover from an earlier dinner. **Oysters** were harvested off the south-east coast of England and were not considered a delicacy at the time. **Game birds** such as partridges had to be hung for some days before eating and could 'smell high'. An invalid or person with a delicate stomach (such as Mr Woodhouse in *Emma*) would eat **gruel**, a light hot dish of oatmeal in water or milk with added sugar or spices.

In the country among the middling classes **dinner**, the main meal of the day, would occur between 3 and 5 pm, but would be much later in the upper ranks. Where the social climber Tom Musgrave insists he eats dinner at 8 o'clock, the poorer Watsons dine at 3 and are served by their old nurse. They assemble round the fire for dessert, probably of dried fruit and sweets. **Tea** was made where it was drunk and poured from a teapot into a wide cup without a handle.

MONEY AND PROFESSIONS

A man of **independence** was one who had his own income; £800–900 per annum would support a young man and a modestly genteel family, but would not be enough for a fashionable establishment. Young women brought **portions**, dowries or fortunes to the men they married: £10,000 was a significant fortune for a gentleman's daughter and £6,000 a considerable one for an attorney's.

A **half crown** was a silver coin worth two shillings and sixpence. Silver was scarce during the French Wars and counterfeiting was common and severely punished.

Gentlemen without an estate or large income had to work in one of the professions. **The Church** was respectable but not lucrative if the parish were poor, like Mr Watson's. Many **livings** (the position of a clergyman) were in the gift of landowners: here Mr Howard has a living from the Osbornes, for whom he has previously worked as a tutor.

An **attorney** was respectable but not quite genteel, unless he were well connected like John Knightley in *Emma*, while an **apothecary** or **surgeon-apothecary** was a useful member of a rural community but with less status than the London physician. Both attorney and apothecary had opportunities to become rich and move up the social scale, as happens in *Emma*, to the heroine's consternation.

A man might also go into politics and become a **Member of Parliament**, again usually with the patronage of a major landowner. As a baron, Lord Osborne would sit in the House of Lords, but would still wish to keep in with the borough so that he could use his influence over the election of an MP.

Because of its glamorous uniform of red coat and **cockade** (knot of ribbons or rosette worn as a badge of office), the **army** was considered the profession most captivating to young ladies – as Mrs Bennet declares in *Pride and Prejudice*.

None of these professions was of course open to the educated woman, whose main options outside the family would be as companion, teacher or governess.

NOTES TO 'THE WATSONS'

PLACES

Using initials for a town in a novel might suggest or disguise a real place. The habit is mocked in *Childhood Writings*. Here the likely possibility is **Dorking** in Surrey. **Chichester** is a cathedral city inland from the south coast about thirty-five miles from Dorking; **Croydon**, now part of London, was then a small market town fifteen or so miles northeast of Dorking; and **Guilford** (Guildford) a small market town about eleven miles west of Dorking.

In **London**, the fashionable **Bedford Coffee House** was close to Covent Garden Theatre and was frequented by actors, authors and literati as well as would-be men-about-town such as John Thorpe in *Northanger Abbey*.

Bath was a favoured resort for the sick who came to drink and bathe in its medicinal waters. The old or **Lower Assembly Rooms** built in 1708 were in the centre of the town near the river while the new ones, opened in 1771, were in the higher part to the north. Stanton and Wickstead are fictional villages.

SOCIAL CUSTOMS

Formal visiting was essential between distant members of a family and among the upper orders in an area. Once a visit had been made, a return visit was required by the head of the household. An unscheduled visit, especially after fourteen years of indifference, as in the case of the Osbornes and the Watsons, was an impropriety; nonetheless it demanded a return visit.

Once acquainted, women curtseyed to each other – a **jerking curtsey** would be the slightest possible courteous acknowledgement of another person.

Both sexes played **cards** in private houses. **Whist** required two pairs of players and considerable attention to the cards. Men could attend all-male **whist clubs**, often held at local inns. See also *Emma*, where the club is frequented by the gentlemen and 'half-gentlemen' of Highbury. The whist club in 'The Watsons' meets three times a week. Other card games included **vingt-un** and the noisy round game of **speculation**, in both of which individual players gambled with **fish** or counters. Fashionable **cassino** required two to four players. **Cribbage**, usually for two players, was scored with a combination of cards, the score being kept by sticks in holes on a board. A **rubber** was three rounds of the same game.

Rich young men in the country **hunted** and kept hounds and expensive hunters for the purpose. In Austen's published novels hunting is important to charming but unprincipled young men: Henry Crawford in *Mansfield Park* and Willoughby in *Sense and Sensibility*. Local people would often gather to watch the hunters drink a **stirrup cup** (usually of port or sherry) to the hunt's success before they set off together. To **throw off** was to free the hounds from their leashes, so beginning the hunt.

SANDITON

PREFACE TO 'SANDITON'

'Sanditon' eschews the country-village setting which Jane Austen declared was, for a novelist, 'the very thing to work on'. Instead, the story takes place in a developing English seaside resort on the Sussex coast full of would-be entrepreneurs and restless health tourists. The fragment is an exuberant mockery of hypochondriacs whose weaknesses are here rendered with zest, as well as a satire on the people who exploit their needs and neuroses. Comically muddled minds match erratically demanding bodies: the world presented in 'Sanditon' is absurd, unsettled and unsettling.

While there are young people competing for marriage partners as in every Austen work, the fragment primarily presents an array of eccentric characters and caricatures, at the centre of which is the Parker family. Tom Parker is the enthusiastic promoter and puffer of the new resort. He is visited there by his three siblings: the madly officious Diana, the much-tortured invalid Susan and the indolent, guzzling Arthur. The trio self-diagnose and self-medicate with gusto, and together offer a droll commentary on the new leisure pursuit of invalidism, the rationale for the new resort.

Poignantly the description of the energetically ailing Diana Parker recalls Jane Austen's own state as she was writing. Diana can hardly crawl from her 'Bed to the Sofa' and is 'bilious', a fashionable term for an ailment that made a sufferer yellowish; when Jane Austen determined this was her complaint, she added the term 'anti-bilious' to her list of medical conditions for which the Sanditon air was beneficial according to Tom Parker. Five days after abandoning her novel in its twelfth chapter, Austen wrote that she was herself turning 'every wrong colour'; several weeks later she was living 'chiefly on the sofa'.

Contrasting with the afflicted Parker sisters are two robust characters. The first is Tom Parker's partner in the commercial project: canny, parsimonious Lady Denham, the last in Jane Austen's line of rich and/or mean-spirited older women: Mrs Ferrars, Lady Catherine de Bourgh, Mrs Churchill and Emma Watson's aunt. Unusually, these women have money and property at their disposal and they use it to control the young of both sexes.

The second robust character is the heroine, the supremely healthy Charlotte Heywood, a 'sober-minded', rather censorious young woman, who is visiting Sanditon as Tom Parker's guest. Most of the time she acts less like a novel heroine and more like the detached observer in satire, noting with 'the calmness of amused Curiosity' the absurdities of the men and women she is meeting in the flimsy, unfinished town.

Charlotte enjoys reading romantic novels but is firm in separating fact from fiction. By contrast, Lady Denham's preposterous nephew Sir Edward appears crazed by fictional plots of seduction and abduction, fancying himself the witty rapist Lovelace in Samuel Richardson's *Clarissa*.

One last intriguing character is the rich and delicate Miss Lambe. Described as 'half-mulatto', she is an heiress from the West Indies who has been brought to the seaside for her health. The only mixed-race person in Austen's oeuvre, she is entirely silent in the fragment.

Where would the novel have gone had Jane Austen had time to continue it? Would the resort of Sanditon have failed or been rescued by the third, more sensible Parker brother? Would the moderately good all achieve marriage? Finally, how much of this fragment would have survived if the novel had been prepared for publication? Is it possible that Austen wrote her first drafts in this exuberant style, then let her creations develop into the rounded characters now so familiar to us? The fragment suggests many intriguing possibilities.

SANDITON

CHAPTER 1

A GENTLEMAN AND lady travelling from Tunbridge towards that part of the Sussex coast which lies between Hastings and East Bourne, being induced by business to quit the high road, and attempt a very rough lane, were overturned in toiling up its long ascent—half rock, half sand. The accident happened just beyond the only gentleman's house near the lane—a house, which their driver, on being first required to take that direction, had conceived to be necessarily their object, and had with most unwilling looks been constrained to pass by—. He had grumbled and shaken his shoulders so much indeed, and pitied and cut his horses so sharply, that he might have been open to the suspicion of overturning them on purpose (especially as the carriage was not his master's) if the road had not indisputably become considerably worse than before, as soon as the premises of the said house were left behind—expressing with a most intelligent portentous countenance that beyond it no wheels but cart wheels could safely proceed.

The severity of the fall was broken by their slow pace and the narrowness of the lane, and the gentleman having scrambled out and helped out his companion, they neither of them at first felt more than shaken and bruised. But the gentleman had in the course of the extrication sprained his foot—and soon becoming sensible of it was obliged in a few moments to cut short both his remonstrance to the driver and his congratulations to his wife and himself—and sit down on the bank, unable to stand.—

"There is something wrong here," said he—putting his hand to his ancle—"But never mind, my dear—(looking up at her with a smile)—it could not have happened, you know, in a better place.—Good out of evil—. The very thing perhaps to be wished for. We shall soon get relief.—*There*, I fancy lies my cure"—pointing to the neat-looking end of a cottage, which was seen romantically situated among wood on a high eminence at some little distance.—"Does not *that* promise to be the very place?—"

His wife fervently hoped it was—but stood, terrified and anxious, neither able to do or suggest anything—and receiving her first real comfort from the sight of several persons now coming to their assistance. The accident had been discerned from a hayfield adjoining the house they had passed—and the persons who approached were a well-looking, hale, gentlemanlike man, of middle age, the proprietor of the place, who happened to be among his haymakers at the time, and three or four of the ablest of them summoned to attend their master—to say nothing of all the rest of the field, men, women and children—not very far off.—Mr. Heywood, such was the name of the said proprietor, advanced with a very civil salutation—much concern for the accident—some surprise at any body's attempting that road in a carriage—and ready offers of assistance. His courtesies were received with good breeding and gratitude and while one or two of the men lent their help to the driver in getting the carriage upright again, the traveller said—

"You are extremely obliging Sir, and I take you at your word.—The injury to my leg is I dare say very trifling, but it is always best in these cases to have a surgeon's opinion without loss of time; and as the road does not seem at present in a favourable state for my getting up to his house myself, I will thank you to send off one of these good people for the surgeon."

"The surgeon Sir!"—replied Mr. Heywood.—"I am afraid you will find no surgeon at hand here, but I dare say we shall do very well without him."—

"Nay Sir, if *he* is not in the way his partner will do just as well—or rather better—. I would rather see his partner indeed—I would prefer the attendance of his partner.—One of these good people can be with him in three minutes I am sure. I need not ask whether

I see the house (looking towards the cottage); for excepting your own, we have passed none in this place, which can be the abode of a gentleman."—

Mr. Heywood looked very much astonished and replied—

"What Sir! are you expecting to find a surgeon in that cottage?—we have neither surgeon nor partner in the parish I assure you."—

"Excuse me Sir"—replied the other. "I am sorry to have the appearance of contradicting you—but though from the extent of the parish or some other cause you may not be aware of the fact—Stay—can I be mistaken in the place?—Am I not in Willingden?—Is not this Willingden?"

"Yes Sir, this is certainly Willingden."

"Then Sir, I can bring proof of your having a surgeon in the parish—whether you may know it or not. Here Sir—(taking out his pocket book—) if you will do me the favour of casting your eye over these advertisements, which I cut out myself from the Morning Post and the Kentish Gazette, only yesterday morning in London—I think you will be convinced that I am not speaking at random. You will find it an advertisement, Sir, of the dissolution of a partnership in the medical line—in your own parish—extensive business—undeniable character—respectable references—wishing to form a separate establishment.—You will find it at full length Sir"—offering him the two little oblong extracts.—

"Sir"—said Mr. Heywood with a good humoured smile—"if you were to shew me all the newspapers that are printed in one week throughout the kingdom, you would not persuade me of there being a surgeon in Willingden—for having lived here ever since I was born, man and boy fifty-seven years, I think I must have *known* of such a person, at least I may venture to say that he has not *much business*.—To be sure, if gentlemen were to be often attempting this lane in postchaises, it might not be a bad speculation for a surgeon to get a house at the top of the hill.—But as to that cottage, I can assure you Sir that it is in fact—(in spite of its spruce air at this distance—) as indifferent a double tenement as any in the parish, and that my shepherd lives at one end, and three old women at the other."

He took the pieces of paper as he spoke—and having looked them over, added—"I believe I can explain it Sir.—Your mistake is in the place.—There are two Willingdens in this country*—and your advertisements refer to the other—which is Great Willingden, or Willingden Abbots, and lies seven miles off, on the other side of Battle—quite down in the Weald. And *we* Sir—(speaking rather proudly) are not in the Weald."—

"Not *down* in the Weald I am sure Sir," replied the traveller, pleasantly. "It took us half an hour to climb your hill.—Well Sir—I dare say it is as you say and I have made an abominably stupid blunder.—All done in a moment;—the advertisements did not catch my eye till the last half hour of our being in town—; when everything was in the hurry and confusion which always attend a short stay there.—One is never able to complete anything in the way of business you know till the carriage is at the door—and accordingly satisfying myself with a brief enquiry, and finding we were actually to pass within a mile or two of a *Willingden*, I sought no farther . . . My dear—(to his wife) I am very sorry to have brought you into this scrape. But do not be alarmed about my leg. It gives me no pain while I am quiet,—and as soon as these good people have succeeded in setting the carriage to rights and turning the horses round, the best thing we can do will be to measure back our steps into the turnpike road and proceed to Hailsham, and so home, without attempting anything farther.—Two hours take us home, from Hailsham—and when once at home, we have our remedy at hand you know.—A little of our own bracing sea air will soon set me on my feet again.—Depend upon it my dear, it is exactly a case for the sea. Saline air and immersion will be the very thing.—My sensations tell me so already."—

In a most friendly manner Mr. Heywood here interposed, entreating them not to think of proceeding till the ancle had been examined, and some refreshment taken, and very cordially pressing them to make use of his house for both purposes.—

---

* **Country**: County.

"We are always well stocked," said he, "with all the common remedies for sprains and bruises—and I will answer for the pleasure it will give my wife and daughters to be of service to you and this lady in every way in their power.—"

A twinge or two in trying to move his foot disposed the traveller to think rather more as he had done at first of the benefit of immediate assistance—and consulting his wife in the few words of "Well my dear, I believe it will be better for us"—turned again to Mr. Heywood—and said—"Before we accept your hospitality Sir,—and in order to do away any unfavourable impression which the sort of wild goose-chase you find me in, may have given rise to—allow me to tell you who we are. My name is Parker.—Mr. Parker of Sanditon;—this lady, my wife Mrs. Parker.—We are on our road home from London.—*My* name perhaps—though I am by no means the first of my family, holding landed property in the parish of Sanditon, may be unknown at this distance from the coast—but Sanditon itself—everybody has heard of Sanditon,—the favourite—for a young and rising bathing-place, certainly the favourite spot of all that are to be found along the coast of Sussex;—the most favoured by Nature, and promising to be the most chosen by man."—

"Yes—I have heard of Sanditon," replied Mr. Heywood.—"Every five years, one hears of some new place or other starting up by the sea, and growing the fashion.—How they can half of them be filled, is the wonder! *Where* people can be found with money or time to go to them!—Bad things for a country;—sure to raise the price of provisions and make the poor good for nothing—as I dare say you find, Sir."

"Not at all Sir, not at all"—cried Mr. Parker eagerly. "Quite the contrary I assure you.—A common idea—but a mistaken one. It may apply to your large, overgrown places, like Brighton, or Worthing, or East Bourne—but *not* to a small village like Sanditon, precluded by its size from experiencing any of the evils of civilization, while the growth of the place, the buildings, the nursery grounds, the demand for every thing, and the sure resort of the very best company, those regular, steady, private families of thorough gentility and character, who are a blessing every where, excite the industry of the poor and diffuse comfort and improvement among them of every sort.—No Sir, I assure you, Sanditon is not a place—"

"I do not mean to take exceptions to *any* place in particular Sir," answered Mr. Heywood.—"I only think our coast is too full of them altogether.—But had we not better try to get you"—

"Our coast too full"—repeated Mr. Parker.—"On that point perhaps we may not totally disagree;—at least there are *enough*. Our coast is abundant enough; it demands no more.—Everybody's taste and every body's finances may be suited—and those good people who are trying to add to the number are in my opinion excessively absurd, and must soon find themselves the dupes of their own fallacious calculations.—Such a place as Sanditon Sir, I may say was wanted, was called for.—Nature had marked it out—had spoken in most intelligible characters—the finest, purest sea breeze on the coast—acknowledged to be so—excellent bathing—fine hard sand—deep water ten yards from the shore—no mud—no weeds—no slimy rocks—never was there a place more palpably designed by Nature for the resort of the invalid—the very spot which thousands seemed in need of—the most desirable distance from London! One complete, measured mile nearer than East Bourne. Only conceive Sir, the advantage of saving a whole mile, in a long journey. But Brinshore Sir, which I dare say you have in your eye—the attempts of two or three speculating people about Brinshore, this last year, to raise that paltry hamlet, lying as it does between a stagnant marsh, a bleak moor and the constant effluvia of a ridge of putrifying sea weed, can end in nothing but their own disappointment. What in the name of common sense is to *recommend* Brinshore?—A most insalubrious air—roads proverbially detestable—water brackish beyond example, impossible to get a good dish of tea within three miles of the place—and as for the soil—it is so cold and ungrateful that it can hardly be made to yield a cabbage.—Depend upon it Sir, that this is a faithful description of Brinshore—not in the smallest degree exaggerated—and if you have heard it differently spoken of—"

"Sir, I never heard it spoken of in my life before," said Mr. Heywood. "I did not know there was such a place in the world."—

"You did not!—There my dear—(turning with exultation to his wife)—you see how it is. So much for the celebrity of Brinshore!—This gentleman did not know there was such a place in the world.—Why, in truth Sir, I fancy we may apply to Brinshore, that line of the poet Cowper in his description of the religious cottager, as opposed to Voltaire—'*She*, never heard of half a mile from home'."—

"With all my heart Sir—apply any verses you like to it—but I want to see something applied to your leg—and I am sure by your lady's countenance that she is quite of my opinion and thinks it a pity to lose any more time.—And here come my girls to speak for themselves and their mother—(two or three genteel looking young women, followed by as many maid servants, were now seen issuing from the house)—I began to wonder the bustle should not have reached *them*.—A thing of this kind soon makes a stir in a lonely place like ours.—Now Sir, let us see how you can be best conveyed into the house."—

The young ladies approached and said every thing that was proper to recommend their father's offers; and in an unaffected manner calculated to make the strangers easy—and as Mrs. Parker was exceedingly anxious for relief—and her husband, by this time, not much less disposed for it—a very few civil scruples were enough—especially as the carriage being now set up, was discovered to have received such injury on the fallen side as to be unfit for present use.—Mr. Parker was therefore carried into the house, and his carriage wheeled off to a vacant barn.—

CHAPTER 2

THE ACQUAINTANCE, thus oddly begun, was neither short nor unimportant. For a whole fortnight the travellers were fixed at Willingden, Mr. Parker's sprain proving too serious for him to move sooner.—He had fallen into very good hands.

The Heywoods were a thoroughly respectable family, and every possible attention was paid in the kindest and most unpretending manner, to both husband and wife. *He* was waited on and nursed, and *she* cheered and comforted with unremitting kindness—and as every office of hospitality and friendliness was received as it ought—as there was not more good will on one side than gratitude on the other—nor any deficiency of generally pleasant manners on either, they grew to like each other in the course of that fortnight, exceedingly well.—

Mr. Parker's character and history were soon unfolded. All that he understood of himself, he readily told, for he was very openhearted;—and where he might be himself in the dark, his conversation was still giving information, to such of the Heywoods as could observe.—By such he was perceived to be an enthusiast;—on the subject of Sanditon, a complete enthusiast.—Sanditon,—the success of Sanditon as a small, fashionable bathing place was the object, for which he seemed to live. A very few years ago, and it had been a quiet village of no pretensions; but some natural advantages in its position and some accidental circumstances having suggested to himself, and the other principal land holder, the probability of its becoming a profitable speculation, they had engaged in it, and planned and built, and praised and puffed, and raised it to a something of young renown—and Mr. Parker could now think of very little besides.—

The facts, which in more direct communication he laid before them, were that he was about five and thirty—had been married,—very happily married seven years—and had four sweet children at home;—that he was of a respectable family, and easy though not large fortune;—no profession—succeeding as eldest son to the property which two or three generations had been holding and accumulating before him;—that he had two brothers and two sisters—all single and all independent—the eldest of the two former indeed, by collateral inheritance, quite as well provided for as himself.—His object in quitting the high road, to hunt for an advertising surgeon, was also plainly stated;—it had not proceeded from any intention of spraining his ancle or doing himself any other injury for the good of such surgeon—nor (as Mr. Heywood had been apt to suppose) from any design of entering into partnership with him—; it was merely in consequence of a wish to establish some medical man at Sanditon, which the nature of the advertisement induced him to expect to accomplish in Willingden.—He was convinced that the advantage of a medical man at hand would very materially promote the rise and prosperity of the place—would in fact tend to bring a prodigious influx;—nothing else was wanting. He had *strong* reason to believe that *one* family had been deterred last year from trying Sanditon on that account—and probably very many more—and his own sisters, who were sad invalids, and whom he was very anxious to get to Sanditon this summer, could hardly be expected to hazard themselves in a place where they could not have immediate medical advice.—

Upon the whole, Mr. Parker was evidently an amiable family-man, fond of wife, children, brothers and sisters—and generally kind-hearted;—liberal, gentlemanlike, easy to please;—of a sanguine turn of mind, with more imagination than judgement. And Mrs. Parker was as evidently a gentle, amiable, sweet tempered woman, the properest wife in the world for a man of strong understanding, but not of capacity to supply the cooler reflection which her own husband sometimes needed, and so entirely waiting to be guided on every occasion, that whether he were risking his fortune or spraining his ancle, she remained equally useless.— Sanditon was a second wife and four children to him—hardly less dear—and certainly more engrossing.—He could talk of it for ever.—It had indeed the highest claims;—not only those of birth place, property, and home,—it was his mine, his lottery, his speculation and his hobby horse; his occupation, his hope and his futurity.—He was extremely desirous of drawing his good friends at Willingden thither; and his endeavours in the cause were as grateful and disinterested as they were warm.—He wanted to secure the promise of a visit—to get as many of the family as his own house would contain, to follow him to Sanditon as soon as possible—and healthy as they all undeniably were—foresaw that every one of them would be benefited by the sea.—He held it indeed as certain, that no person could be really well, no person (however upheld for the present by fortuitous aids of exercise and spirits in a semblance of health) could be really in a state of secure and permanent health without spending at least six weeks by the sea every year.—The sea air and sea bathing together were nearly infallible, one or the other of them being a match for every disorder, of the stomach, the lungs or the blood; they were anti-spasmodic, anti-pulmonary, anti-sceptic, antibilious and anti-rheumatic. Nobody could catch cold by the sea, nobody wanted appetite by the sea, nobody wanted spirits, nobody wanted strength.—They were healing, softing, relaxing—fortifying and bracing—seemingly just as was wanted—sometimes one, sometimes the other.—If the sea breeze failed, the sea-bath was the certain corrective;—and where bathing disagreed, the sea breeze alone was evidently designed by Nature for the cure.—

His eloquence however could not prevail. Mr. and Mrs. Heywood never left home. Marrying early and having a very numerous family, their movements had been long limited to one small circle; and they were older in habits than in age.—Excepting two journeys to London in the year, to receive his dividends, Mr. Heywood went no farther than his feet or his well-tried old horse could carry him, and Mrs. Heywood's adventurings were only now and then to visit her neighbours, in the old coach which had been new when they married and fresh lined on their eldest son's coming of age ten years ago.—

They had very pretty property—enough, had their family been of reasonable limits, to have allowed them a very gentlemanlike share of luxuries and change—enough for them to have indulged in a new carriage and better roads, an occasional month at Tunbridge Wells, and symptoms of the gout and a winter at Bath;—but the maintenance, education and fitting out of fourteen children demanded a very quiet, settled, careful course of life—and obliged them to be stationary and healthy at Willingden. What prudence had at first enjoined, was now rendered pleasant by habit. They never left home, and they had a gratification in saying so.—But very far from wishing their children to do the same, they were glad to promote *their* getting out into the world, as much as possible. *They* staid at home, that their children *might* get out;—and while making that home extremely comfortable, welcomed every change from it which could give useful connections or respectable acquaintance to sons or daughters. When Mr. and Mrs. Parker therefore ceased from soliciting a family-visit, and bounded their views to carrying back one daughter with them, no difficulties were started. It was general pleasure and consent.—

Their invitation was to Miss Charlotte Heywood, a very pleasing young woman of two and twenty, the eldest of the daughters at home, and the one who under her mother's directions had been particularly useful and obliging to them; who had attended them most, and knew them best.—Charlotte was to go,—with excellent health, to bathe and be better if she could—to receive every possible pleasure which Sanditon could be made to supply by the gratitude of those she went with—and to buy new parasols, new gloves, and new brooches, for her sisters and herself at the library, which Mr. Parker was anxiously wishing to support.—All that Mr. Heywood himself could be persuaded to promise was, that he would send everyone to Sanditon, who asked his advice, and that nothing should ever induce him (as far as the future could be answered for) to spend even five shillings at Brinshore.—

CHAPTER 3

EVERY NEIGHBOURHOOD should have a great lady.—The great lady of Sanditon was Lady Denham; and in their journey from Willingden to the coast Mr. Parker gave Charlotte a more detailed account of her than had been called for before.—She had been necessarily often mentioned at Willingden,—for being his colleague in speculation, Sanditon itself could not be talked of long, without the introduction of Lady Denham, and that she was a very rich old lady, who had buried two husbands, who knew the value of money, was very much looked up to and had a poor cousin living with her, were facts already well known, but some further particulars of her history and her character served to lighten the tediousness of a long hill, or a heavy bit of road, and to give the visiting young lady a suitable knowledge of the person with whom she might now expect to be daily associating.—

Lady Denham had been a rich Miss Brereton, born to wealth but not to education. Her first husband had been a Mr. Hollis, a man of considerable property in the country, of which a large share of the parish of Sanditon, with manor and mansion house, made a part. He had been an elderly man when she married him;—her own age about thirty.—Her motives for such a match could be little understood at the distance of forty years, but she had so well nursed and pleased Mr. Hollis, that at his death he left her everything—all his estates, and all at her disposal. After a widowhood of some years, she had been induced to marry again. The late Sir Harry Denham, of Denham Park in the neighbourhood of Sanditon, had succeeded in removing her and her large income to his own domains, but he could not succeed in the views of permanently enriching his family, which were attributed to him. She had been too wary to put anything out of her own power—and when on Sir Harry's decease she returned again to her own house at Sanditon, she was said to have made this boast to a friend, "that though she had *got* nothing but her title from the family, still she had *given* nothing for it."—For the title, it was to be supposed that she had married—and Mr. Parker acknowledged there being just such a degree of value for it apparent now, as to give her conduct that natural explanation.

"There is at times," said he—"a little self-importance—but it is not offensive;—and there are moments, there are points, when her love of money is carried greatly too far. But she is a good-natured woman, a very good-natured woman—a very obliging, friendly neighbour; a cheerful, independent, valuable character—and her faults may be entirely imputed to her want of education. She has good natural sense, but quite uncultivated.—She has a fine active mind, as well as a fine healthy frame for a woman of seventy, and enters into the improvement of Sanditon with a spirit truly admirable—though now and then, a littleness *will* appear. She cannot look forward quite as I would have her—and takes alarm at a trifling present expence, without considering what returns it *will* make her in a year or two.

"That is—we think *differently*, we now and then see things *differently*, Miss Heywood.—Those who tell their own story you know must be listened to with caution.—When you see us in contact, you will judge for yourself."—

Lady Denham was indeed a great lady beyond the common wants of society—for she had many thousands a year to bequeath, and three distinct sets of people to be courted by: her own relations, who might very reasonably wish for her original thirty thousand pounds among them, the legal heirs of Mr. Hollis, who must hope to be more endebted to *her* sense of justice than he had allowed them to be to *his*, and those members of the Denham family, whom her second husband had hoped to make a good bargain for.—By all of these, or by branches of them, she had no doubt been long, and still continued to be, well attacked;—and of these three divisions, Mr. Parker did not hesitate to say that Mr. Hollis's kindred were the *least* in favour and Sir Harry Denham's the *most*.—The former he believed had done themselves irremediable harm by expressions of very unwise and unjustifiable resentment at the time of Mr. Hollis's death;—the latter, to the advantage of being the remnant of a connection which she certainly valued, joined those of having been known to her from their childhood and of being always at hand to preserve their interest by reasonable attention. Sir Edward, the present baronet, nephew to Sir Harry, resided constantly at Denham Park; and Mr. Parker had little doubt that he and his sister Miss Denham, who lived with him, would be principally remembered in her will. He sincerely hoped it.—Miss Denham had a very small provision—and her brother was a poor man for his rank in society.

"He is a warm friend to Sanditon"—said Mr. Parker—"and his hand would be as liberal as his heart, had he the power.—He would be a noble coadjutor!—As it is, he does what he can—and is running up a tasteful little cottage ornée, on a strip of waste ground Lady

Denham has granted him—which I have no doubt we shall have many a candidate for, before the end even of *this* season."

Till within the last twelvemonth, Mr. Parker had considered Sir Edward as standing without a rival, as having the fairest chance of succeeding to the greater part of all that she had to give—but there was now another person's claims to be taken into the account, those of the young female relation, whom Lady Denham had been induced to receive into her family. After having always protested against any such addition, and long and often enjoyed the repeated defeats she had given to every attempt of her relations to introduce this young lady or that young lady as a companion at Sanditon House, she had brought back with her from London last Michaelmas a Miss Brereton, who bid fair by her merits to vie in favour with Sir Edward, and to secure for herself and her family that share of the accumulated property which they had certainly the best right to inherit.—

Mr. Parker spoke warmly of Clara Brereton, and the interest of his story increased very much with the introduction of such a character. Charlotte listened with more than amusement now;—it was solicitude and enjoyment, as she heard her described to be lovely, amiable, gentle, unassuming, conducting herself uniformly with great good sense, and evidently gaining by her innate worth on the affections of her patroness.—Beauty, sweetness, poverty and dependance, do not want the imagination of a man to operate upon. With due exceptions—woman feels for woman very promptly and compassionately. He gave the particulars which had led to Clara's admission at Sanditon, as no bad exemplification of that mixture of character, that union of littleness with kindness with good sense with even liberality, which he saw in Lady Denham.—After having avoided London for many years, and principally on account of these very cousins, who were continually writing, inviting and tormenting her, and whom she was determined to keep at a distance, she had been obliged to go there last Michaelmas with the certainty of being detained at least a fortnight.—She had gone to an hotel—living, by her own account, as prudently as possible, to defy the reputed expensiveness of such a home, and at the end of three days calling for her bill, that she might judge of her state.—Its amount was such as determined her on staying not another hour in the house, and she was preparing in all the anger and perturbation which a belief of very gross imposition *there*, and an ignorance of *where* to go for better usage, to leave the hotel at all hazards, when the cousins, the politic and lucky cousins, who seemed always to have a spy on her, introduced themselves at this important moment, and learning her situation, persuaded her to accept such a home for the rest of her stay as their humbler house in a very inferior part of London could offer.—

She went; was delighted with her welcome and the hospitality and attention she received from every body—found her good cousins the Breretons beyond her expectation worthy people—and finally was impelled, by a personal knowledge of their narrow income and pecuniary difficulties, to invite one of the girls of the family to pass the winter with her. The invitation was to *one*, for six months—with the probability of another being then to take her place;—but in *selecting* the one, Lady Denham had shewn the good part of her character—for passing by the actual *daughters* of the house, she had chosen Clara, a niece—more helpless and more pitiable of course than any—and dependant on poverty—an additional burden on an encumbered circle—and one who had been so low in every worldly view, as with all her natural endowments and powers to have been preparing for a situation little better than a nursery maid.—

Clara had returned with her—and by her good sense and merit had now, to all appearance, secured a very strong hold in Lady Denham's regard. The six months had long been over—and not a syllable was breathed of any change, or exchange.—She was a general favourite;—the influence of her steady conduct and mild, gentle temper was felt by everybody. The prejudices which had met her at first in some quarters were all dissipated. She was felt to be worthy of trust—to be the very companion who would guide and soften Lady Denham—who would enlarge her mind and open her hand.—She was as thoroughly amiable as she was lovely—and since having had the advantage of their Sanditon breezes, that loveliness was complete.

CHAPTER 4

"AND WHOSE VERY snug-looking place is this?"—said Charlotte, as in a sheltered dip within two miles of the sea, they passed close by a moderate-sized house, well fenced and planted, and rich in the garden, orchard and meadows which are the best embellishments of such a dwelling. "It seems to have as many comforts about it as Willingden."—

"Ah!"—said Mr. Parker.—"This is my old house—the house of my forefathers—the house where I and all my brothers and sisters were born and bred—and where my own three eldest children were born—where Mrs. Parker and I lived till within the last two years—till our new house was finished.—I am glad you are pleased with it.—It is an honest old place—and Hillier keeps it in very good order. I have given it up you know to the man who occupies the chief of my land. *He* gets a better house by it—and I, a rather better situation!—One other hill brings us to Sanditon—modern Sanditon—a beautiful spot.—Our ancestors, you know, always built in a hole.—Here were we, pent down in this little contracted nook, without air or view, only one mile and three quarters from the noblest expanse of ocean between the South Foreland and the Land's End, and without the smallest advantage from it. You will not think I have made a bad exchange, when we reach Trafalgar House—which, by the bye, I almost wish I had not named Trafalgar—for Waterloo is more the thing now. However, Waterloo is in reserve—and if we have encouragement enough this year for a little Crescent to be ventured on—(as I trust we shall) then we shall be able to call it Waterloo Crescent—and the name joined to the form of the building, which always takes, will give us the command of lodgers—. In a good season we should have more applications than we could attend to."—

"It was always a very comfortable house"—said Mrs. Parker—looking at it through the back window with something like the fondness of regret.—"And such a nice garden—such an excellent garden."

"Yes, my love, but *that* we may be said to carry with us.—*It* supplies us, as before, with all the fruit and vegetables we want; and we have in fact all the comfort of an excellent kitchen garden, without the constant eyesore of its formalities, or the yearly nuisance of its decaying vegetation.—Who can endure a cabbage bed in October?"

"Oh! dear—yes.—We are quite as well off for gardenstuff as ever we were—for if it is forgot to be brought at any time, we can always buy what we want at Sanditon House.—The gardener there is glad enough to supply us—. But it was a nice place for the children to run about in. So shady in summer!"

"My dear, we shall have shade enough on the hill and more than enough in the course of a very few years—. The growth of my plantations is a general astonishment. In the mean while we have the canvas awning, which gives us the most complete comfort within doors—and you can get a parasol at Whitby's for little Mary at any time, or a large bonnet at Jebbs'.—And as for the boys, I must say I would rather *them* run about in the sunshine than not. I am sure we agree, my dear, in wishing our boys to be as hardy as possible."—

"Yes indeed, I am sure we do—and I will get Mary a little parasol, which will make her as proud as can be. How grave she will walk about with it, and fancy herself quite a little woman.—Oh! I have not the smallest doubt of our being a great deal better off where we are now. If we any of us want to bathe, we have not a quarter of a mile to go.—But you know (still looking back) one loves to look at an old friend, at a place where one has been happy.—The Hilliers did not seem to feel the storms last winter at all.—I remember seeing Mrs. Hillier after one of those dreadful nights, when *we* had been literally rocked in our bed, and she did not seem at all aware of the wind being anything more than common."

"Yes, yes—that's likely enough. *We* have all the grandeur of the storm, with less real danger, because the wind meeting with nothing to oppose or confine it around our house, simply rages and passes on—while down in this gutter—nothing is known of the state of the air, below the tops of the trees—and the inhabitants may be taken totally unawares, by one of those dreadful currents which should do more mischief in a valley, when they *do* arise, than an open country ever experiences in the heaviest gale.— But my dear love—as to gardenstuff;—you were saying that any accidental omission is supplied in a moment by Lady Denham's gardener—but it occurs to me that we ought to go elsewhere upon such occasions—and that old Stringer and his son have a higher claim. I encouraged him to set up—and am afraid he does not do very well—that is, there has not been time enough yet.—He *will* do very well beyond a doubt—but at first it is up hill work; and therefore we must give him what help we can—and when any vegetables or fruit happen to be wanted,—and it will not be amiss to have them often wanted, to have something or other forgotten most days—just to have a nominal supply you know, that poor old Andrew may not lose his daily job—but in fact to buy the chief of our consumption of the Stringers.—"

"Very well my love, that can be easily done—and cook will be satisfied—which will be a great comfort, for she is always complaining of old Andrew now, and says he never brings her what she wants.—There—now the old house is quite left behind.—What is it, your brother Sidney says about its being a hospital?"

"Oh! my dear Mary, merely a joke of his. He pretends to advise me to make a hospital of it. He pretends to laugh at my improvements. Sidney says any thing you know. He has always said what he chose of and to us all. Most families have such a member among them I believe Miss Heywood.—There is a someone in most families privileged by superior abilities or spirits to say anything.—In ours, it is Sidney; who is a very clever young man, and with great powers of pleasing.—He lives too much in the world to be settled; that is his only fault.—He is here and there and every where. I wish we may get him to Sanditon. I should like to have you acquainted with him.—And it would be a fine thing for the place!—Such a young man as Sidney, with his neat equipage and fashionable air.—You and I Mary, know what effect it might have: many a respectable family, many a careful mother, many a pretty daughter, might it secure us, to the prejudice of East Bourne and Hastings."—

They were now approaching the church and real village of Sanditon, which stood at the foot of the hill they were afterwards to ascend—a hill, whose side was covered with the woods and enclosures of Sanditon House and whose height ended in an open down where the new buildings might soon be looked for. A branch only, of the valley, winding more obliquely towards the sea, gave a passage to an inconsiderable stream, and formed at its mouth a third habitable division, in a small cluster of fisherman's houses.—

The village contained little more than cottages, but the spirit of the day had been caught, as Mr. Parker observed with delight to Charlotte, and two or three of the best of them were smartened up with a white curtain and "Lodgings to let"—, and farther on, in the little green court of an old farm house, two females in elegant white were actually to be seen with their books and camp stools—and in turning the corner of the baker's shop, the sound of a harp might be heard through the upper casement.— Such sights and sounds were highly blissful to Mr. Parker.—Not that he had any personal concern in the success of the village itself; for considering it as too remote from the beach, he had done nothing there—but it was a most valuable proof of the increasing fashion of the place altogether. If the *village* could attract, the hill might be nearly full.—He anticipated an amazing season.—At the same time last year (late in July) there had not been a single lodger in the village!—nor did he remember any during the whole summer, excepting one family of children who came from London for sea air after the hooping cough, and whose mother would not let them be nearer the shore for fear of their tumbling in.—

"Civilization, civilization indeed!"—cried Mr. Parker, delighted—. "Look my dear Mary—Look at William Heeley's windows.—Blue shoes, and nankin boots!—Who would have expected such a sight at a shoemaker's in old Sanditon!—This is new within the month. There was no blue shoe when we passed this way a month ago.—Glorious indeed!—Well, I think I *have* done something in my day.—Now, for our hill, our health-breathing hill.—"

In ascending, they passed the lodge-gates of Sanditon House, and saw the top of the house itself among its groves. It was the last building of former days in that line of the parish. A little higher up, the modern began; and in crossing the down, a Prospect House, a Bellevue Cottage, and a Denham Place were to be looked at by Charlotte with the calmness of amused curiosity, and by Mr. Parker with the eager eye which hoped to see scarcely any empty houses.—More bills at the window than he had calculated on;—and a smaller shew of company on the hill—fewer carriages, fewer walkers. He had fancied it just the time of day for them to be all returning from their airings to dinner.—But the sands and the terrace always attracted some—and the tide must be flowing—about half-tide now.—He longed to be on the sands, the cliffs, at his own house and every where out of his house at once. His spirits rose with the very sight of the sea and he could almost feel his ancle getting stronger already.—

Trafalgar House, on the most elevated spot on the down, was a light elegant building, standing in a small lawn with a very young plantation round it, about an hundred yards from the brow of a steep, but not very lofty cliff—and the nearest to it, of every building, excepting one short row of smart-looking houses, called the Terrace, with a broad walk in front, aspiring to be the Mall of the place. In this row were the best milliner's shop and the library—a little detached from it, the hotel and billiard room.—Here began the descent to the beach, and to the bathing machines—and this was therefore the favourite spot for beauty and fashion.—At Trafalgar House, rising at a little distance behind the Terrace, the travellers were safely set down, and all was happiness and joy between papa and mama and their children; while Charlotte, having received possession of her apartment, found amusement enough in standing at her ample, Venetian window, and looking over the miscellaneous foreground of unfinished buildings, waving linen, and tops of houses, to the sea, dancing and sparkling in sunshine and freshness.—

CHAPTER 5

WHEN THEY MET before dinner, Mr. Parker was looking over letters.—

"Not a line from Sidney!"—said he.—"He is an idle fellow.—I sent him an account of my accident from Willingden, and thought he would have vouchsafed me an answer.—But perhaps it implies that he is coming himself.—I trust it may.—But here is a letter from one of my sisters. *They* never fail me.—Women are the only correspondents to be depended on.—Now Mary, (smiling at his wife)—before I open it, what shall we guess as to the state of health of those it comes from—or rather what would Sidney say if he were here?—Sidney is a saucy fellow, Miss Heywood.—And you must know, he will have it there is a good deal of imagination in my two sisters' complaints—but it really is not so—or very little.—They have wretched health, as you have heard us say frequently, and are subject to a variety of very serious disorders.—Indeed, I do not believe they know what a day's health is;—and at the same time, they are such excellent useful women and have so much energy of character that, where any good is to be done, they force themselves on exertions which, to those who do not thoroughly know them, have an extraordinary appearance.—But there is really no affectation about them. They have only weaker constitutions and stronger minds than are often met with, either separate or together.—And our youngest brother, who lives with them, and who is not much above twenty, I am sorry to say, is almost as great an invalid as themselves.—He is so delicate that he can engage in no profession.—Sidney laughs at him—but it really is no joke—though Sidney often makes me laugh at them all in spite of myself.—Now, if he were here, I know he would be offering odds, that either Susan, Diana or Arthur would appear by this letter to have been at the point of death within the last month.—"

Having run his eye over the letter, he shook his head and began:—

"No chance of seeing them at Sanditon I am sorry to say.—A very indifferent account of them indeed. Seriously, a *very* indifferent account.—Mary, you will be quite sorry to hear how ill they have been and are.—Miss Heywood, if you will give me leave, I will read Diana's letter aloud.—I like to have my friends acquainted with each other—and I am afraid this is the only sort of acquaintance I shall have the means of accomplishing between you.—And I can have no scruple on Diana's account—for her letters shew her exactly as she is, the most active, friendly, warm-hearted being in existence, and therefore must give a good impression."

He read.—

"My dear Tom, We were all much grieved at your accident, and if you had not described yourself as fallen into such very good hands, I should have been with you at all hazards the day after the receipt of your letter, though it found me suffering under a more severe attack than usual of my old grievance, spasmodic bile, and hardly able to crawl from my bed to the sofa.—But how were you treated?—Send me more particulars in your next.—If indeed a simple sprain, as you denominate it, nothing would have been so judicious as friction, friction by the hand alone, supposing it could be applied *instantly*.—Two years ago I happened to be calling on Mrs. Sheldon when her coachman sprained his foot as he was cleaning the carriage and could hardly limp into the house—but by the immediate use of friction alone, steadily persevered in (and I rubbed his ancle with my own hand for six hours without intermission)—he was well in three days.—Many thanks my dear Tom, for the kindness with respect to us, which had so large a share in bringing on your accident.—But pray: never run into peril again, in looking for an apothecary on our account, for had you the most experienced man in his line settled at Sanditon, it would be no recommendation to us. We have entirely done with the whole medical tribe. We have consulted physician after physician in vain, till we are quite convinced that they can do nothing for us and that we must trust to our own knowledge of our own wretched constitutions for any relief.—But if you think it advisable for the interest of the *place*, to get a medical man there, I will undertake the commission with pleasure, and have no doubt of succeeding.—I could soon put the necessary irons in the fire.— As for getting to Sanditon myself, it is quite an impossibility. I grieve to say that I dare not attempt it, but my feelings tell me too plainly that in my present state, the sea air would probably be the death of me.—And neither of my dear companions will leave me, or I would promote their going down to you for a fortnight. But in truth, I doubt whether Susan's nerves would be equal to the effort. She has been suffering much from the headache and six leeches a day for ten days together relieved her so little that we thought it right to change our measures—and being convinced on examination that much of the evil lay in her gum, I persuaded her to attack the disorder there. She has accordingly had three teeth drawn, and is decidedly better, but her nerves are a good deal deranged. She can only speak in a whisper—and fainted away twice this morning on poor Arthur's trying to suppress a cough. He, I am happy to say, is tolerably well—though more languid than I like—and I fear for his liver.—I have heard nothing of Sidney since your being together in town, but conclude his scheme to the Isle of Wight has not taken place, or we should have seen him in his way.—Most sincerely do we wish you a good season at Sanditon, and though we cannot contribute to your beau monde in person, we are doing our utmost to send you company worth having; and think we may safely reckon on securing you two large families, one a rich West Indian from Surry, the other a most respectable girls boarding school, or academy, from Camberwell.—I will not tell you how many people I have employed in the business—Wheel within wheel.—But success more than repays.—Yours most affec^{ly}—&c."

"Well"—said Mr. Parker as he finished.—"Though I dare say Sidney might find something extremely entertaining in this letter and make us laugh for half an hour together, I declare *I* by myself can see nothing in it but what is either very pitiable or very creditable.—With all their sufferings, you perceive how much they are occupied in promoting the good of others!—So anxious for Sanditon! Two large families—one, for Prospect House probably, the other, for No. 2 Denham Place—or the end house of the Terrace,—and extra beds at the hotel.—I told you my sisters were excellent women, Miss Heywood—."

"And I am sure they must be very extraordinary ones,"—said Charlotte. "I am astonished at the cheerful style of the letter, considering the state in which both sisters appear to be.—Three teeth drawn at once!—frightful!—Your sister Diana seems almost as ill as possible, but those three teeth of your sister Susan's are more distressing than all the rest.—"

"Oh!—they are so used to the operation—to every operation—and have such fortitude!—"

"Your sisters know what they are about, I dare say, but their measures seem to touch on extremes.—I feel that in any illness, *I* should be so anxious for professional advice, so very little venturesome for myself, or any body I loved!—But then, *we* have been so healthy a family, that I can be no judge of what the habit of self-doctoring may do.—"

"Why to own the truth," said Mrs. Parker—"I *do* think the Miss Parkers carry it too far sometimes—and so do you my love, you know.—You often think they would be better, if they would leave themselves more alone—and especially Arthur. I know you think it a great pity they should give *him* such a turn for being ill.—"

"Well, well—my dear Mary—I grant you, it *is* unfortunate for poor Arthur, that at his time of life he should be encouraged to give way to indisposition. It *is* bad;—it *is* bad that he should be fancying himself too sickly for any profession—and sit down at one and twenty, on the interest of his own little fortune, without any idea of attempting to improve it, or of engaging in any occupation that may be of use to himself or others.—But let us talk of pleasanter things.—These two large families are just what we wanted.—But—here is something at hand, pleasanter still—Morgan, with his 'Dinner on Table.'"—

CHAPTER 6

THE PARTY WERE very soon moving after dinner. Mr. Parker could not be satisfied without an early visit to the library, and the library subscription book, and Charlotte was glad to see as much, and as quickly as possible, where all was new. They were out in the very quietest part of a watering-place day, when the important business of dinner or of sitting after dinner was going on in almost every inhabited lodging;—here and there a solitary elderly man might be seen, who was forced to move early and walk for health—but in general, it was a thorough pause of company, it was emptiness and tranquillity on the Terrace, the cliffs, and the sands.—The shops were deserted—the straw hats and pendant lace seemed left to their fate both within the house and without, and Mrs. Whilby at the library was sitting in her inner room, reading one of her own novels, for want of employment.—

The list of subscribers was but commonplace. The Lady Denham, Miss Brereton, Mr. and Mrs. Parker, Sir Edward Denham and Miss Denham, whose names might be said to lead off the season, were followed by nothing better than—Mrs. Mathews—Miss Mathews, Miss E. Mathews, Miss H. Mathews.—Dr. and Mrs. Brown—Mr. Richard Pratt.—Lieutenant Smith R. N. Captain Little,—Limehouse.—Mrs. Jane Fisher. Miss Fisher. Miss Scroggs.—Rev. Mr. Hankins. Mr. Beard—solicitor, Grays Inn.—Mrs. Davis. And Miss Merryweather.—Mr. Parker could not but feel that the list was not only without distinction, but less numerous than he had hoped. It was but July however, and August and September were the months;—and besides, the promised large families from Surry and Camberwell were an ever-ready consolation.—

Mrs. Whitby came forward without delay from her literary recess, delighted to see Mr. Parker again, whose manners recommended him to every body, and they were fully occupied in their various civilities and communications, while Charlotte, having added her name to the list as the first offering to the success of the season, was busy in some immediate purchases for the further good of everybody, as soon as Miss Whitby could be hurried down from her toilette, with all her glossy curls and smart trinkets to wait on her.—The library, of course, afforded every thing; all the useless things in the world that could not be done without, and among so many pretty temptations, and with so much good will for Mr. Parker to encourage expenditure, Charlotte began to feel that she must check herself—or rather she reflected that at two and twenty there could be no excuse for her doing otherwise— and that it would not do for her to be spending all her money the very first evening. She took up a book; it happened to be a volume of *Camilla*. She had not Camilla's youth, and had no intention of having her distress,—so, she turned from the drawers of rings and brooches, repressed farther solicitation and paid for what she bought.—

For her particular gratification, they were then to take a turn on the cliff—but as they quitted the library they were met by two ladies whose arrival made an alteration necessary, Lady Denham and Miss Brereton.—They had been to Trafalgar House, and been directed thence to the library, and though Lady Denham was a great deal too active to regard the walk of a mile as anything requiring rest, and talked of going home again directly, the Parkers knew that to be pressed into their house, and obliged to take her tea with them, would suit her best,—and therefore the stroll on the cliff gave way to an immediate return home.—

"No, no," said her ladyship—"I will not have you hurry your tea on my account.—I know you like your tea late.—My early hours are not to put my neighbours to inconvenience. No, no, Miss Clara and I will get back to our own tea.—We came out with no other thought.—We wanted just to see you and make sure of your being really come—, but we get back to our own tea."—

She went on however towards Trafalgar House and took possession of the drawing room very quietly—without seeming to hear a word of Mrs. Parker's orders to the servant as they entered, to bring tea directly.

Charlotte was fully consoled for the loss of her walk, by finding herself in company with those, whom the conversation of the morning had given her a great curiosity to see. She observed them well.—Lady Denham was of middle height, stout, upright and alert in her motions with a shrewd eye, and self-satisfied air—but not an unagreeable countenance—and though her manner was rather downright and abrupt, as of a person who valued herself on being free-spoken, there was a good humour and cordiality about her—a civility and readiness to be acquainted with Charlotte herself, and a heartiness of welcome towards her old friends, which was inspiring the good will she seemed to feel;—and as for Miss Brereton, her appearance so completely justified Mr. Parker's praise that Charlotte thought she had never beheld a more lovely, or more interesting young woman.—Elegantly tall, regularly handsome, with great delicacy of complexion and soft blue eyes, a sweetly modest and yet naturally graceful address, Charlotte could see in her only the most perfect representation of whatever heroine might be most beautiful and bewitching, in all the numerous volumes they had left behind them on Mrs. Whilby's shelves.—Perhaps it might be partly owing to her having just issued from a circulating library—but she could not separate the idea of a complete heroine from Clara Brereton. Her situation with Lady Denham so very much in favour of it!—She seemed placed with her on purpose to be ill-used.—Such poverty and dependence, joined to such beauty and merit, seemed to leave no choice in the business.—These feelings were not the result of any spirit of romance in Charlotte herself. No, she was a very sober-minded young lady, sufficiently well-read in novels to supply her imagination with amusements, but not at all unreasonably influenced by them; and while she pleased herself the first five minutes with fancying the persecutions which *ought* to be the lot of the interesting Clara, especially in the form of the most barbarous conduct on Lady Denham's side, she found no reluctance to admit, from subsequent observation, that they appeared to be on very comfortable terms.—She could see nothing worse in Lady Denham, than the sort of old-fashioned formality of always calling her *Miss Clara*—nor anything objectionable in the degree of observance and attention which Clara paid.—On one side it seemed protecting kindness, on the other grateful and affectionate respect.—

The conversation turned entirely upon Sanditon, its present number of visitants and the chances of a good season. It was evident that Lady Denham had more anxiety, more fears of loss, than her coadjutor. She wanted to have the place fill faster, and seemed to have many harassing apprehensions of the lodgings being in some instances underlet.—Miss Diana Parker's two large families were not forgotten.

"Very good, very good," said her Ladyship.—"A West Indy family and a school. That sounds well. That will bring money."—

"No people spend more freely, I believe, than West Indians," observed Mr. Parker.—

"Aye—so I have heard—and because they have full purses, fancy themselves equal, may be, to your old country families. But then, they who scatter their money so freely, never think of whether they may not be doing mischief by raising the price of things—and I have heard that's very much the case with your West-ingines—and if they come among us to raise the price of our necessaries of life, we shall not much thank them Mr. Parker."—

"My dear madam, they can only raise the price of consumable articles, by such an extraordinary demand for them and such a diffusion of money among us, as must do us more good than harm.—Our butchers and bakers and traders in general cannot get rich without bringing prosperity to *us*.—If *they* do not gain, our rents must be insecure—and in proportion to their profit must be ours eventually in the increased value of our houses."

"Oh!—well.—But I should not like to have butcher's meat raised, though—and I shall keep it down as long as I can.—Aye—that young lady smiles I see;—I dare say she thinks me an odd sort of a creature,—but *she* will come to care about such matters herself in time. Yes, yes, my dear, depend upon it, you will be thinking of the price of butcher's meat in time—though you may not happen to have quite such a servants' hall to feed, as I have.—And I do believe *those* are best off, that have fewest servants.—I am not a woman of parade, as all the world knows, and if it was not for what I owe to poor Mr. Hollis's memory, I should never keep up Sanditon House as I do;—it is not for my own pleasure.—Well Mr. Parker—and the other is a boarding school, a French boarding school, is it?—No harm in that.—They'll stay their six weeks.—And out of such a number, who knows but some may be consumptive and want asses' milk—and I have two milch asses at this present time.—But perhaps the little Misses may hurt the furniture.—I hope they will have a good sharp governess to look after them."—

Poor Mr. Parker got no more credit from Lady Denham than he had from his sisters, for the object which had taken him to Willingden.

"Lord! my dear Sir," she cried, "how could you think of such a thing? I am very sorry you met with your accident, but upon my word you deserved it.—Going after a doctor!—Why, what should we do with a doctor here? It would be only encouraging our servants and the poor to fancy themselves ill, if there was a doctor at hand.—Oh! pray, let us have none of the tribe at Sanditon. We go on very well as we are. There is the sea and the Downs and my milch-asses—and I have told Mrs. Whilby that if any body enquires for a chamber horse, they may be supplied at a fair rate—(poor Mr. Hollis's chamber horse, as good as new)—and what can people want for, more?—Here have I lived seventy good years in the world and never took physic above twice—and never saw the face of a doctor in all my life, on my *own* account.—And I verily believe if my poor dear Sir Harry had never seen one neither, he would have been alive now.—Ten fees, one after another, did the man take who sent *him* out of the world.—I beseech you Mr. Parker, no doctors here."—

The tea things were brought in.—

"Oh! my dear Mrs. Parker—you should not indeed—why would you do so? I was just upon the point of wishing you good evening. But since you are so very neighbourly, I believe Miss Clara and I must stay."—

CHAPTER 7

THE POPULARITY of the Parkers brought them some visitors the very next morning;—amongst them, Sir Edward Denham and his sister, who having been at Sanditon House drove on to pay their compliments; and the duty of letter-writing being accomplished, Charlotte was settled with Mrs. Parker in the drawing room in time to see them all.—The Denhams were the only ones to excite particular attention. Charlotte was glad to complete her knowledge of the family by an introduction to them, and found them, the better half at least—(for while single, the *gentleman* may sometimes be thought the better half, of the pair)—not unworthy notice.—Miss Denham was a fine young woman, but cold and reserved, giving the idea of one who felt her consequence with pride and her poverty with discontent, and who was immediately gnawed by the want of an handsomer equipage than the simple gig in which they travelled, and which their groom was leading about still in her sight.—Sir Edward was much her superior in air and manner;—certainly handsome, but yet more to be remarked for his very good address and wish of paying attention and giving pleasure.—He came into the room remarkably well, talked much—and very much to Charlotte, by whom he chanced to be placed—and she soon perceived that he had a fine countenance, a most pleasing gentleness of voice, and a great deal of conversation. She liked him.—Sober-minded as she was, she thought him agreeable, and did not quarrel with the suspicion of his finding her equally so, which *would* arise, from his evidently disregarding his sister's motion to go, and persisting in his station and his discourse.—I make no apologies for my heroine's vanity.—If there are young ladies in the world at her time of life, more dull of fancy and more careless of pleasing, I know them not, and never wish to know them.—

At last, from the low French windows of the drawing room which commanded the road and all the paths across the Down, Charlotte and Sir Edward, as they sat, could not but observe Lady

Denham and Miss Brereton walking by—and there was instantly a slight change in Sir Edward's countenance—with an anxious glance after them as they proceeded—followed by an early proposal to his sister—not merely for moving, but for walking on together to the Terrace—which altogether gave an hasty turn to Charlotte's fancy, cured her of her half-hour's fever, and placed her in a more capable state of judging, when Sir Edward was gone, of *how* agreeable he had actually been.—"Perhaps there was a good deal in his air and address; and his title did him no harm."

She was very soon in his company again. The first object of the Parkers, when their house was cleared of morning visitors, was to get out themselves;—the Terrace was the attraction to all;—every body who walked must begin with the Terrace, and there, seated on one of the two green benches by the gravel walk, they found the united Denham party;—but though united in the gross, very distinctly divided again—the two superior ladies being at one end of the bench, and Sir Edward and Miss Brereton at the other.—

Charlotte's first glance told her that Sir Edward's air was that of a lover.—There could be no doubt of his devotion to Clara.— How Clara received it, was less obvious—but she was inclined to think not very favourably; for though sitting thus apart with him (which probably she might not have been able to prevent) her air was calm and grave.—That the young lady at the other end of the bench was doing penance, was indubitable. The difference in Miss Denham's countenance, the change from Miss Denham sitting in cold grandeur in Mrs. Parker's drawing-room to be kept from silence by the efforts of others, to Miss Denham at Lady Denham's elbow, listening and talking with smiling attention or solicitous eagerness, was very striking—and very amusing—or very melancholy, just as satire or morality might prevail.—Miss Denham's character was pretty well decided with Charlotte.

Sir Edward's required longer observation. He surprised her by quitting Clara immediately on their all joining and agreeing to walk, and by addressing his attentions entirely to herself.—Stationing himself close by her, he seemed to mean to detach her as much as possible from the rest of the party and to give her the whole of his conversation. He began, in a tone of great taste and feeling, to talk of the sea and the sea shore—and ran with energy through all the usual phrases employed in praise of their sublimity, and descriptive of the *undescribable* emotions they excite in the mind of sensibility.—The terrific grandeur of the ocean in a storm, its glassy surface in a calm, its gulls and its samphire, and the deep fathoms of its abysses, its quick vicissitudes, its direful deceptions, its mariners tempting it in sunshine and overwhelmed by the sudden tempest, all were eagerly and fluently touched;—rather common-place perhaps—but doing very well from the lips of a handsome Sir Edward,—and she could not but think him a man of feeling—till he began to stagger her by the number of his quotations, and the bewilderment of some of his sentences.—

"Do you remember," said he, "Scott's beautiful lines on the sea?—Oh! what a description they convey!—They are never out of my thoughts when I walk here.—That man who can read them unmoved must have the nerves of an assassin!—Heaven defend me from meeting such a man un-armed."—

"What description do you mean?"—said Charlotte. "I remember none at this moment, of the sea, in either of Scott's poems."—

"Do not you indeed?—Nor can I exactly recall the beginning at this moment.—But—you cannot have forgotten his description of woman.—

'Oh! Woman in our hours of ease'——

Delicious! Delicious!—Had he written nothing more, he would have been immortal. And then again, that unequalled, unrivalled address to parental affection—

> 'Some feelings are to mortals given
> With less of earth in them than heaven' &c.

But while we are on the subject of poetry, what think you Miss Heywood of Burns's lines to his Mary?—Oh! there is pathos to madden one!—If ever there was a man who *felt*, it was Burns.—Montgomery has all the fire of poetry, Wordsworth has the true soul of it—Campbell in his pleasures of hope has touched the extreme of our sensations—'Like angel's visits, few and far between'. Can you conceive any thing more subduing, more melting, more fraught with the deep sublime than that line?—But Burns—I confess my sense of his pre-eminence Miss Heywood.—If Scott *has* a fault, it is the want of passion.—Tender, elegant, descriptive—but *tame.*— The man who cannot do justice to the attributes of woman is my contempt.—Sometimes indeed a flash of feeling seems to irradiate him—as in the lines we were speaking of—'Oh! Woman in our hours of ease'—. But Burns is always on fire.—His soul was the altar in which lovely woman sat enshrined, his spirit truly breathed the immortal incense which is her due.—"

"I have read several of Burns's poems with great delight," said Charlotte as soon as she had time to speak, "but I am not poetic enough to separate a man's poetry entirely from his character;— and poor Burns's known irregularities greatly interrupt my enjoyment of his lines.—I have difficulty in depending on the *truth* of his feelings as a lover. I have not faith in the *sincerity* of the affections of a man of his description. He felt and he wrote and he forgot."

"Oh! no no—" exclaimed Sir Edward in an extasy. "He was all ardour and truth!—His genius and his susceptibilities might lead him into some aberrations.—But who is perfect?—It were hyper-criticism, it were pseudo-philosophy to expect from the soul of high toned genius, the grovellings of a common mind.—The coruscations of talent, elicited by impassioned feeling in the breast of man, are perhaps incompatible with some of the prosaic decencies of life;—nor can you, loveliest Miss Heywood—(speaking with an air of deep sentiment)—nor can any woman be a fair judge of what a man may be propelled to say, write or do, by the sovereign impulses of illimitable ardour."

This was very fine;—but if Charlotte understood it at all, not very moral—and being moreover by no means pleased with his extraordinary stile of compliment, she gravely answered,

"I really know nothing of the matter.—This is a charming day. The wind I fancy must be southerly."

"Happy, happy wind, to engage Miss Heywood's thoughts!—"

She began to think him downright silly.—His chusing to walk with her, she had learnt to understand. It was done to pique Miss Brereton. She had read it, in an anxious glance or two on his side—but why he should talk so much nonsense, unless he could do no better, was unintelligible.—He seemed very sentimental, very full of some feelings or other, and very much addicted to all the newest-fashioned hard words—had not a very clear brain she presumed, and talked a good deal by rote.—The future might explain him further—but when there was a proposition for going into the library she felt that she had had quite enough of Sir Edward for one morning, and very gladly accepted Lady Denham's invitation of remaining on the Terrace with her.—

The others all left them, Sir Edward with looks of very gallant despair in tearing himself away, and they united their agreeableness—that is, Lady Denham, like a true great lady, talked and talked only of her own concerns, and Charlotte listened—amused in considering the contrast between her two companions.— Certainly, there was no strain of doubtful sentiment, nor any phrase of difficult interpretation, in Lady Denham's discourse. Taking hold of Charlotte's arm with the ease of one who felt that any notice from her was an honour, and communicative, from the influence of the same conscious importance or a natural love of talking, she immediately said in a tone of great satisfaction—and with a look of arch sagacity—

"Miss Esther wants me to invite her and her brother to spend a week with me at Sanditon House, as I did last summer.—But I shan't.—She has been trying to get round me every way, with her praise of this, and her praise of that; but I saw what she was about.—I saw through it all.—I am not very easily taken in my dear."

Charlotte could think of nothing more harmless to be said, than the simple enquiry of—"Sir Edward and Miss Denham?"—

"Yes, my dear. *My young folks*, as I call them sometimes, for I take them very much by the hand. I had them with me last summer about this time, for a week; from Monday to Monday; and very delighted and thankful they were.—For they are very good young people my dear. I would not have you think that

I *only* notice them for poor dear Sir Harry's sake. No, no; they are very deserving themselves, or trust me, they would not be so much in *my* company.—I am not the woman to help any body blindfold.—I always take care to know what I am about and who I have to deal with, before I stir a finger.—I do not think I was ever over-reached in my life; and that is a good deal for a woman to say that has been married twice.—Poor dear Sir Harry (between ourselves) thought at first to have got more.—But (with a bit of a sigh) he is gone, and we must not find fault with the dead. Nobody could live happier together than us—and he was a very honourable man, quite the gentleman of ancient family.—And when he died, I gave Sir Edward his gold watch.—"

She said this with a look at her companion which implied its right to produce a great impression—and seeing no rapturous astonishment in Charlotte's countenance, added quickly—

"He did not bequeath it to his nephew, my dear—it was no bequest. It was not in the will. He only told me, and *that* but once, that he should wish his nephew to have his watch; but it need not have been binding, if I had not chose it.—"

"Very kind indeed! very handsome!"—said Charlotte, absolutely forced to affect admiration.—

"Yes, my dear—and it is not the *only* kind thing I have done by him.—I have been a very liberal friend to Sir Edward. And poor young man, he needs it bad enough;—for though I am *only* the *dowager* my dear, and he is the *heir*, things do not stand between us in the way they commonly do between those two parties.—Not a shilling do I receive from the Denham estate. Sir Edward has no payments to make *me*. He don't stand uppermost, believe me.—It is *I* that help *him*."

"Indeed!—He is a very fine young man;—particularly elegant in his address."—

This was said chiefly for the sake of saying something—but Charlotte directly saw that it was laying her open to suspicion by Lady Denham's giving a shrewd glance at her and replying—

"Yes, yes, he is very well to look at—and it is to be hoped some lady of large fortune will think so—for Sir Edward *must* marry for money.—He and I often talk that matter over.—A handsome young fellow like him, will go smirking and smiling about and paying girls compliments, but he knows he *must* marry for money.—And Sir Edward is a very steady young man in the main, and has got very good notions."

"Sir Edward Denham," said Charlotte, "with such personal advantages may be almost sure of getting a woman of fortune, if he chuses it."—

This glorious sentiment seemed quite to remove suspicion. "Aye my dear—that's very sensibly said," cried Lady Denham. "And if we could but get a young heiress to Sanditon! But heiresses are monstrous scarce! I do not think we have had an heiress here, or even a co, since Sanditon has been a public place. Families come after families, but as far as I can learn, it is not one in an hundred of them that have any real property, landed or funded.—An income perhaps, but no property. Clergymen may be, or lawyers from town, or half pay officers, or widows with only a jointure. And what good can such people do anybody?—except just as they take our empty houses—and (between ourselves) I think they are great fools for not staying at home. Now, if we could get a young heiress to be sent here for her health—(and if she was ordered to drink asses' milk I could supply her)—and as soon as she got well, have her fall in love with Sir Edward!"—

"That would be very fortunate indeed."

"And Miss Esther must marry somebody of fortune too—she must get a rich husband. Ah! young ladies that have no money are very much to be pitied!—But—" after a short pause—"if Miss Esther thinks to talk me into inviting them to come and stay at Sanditon House, she will find herself mistaken.—Matters are altered with me since last summer you know—. I have Miss Clara with me now, which makes a great difference."

She spoke this so seriously that Charlotte instantly saw in it the evidence of real penetration and prepared for some fuller remarks—but it was followed only by—

"I have no fancy for having my house as full as an hotel. I should not chuse to have my two housemaids' time taken up all the morning, in dusting out bed rooms.—They have Miss Clara's room to put to rights as well as my own every day.—If they had hard places, they would want higher wages.—"

For objections of this nature, Charlotte was not prepared, and she found it so impossible even to affect sympathy, that she could say nothing.—Lady Denham soon added, with great glee—

"And besides all this my dear, am I to be filling my house to the prejudice of Sanditon?—If people want to be by the sea, why don't they take lodgings?—Here are a great many empty houses—three on this very terrace; no fewer than three lodging papers staring us in the face at this very moment, Numbers 3, 4 and 8. 8, the corner house, may be too large for them, but either of the two others are nice little snug houses, very fit for a young gentleman and his sister.—And so, my dear, the next time Miss Esther begins talking about the dampness of Denham Park, and the good bathing always does her, I shall advise them to come and take one of these lodgings for a fortnight.—Don't you think that will be very fair?—Charity begins at home you know."—

Charlotte's feelings were divided between amusement and indignation—but indignation had the larger and the increasing share.—She kept her countenance and she kept a civil silence. She could not carry her forbearance farther; but without attempting to listen longer, and only conscious that Lady Denham was still talking on in the same way, allowed her thoughts to form themselves into such a meditation as this:—

"She is thoroughly mean. I had not expected any thing so bad.— Mr. Parker spoke too mildly of her.—His judgement is evidently not to be trusted.—His own good nature misleads him. He is too kind hearted to see clearly.—I must judge for myself.—And their very *connection* prejudices him.—He has persuaded her to engage in the same speculation—and because their object in that line is the same, he fancies she feels like him in others.—But she is very, very mean.—I can see no good in her.—Poor Miss Brereton!—And she makes every body mean about her.—This poor Sir Edward and his sister,—how far nature meant them to be respectable I can not tell,—but they are *obliged* to be mean in their servility to her.—And

I am mean too, in giving her my attention, with the appearance of coinciding with her.—Thus it is, when rich people are sordid."—

CHAPTER 8

THE TWO LADIES continued walking together till rejoined by the others, who as they issued from the library were followed by a young Whilby running off with five volumes under his arm to Sir Edward's gig—and Sir Edward, approaching Charlotte, said, "You may perceive what has been our occupation. My sister wanted my counsel in the selection of some books.—We have many leisure hours, and read a great deal.—I am no indiscriminate novel-reader. The mere trash of the common circulating library, I hold in the highest contempt. You will never hear me advocating those puerile emanations which detail nothing but discordant principles incapable of amalgamation, or those vapid tissues of ordinary occurrences from which no useful deductions can be drawn.—In vain may we put them into a literary alembic;*—we distil nothing which can add to science.†—You understand me I am sure?"

"I am not quite certain that I do.—But if you will describe the sort of novels which you *do* approve, I dare say it will give me a clearer idea."

"Most willingly, fair questioner.—The novels which I approve are such as display human nature with grandeur—such as shew her in the sublimities of intense feeling—such as exhibit the progress of strong passion from the first germ of incipient susceptibility to the utmost energies of reason half-dethroned,—where we see the strong spark of woman's captivations elicit such fire in the soul of man as leads him—(though at the risk of some aberration from the strict line of primitive obligations)—to hazard all, dare all, achieve all, to obtain her.—Such are the works which I peruse with delight, and I hope I may say, with amelioration. They hold forth

* **Alembic**: a glass vessel, traditionally used for distilling chemicals, but gaining a figurative meaning towards the end of the eighteenth century.
† **Science**: general knowledge.

the most splendid portraitures of high conceptions, unbounded views, illimitable ardour, indomptible decision—and even when the event is mainly anti-prosperous to the high-toned machinations of the prime character, the potent, pervading hero of the story, it leaves us full of generous emotions for him;—our hearts are paralized—. 'Twere pseudo-philosophy to assert that we do not feel more enwrapped by the brilliancy of his career, than by the tranquil and morbid virtues of any opposing character. Our approbation of the latter is but eleemosynary.*—These are the novels which enlarge the primitive capabilities of the heart, and which it cannot impugn the sense, or be any dereliction of the character, of the most anti-puerile man, to be conversant with."—

"If I understand you aright—" said Charlotte—"our taste in novels is not at all the same."

And here they were obliged to part—Miss Denham being too much tired of them all, to stay any longer.—The truth was that Sir Edward, whom circumstances had confined very much to one spot, had read more sentimental novels than agreed with him. His fancy had been early caught by all the impassioned and most exceptionable parts of Richardson's; and such authors as have since appeared to tread in Richardson's steps, so far as man's determined pursuit of woman in defiance of every opposition of feeling and convenience is concerned, had since occupied the greater part of his literary hours, and formed his character.—With a perversity of judgement, which must be attributed to his not having by nature a very strong head, the graces, the spirit, the ingenuity, and the perseverance, of the villain of the story outweighed all his absurdities and all his atrocities with Sir Edward. With him, such conduct was genius, fire and feeling.—It interested and inflamed him; and he was always more anxious for its success and mourned over its discomfitures with more tenderness than could ever have been contemplated by the authors.—Though he owed many of his ideas to this sort of reading, it were unjust to say that he read nothing else, or that his language were not formed on a more

---

* **Eleemosynary**: given or received as an act of charity.

general knowledge of modern literature.—He read all the essays, letters, tours and criticisms of the day—and with the same ill-luck which made him derive only false principles from lessons of morality, and incentives to vice from the history of its overthrow, he gathered only hard words and involved sentences from the style of our most approved writers.—

Sir Edward's great object in life was to be seductive.—With such personal advantages as he knew himself to possess, and such talents as he did also give himself credit for, he regarded it as his duty.—He felt that he was formed to be a dangerous man—quite in the line of the Lovelaces.—The very name of Sir Edward, he thought, carried some degree of fascination with it.—To be generally gallant and assiduous about the fair, to make fine speeches to every pretty girl, was but the inferior part of the character he had to play.—Miss Heywood, or any other young woman with any pretensions to beauty, he was entitled (according to his own views of society) to approach with high compliment and rhapsody on the slightest acquaintance; but it was Clara alone on whom he had serious designs; it was Clara whom he meant to seduce.—Her seduction was quite determined on. Her situation in every way called for it. She was his rival in Lady Denham's favour, she was young, lovely and dependant.—He had very early seen the necessity of the case, and had now been long trying with cautious assiduity to make an impression on her heart, and to undermine her principles.—

Clara saw through him, and had not the least intention of being seduced—but she bore with him patiently enough to confirm the sort of attachment which her personal charms had raised.—A greater degree of discouragement indeed would not have affected Sir Edward—. He was armed against the highest pitch of disdain or aversion.—If she could not be won by affection, he must carry her off. He knew his business.—Already had he had many musings on the subject. If he *were* constrained so to act, he must naturally wish to strike out something new, to exceed those who had gone before him—and he felt a strong curiosity to ascertain whether the neighbourhood of Tombuctoo might not afford some solitary house adapted for Clara's reception;—but the expence alas! of measures in that masterly stile was ill-suited to his purse, and prudence obliged him to prefer the quietest sort of ruin and disgrace for the object of his affections, to the more renowned.—

CHAPTER 9

ONE DAY, SOON after Charlotte's arrival at Sanditon, she had the pleasure of seeing, just as she ascended from the sands to the Terrace, a gentleman's carriage with post horses standing at the door of the hotel, as very lately arrived, and by the quantity of luggage taking off, bringing, it might be hoped, some respectable family determined on a long residence.—

Delighted to have such good news for Mr. and Mrs. Parker, who had both gone home some time before, she proceeded for Trafalgar House with as much alacrity as could remain, after having been contending for the last two hours with a very fine wind blowing directly on shore; but she had not reached the little lawn, when she saw a lady walking nimbly behind her at no great distance; and convinced that it could be no acquaintance of her own, she resolved to hurry on and get into the house if possible before her. But the stranger's pace did not allow this to be accomplished;—Charlotte was on the steps and had rung, but the door was not opened, when the other crossed the lawn;—and when the servant appeared, they were just equally ready for entering the house.—

The ease of the lady, her "How do you do Morgan?—" and Morgan's looks on seeing her, were a moment's astonishment—but another moment brought Mr. Parker into the hall to welcome the sister he had seen from the drawing room, and she was soon introduced to Miss Diana Parker.

There was a great deal of surprise but still more pleasure in seeing her.—Nothing could be kinder than her reception from both husband and wife. "How did she come? and with whom?—And they were so glad to find her equal to the journey!—And that she was to belong to *them*, was a thing of course."

Miss Diana Parker was about four and thirty, of middling height and slender;—delicate looking rather than sickly; with an agreeable face, and a very animated eye;—her manners resembling her brother's in their ease and frankness, though with more decision and less mildness in her tone. She began an account of herself without delay—thanking them for their invitation, but "*that* was quite out of the question, for they were all three come, and meant to get into lodgings and make some stay."—

"All three come!—What!—Susan and Arthur!—Susan able to come too!—This was better and better."

"Yes—we are actually all come. Quite unavoidable.—Nothing else to be done.—You shall hear all about it.—But my dear Mary, send for the children;—I long to see them."—

"And how has Susan borne the journey?—and how is Arthur?—and why do not we see him here with you?"—

"Susan has borne it wonderfully. She had not a wink of sleep either the night before we set out, or last night at Chichester, and as this is not so common with her as with *me*, I have had a thousand fears for her—but she has kept up wonderfully—had no hysterics of consequence till we came within sight of poor old Sanditon—and the attack was not very violent—nearly over by the time we reached your hotel—so that we got her out of the carriage extremely well, with only Mr. Woodcock's assistance—and when I left her she was directing the disposal of the luggage and helping old Sam uncord the trunks.—She desired her best love, with a thousand regrets at being so poor a creature that she could not come with me. And as for poor Arthur, he would not have been unwilling himself, but there is so much wind that I did not think he could safely venture,—for I am *sure* there is lumbago hanging about him—and so I helped him on with his great coat and sent him off to the Terrace, to take us lodgings.—Miss Heywood must have seen our carriage standing at the hotel.—I knew Miss Heywood the moment I saw her before me on the Down.—My dear Tom I am glad to see you walk so well. Let me feel your ancle.—That's right; all right and clean. The play of your sinews a *very* little affected;—barely perceptible.—Well—now for the explanation of my being here.—I told you in my letter, of the two considerable families I was hoping to secure for you—the West Indians, and the seminary."—

Here Mr. Parker drew his chair still nearer to his sister, and took her hand again most affectionately as he answered "Yes, yes;—how active and how kind you have been!"—

"The West Indians," she continued, "whom I look upon as the *most* desirable of the two—as the best of the good—prove to be a Mrs. Griffiths and her family. I know them only through others.—You must have heard me mention Miss Capper, the particular friend of *my* very particular friend Fanny Noyce;—now, Miss Capper is extremely intimate with a Mrs. Darling, who is on terms of constant correspondence with Mrs. Griffiths herself.—Only a *short* chain, you see, between us, and not a link wanting. Mrs. Griffiths meant to go to the sea, for her young people's benefit—had fixed on the coast of Sussex, but was undecided as to the where, wanted something private, and wrote to ask the opinion of her friend Mrs. Darling.—Miss Capper happened to be staying with Mrs. Darling when Mrs. Griffiths's letter arrived, and was consulted on the question; *she* wrote the same day to Fanny Noyce and mentioned it to her—and Fanny, all alive for *us*, instantly took up her pen and forwarded the circumstance to me—except as to *names*—which have but lately transpired.—There was but *one* thing for *me* to do.—I answered Fanny's letter by the same post and pressed for the recommendation of Sanditon. Fanny had feared your having no house large enough to receive such a family.—But I seem to be spinning out my story to an endless length.—You see how it was all managed. I had the pleasure of hearing soon afterwards by the same simple link of connection that Sanditon *had been* recommended by Mrs. Darling, and that the West Indians were very much disposed to go thither.—This was the state of the case when I wrote to you;—but two days ago—yes, the day before yesterday—I heard again from Fanny Noyce, saying that *she* had heard from Miss Capper, who by a letter from Mrs. Darling understood that Mrs. Griffiths has expressed herself in a letter to Mrs. Darling more doubtingly on the subject of Sanditon.—Am I clear?—I would be anything rather than not clear."—

"Oh! perfectly, perfectly. Well?"—

"The reason of this hesitation, was her having no connections in the place, and no means of ascertaining that she should have good accommodations on arriving there;—and she was particularly careful and scrupulous on all those matters more on account of a certain Miss Lambe, a young lady (probably a niece) under her care, than on her own account or her daughters'.—Miss Lambe has an immense fortune—richer than all the rest—and very delicate health.—One sees clearly enough by all this, the *sort* of woman Mrs. Griffiths must be—as helpless and indolent, as wealth and a hot climate are apt to make us. But we are not all born to equal energy.—What was to be done?—I had a few moments' indecision;—whether to offer to write to *you*,—or to Mrs. Whitby to secure them a house?—but neither pleased me.—I hate to employ others, when I am equal to act myself—and my conscience told me that this was an occasion which called for me. Here was a family of helpless invalids whom I might essentially serve.—I sounded Susan—the same thought had occurred to her.—Arthur made no difficulties—our plan was arranged immediately, we were off yesterday morning at six—, left Chichester at the same hour to day—and here we are.—"

"Excellent!—Excellent!—" cried Mr. Parker.—"Diana, you are unequalled in serving your friends and doing good to all the world.—I know nobody like you.—Mary, my love, is not she a wonderful creature?—Well—and now, what house do you design to engage for them?—What is the size of their family?—"

"I do not at all know—" replied his sister—"have not the least idea;—never heard any particulars;—but I am very sure that the largest house at Sanditon cannot be *too* large. They are more likely to want a second.—I shall take only one however, and that but for a week certain.—Miss Heywood, I astonish you.—You hardly know what to make of me.—I see by your looks, that you are not used to such quick measures."—

The words "Unaccountable officiousness!—Activity run mad!"—had just passed through Charlotte's mind—but a civil answer was easy.

"I dare say I do look surprised," said she—"because these are very great exertions, and I know what invalids both you and your sister are."

"Invalids indeed.—I trust there are not three people in England who have so sad a right to that appellation.—But my dear Miss Heywood, we are sent into this world to be as extensively useful as possible, and where some degree of strength of mind is given, it is not a feeble body which will excuse us—or incline us to excuse ourselves.—The world is pretty much divided between the weak of mind and the strong—between those who can act and those who can not—and it is the bounden duty of the capable to let no opportunity of being useful escape them.—My sister's complaints and mine are happily not often of a nature, to threaten existence *immediately*—and as long as we *can* exert ourselves to be of use to others, I am convinced that the body is the better for the refreshment the mind receives in doing its duty.—While I have been travelling, with this object in view, I have been perfectly well."—

The entrance of the children ended this little panegyric on her own disposition—and after having noticed and caressed them all, she prepared to go.—"Cannot you dine with us?—Is not it possible to prevail on you to dine with us?" was then the cry; and *that* being absolutely negatived, it was "And when shall we see you again? and how can we be of use to you?"—and Mr. Parker warmly offered his assistance in taking the house for Mrs. Griffiths.—

"I will come to you the moment I have dined," said he, "and we will go about together."—

But this was immediately declined.—

"No, my dear Tom, upon no account in the world shall you stir a step on any business of mine.—Your ancle wants rest. I see by the position of your foot, that you have used it too much already.—No, I shall go about my house-taking directly. Our dinner is not ordered till six—and by that time I hope to have completed it. It is now only half past four.—As to seeing *me* again to day—I cannot answer for it; the others will be at the hotel all the evening, and delighted to see you at any time, but as soon as I get back I shall hear what Arthur has done about our own lodgings, and probably the moment dinner is over shall be out again on business relative to them, for we hope to get into some lodgings or other and be settled after breakfast tomorrow.—I have not much confidence in poor Arthur's skill for lodging-taking, but he seemed to like the commission.—"

"I think you are doing too much," said Mr. Parker. "You will knock yourself up. You should not move again after dinner."

"No, indeed you should not—" cried his wife, "for dinner is such a mere *name* with you all, that it can do you no good.—I know what your appetites are."—

"My appetite is very much mended I assure you lately. I have been taking some bitters of my own decocting, which have done wonders. Susan never eats—I grant you—and just at present *I* shall want nothing; I never eat for about a week after a journey—but as for Arthur, he is only too much disposed for food. We are often obliged to check him."—

"But you have not told me anything of the *other* family coming to Sanditon," said Mr. Parker as he walked with her to the door of the house—"the Camberwell seminary; have we a good chance of *them*?—"

"Oh! certain—quite certain.—I had forgotten them for the moment, but I had a letter three days ago from my friend Mrs. Charles Dupuis which assured me of Camberwell. Camberwell will be here to a certainty, and very soon.—*That* good woman (I do not know her name) not being so wealthy and independent as Mrs. Griffiths—can travel and chuse for herself.—I will tell you how I got at *her*. Mrs. Charles Dupuis lives almost next door to a lady, who has a relation lately settled at Clapham, who actually attends the seminary and gives lessons on eloquence and belles lettres to some of the girls.—I got that man a hare from one of Sidney's friends—and he recommended Sanditon—without *my* appearing however—Mrs. Charles Dupuis managed it all."—

CHAPTER 10

IT WAS NOT A WEEK since Miss Diana Parker had been told by her feelings, that the sea air would probably in her present state be the death of her, and now she was at Sanditon, intending to make some stay, and without appearing to have the slightest recollection of having written or felt any such thing.—It was impossible for Charlotte not to suspect a good deal of fancy in such an extraordinary state of health.—Disorders and recoveries so very much out of the common way, seemed more like the amusement of eager minds in want of employment than of actual afflictions and relief. The Parkers were no doubt a family of imagination and quick feelings—and while the eldest brother found vent for his superfluity of sensation as a projector, the sisters were perhaps driven to dissipate theirs in the invention of odd complaints.—The *whole* of their mental vivacity was evidently not so employed; part was laid out in a zeal for being useful.—It should seem that they must either be very busy for the good of others, or else extremely ill themselves.

Some natural delicacy of constitution in fact, with an unfortunate turn for medicine, especially quack medicine, had given them an early tendency, at various times, to various disorders;—the rest of their suffering was from fancy, the love of distinction and the love of the wonderful.—They had charitable hearts and many amiable feelings—but a spirit of restless activity, and the glory of doing more than anybody else, had their share in every exertion of benevolence—and there was vanity in all they did, as well as in all they endured.—

Mr. and Mrs Parker spent a great part of the evening at the hotel; but Charlotte had only two or three views of Miss Diana posting over the Down after a house for this lady whom she had never seen, and who had never employed her. She was not made acquainted with the others till the following day, when, being removed into lodgings and all the party continuing quite well, their brother and sister and herself were entreated to drink tea with them.—They were in one of the Terrace houses—and she found them arranged for the evening in a small neat drawing room, with a beautiful view of the sea if they had chosen it,—but though it had been a very fair English summer-day, not only was there no open window, but the sopha and the table and the establishment in general was all at the other end of the room by a brisk fire.—

Miss Parker—whom, remembering the three teeth drawn in one day, Charlotte approached with a peculiar degree of respectful compassion—was not very unlike her sister in person or manner—though more thin and worn by illness and medicine, more relaxed in air, and more subdued in voice. She talked however, the whole evening, as incessantly as Diana—and excepting that she sat with salts in her hand, took drops two or three times from one, out of the several phials already at home on the mantlepiece, and made a great many odd faces and contortions, Charlotte could perceive no symptoms of illness which she, in the boldness of her own good health, would not have undertaken to cure, by putting out the fire, opening the window, and disposing of the drops and the salts by means of one or the other.

She had had considerable curiosity to see Mr. Arthur Parker; and having fancied him a very puny, delicate-looking young man, the smallest very materially of not a robust family, was astonished to find him quite as tall as his brother and a great deal stouter—broad made and lusty—and with no other look of an invalid, than a sodden[*] complexion.—Diana was evidently the chief of the family; principal mover and actor;—she had been on her feet the whole morning, on Mrs. Griffiths's business or their own, and was still the most alert of the three.—Susan had only superintended their final removal from the hotel, bringing two heavy boxes herself, and Arthur had found the air so cold that he had merely walked from one house to the other as nimbly as he could,—and boasted much of sitting by the fire till he had cooked up a very good one.—

---

[*] **Sodden**: heavy, dull, wanting vivacity.

Diana, whose exercise had been too domestic to admit of calculation, but who, by her own account, had not once sat down during the space of seven hours, confessed herself a little tired. She had been too successful however for much fatigue; for not only had she by walking and talking down a thousand difficulties at last secured a proper house at eight guineas per week for Mrs. Griffiths; she had also opened so many treaties with cooks, housemaids, washerwomen and bathing women, that Mrs. Griffiths would have little more to do on her arrival, than to wave her hand and collect them around her for choice.—Her concluding effort in the cause had been a few polite lines of information to Mrs. Griffiths herself—time not allowing for the circuitous train of intelligence which had been hitherto kept up,—and she was now regaling in the delight of opening the first trenches of an acquaintance with such a powerful discharge of unexpected obligation.

Mr. and Mrs. Parker and Charlotte had seen two post chaises crossing the Down to the hotel as they were setting off—a joyful sight—and full of speculation.—The Miss Parkers and Arthur had also seen something;—they could distinguish from their window that there *was* an arrival at the hotel, but not its amount. Their visitors answered for two hack-chaises.—Could it be the Camberwell seminary?—No—No.—Had there been a third carriage, perhaps it might; but it was very generally agreed that two hack chaises could never contain a seminary.—Mr. Parker was confident of another new family.—

When they were all finally seated, after some removals to look at the sea and the hotel, Charlotte's place was by Arthur, who was sitting next to the fire with a degree of enjoyment which gave a good deal of merit to his civility in wishing her to take his chair.—There was nothing dubious in her manner of declining it, and he sat down again with much satisfaction. She drew back her chair to have all the advantage of his person as a screen, and was very thankful for every inch of back and shoulders beyond her pre-conceived idea.

Arthur was heavy in eye as well as figure, but by no means indisposed to talk;—and while the other four were chiefly engaged together, he evidently felt it no penance to have a fine young woman next to him, requiring in common politeness some attention—as his brother, who felt the decided want of some motive for action, some powerful object of animation for him, observed with considerable pleasure.—Such was the influence of youth and bloom that he began even to make a sort of apology for having a fire.

"We should not have one at home," said he, "but the sea air is always damp. I am not afraid of anything so much as damp.—"

"I am so fortunate," said Charlotte, "as never to know whether the air is damp or dry. It has always some property that is wholesome and invigorating to me.—"

"*I* like the air too, as well as anybody can," replied Arthur; "I am very fond of standing at an open window when there is no wind,—but unluckily a damp air does not like *me*.—It gives me the rheumatism.—You are not rheumatic I suppose?—"

"Not at all."

"That's a great blessing.—But perhaps you are nervous."

"No—I believe not. I have no idea that I am."—

"*I* am very nervous.—To say the truth—nerves are the worst part of my complaints in *my* opinion.—My sisters think me bilious, but I doubt it.—"

"You are quite in the right, to doubt it as long as you possibly can, I am sure.—"

"If I were bilious," he continued, "you know wine would disagree with me, but it always does me good.—The more wine I drink (in moderation) the better I am.—I am always best of an evening.—If you had seen me today before dinner, you would have thought me a very poor creature.—"

Charlotte could believe it—. She kept her countenance however, and said—

"As far as I can understand what nervous complaints are, I have a great idea of the efficacy of air and exercise for them,—daily, regular exercise;—and I should recommend rather more of it to *you* than I suspect you are in the habit of taking.—"

"Oh! I am very fond of exercise myself,"—he replied—"and mean to walk a great deal while I am here, if the weather is temperate.

I shall be out every morning before breakfast—and take several turns upon the Terrace, and you will often see me at Trafalgar House."—

"But you do not call a walk to Trafalgar House much exercise?—"

"Not as to mere distance, but the hill is so steep!—Walking up that hill, in the middle of the day, would throw me into such a perspiration!—You would see me all in a bath, by the time I got there!—I am very subject to perspiration, and there cannot be a surer sign of nervousness.—"

They were now advancing so deep in physics, that Charlotte viewed the entrance of the servant with the tea things as a very fortunate interruption.—It produced a great and immediate change. The young man's attentions were instantly lost. He took his own cocoa from the tray,—which seemed provided with almost as many tea-pots &c as there were persons in company, Miss Parker drinking one sort of herb-tea and Miss Diana another—and turning completely to the fire, sat coddling and cooking it to his own satisfaction and toasting some slices of bread, brought up ready-prepared in the toast rack—and till it was all done, she heard nothing of his voice but the murmuring of a few broken sentences of self-approbation and success.—When his toils were over however, he moved back his chair into as gallant a line as ever, and proved that he had not been working only for himself, by his earnest invitation to her to take both cocoa and toast.—She was already helped to tea—which surprised him—so totally self-engrossed had he been.—

"I thought I should have been in time," said he, "but cocoa takes a great deal of boiling.—"

"I am much obliged to you," replied Charlotte—"but I *prefer* tea."

"Then I will help myself," said he.—"A large dish of rather weak cocoa every evening agrees with me better than anything."—

It struck her however, as he poured out this rather weak cocoa, that it came forth in a very fine, dark coloured stream—and at the same moment, his sisters both crying out—"Oh! Arthur, you get your cocoa stronger and stronger every evening"—, with Arthur's somewhat conscious reply of "*Tis* rather stronger than it should be tonight"—convinced her that Arthur was by no means so fond of being starved as they could desire, or as he felt proper himself.—He was certainly very happy to turn the conversation on dry toast, and hear no more of his sisters.—

"I hope you will eat some of this toast," said he, "I reckon myself a very good toaster; I never burn my toasts—I never put them too near the fire at first—and yet, you see, there is not a corner but what is well browned.—I hope you like dry toast.—"

"With a reasonable quantity of butter spread over it, very much"—said Charlotte—"but not otherwise.—"

"No more do I"—said he, exceedingly pleased.—"We think quite alike there.—So far from dry toast being wholesome, *I* think it a very bad thing for the stomach. Without a little butter to soften it, it hurts the coats of the stomach. I am sure it does.—I will have the pleasure of spreading some for you directly—and afterwards I will spread some for myself.—Very bad indeed for the coats of the stomach—but there is no convincing *some* people.—It irritates and acts like a nutmeg grater.—"

He could not get the command of the butter however, without a struggle, his sisters accusing him of eating a great deal too much, and declaring he was not to be trusted;—and he maintaining that he only ate enough to secure the coats of his stomach;—and besides, he only wanted it now for Miss Heywood.—Such a plea must prevail; he got the butter and spread away for her with an accuracy of judgement which at least delighted himself; but when her toast was done, and he took his own in hand, Charlotte could hardly contain herself as she saw him watching his sisters, while he scrupulously scraped off almost as much butter as he put on, and then seize an odd moment for adding a great dab just before it went into his mouth.—Certainly, Mr. Arthur Parker's enjoyments in invalidism were very different from his sisters'—by no means so spiritualized.—A good deal of earthy dross hung about him. Charlotte could not but suspect him of adopting that line of life, principally for the indulgence of an indolent temper—and to be determined on having no disorders but such as called for warm rooms and good nourishment.—In one particular however, she soon found that he had caught something from *them.*—

"What!" said he—"Do you venture upon two dishes of strong green tea in one evening?—What nerves you must have!—How I envy you.—Now, if *I* were to swallow only one such dish—what do you think its effect would be upon me?—"

"Keep you awake perhaps all night"—replied Charlotte, meaning to overthrow his attempts at surprise, by the grandeur of her own conceptions.—

"Oh! if that were all!—" he exclaimed.—"No—it would act on me like poison and entirely take away the use of my right side, before I had swallowed it five minutes.—It sounds almost incredible—but it has happened to me so often that I cannot doubt it.—The use of my right side is entirely taken away for several hours!"

"It sounds rather odd to be sure"—answered Charlotte coolly—"but I dare say it would be proved to be the simplest thing in the world, by those who have studied right sides and green tea scientifically and thoroughly understand all the possibilities of their action on each other."—

Soon after tea, a letter was brought to Miss Diana Parker from the hotel.—"From Mrs. Charles Dupuis"—said she.—"Some private hand."—And having read a few lines, exclaimed aloud, "Well, this is very extraordinary! very extraordinary indeed!—That both should have the same name.—Two Mrs. Griffiths!—This is a letter of recommendation and introduction to me, of the lady from Camberwell—and *her* name happens to be Griffiths too."—

A few lines more however, and the colour rushed into her cheeks, and with much perturbation she added—"The oddest thing that ever was!—a Miss Lambe too!—a young West Indian of large fortune.—But it *cannot* be the same.—Impossible that it should be the same."—

She read the letter aloud for comfort.—It was merely to "introduce the bearer, Mrs. Griffiths from Camberwell, and the three young ladies under her care, to Miss Diana Parker's notice.—Mrs. Griffiths being a stranger at Sanditon, was anxious for a respectable introduction—and Mrs. Charles Dupuis therefore, at the instance of the intermediate friend, provided her with this letter, knowing that she could not do her dear Diana a greater kindness than by giving her the means of being useful.—Mrs. Griffiths's chief solicitude would be for the accommodation and comfort of one of the young ladies under her care, a Miss Lambe, a young West Indian of large fortune, in delicate health."—"It was very strange!—very remarkable!—very extraordinary," but they were all agreed in determining it to be *impossible* that there should not be two families; such a totally distinct set of people as were concerned in the reports of each made that matter quite certain. There *must* be two families.—Impossible to be otherwise.—"Impossible" and "Impossible", was repeated over and over again with great fervour.—An accidental resemblance of names and circumstances, however striking at first, involved nothing really incredible—and so it was settled.—

Miss Diana herself derived an immediate advantage to counterbalance her perplexity. She must put her shawl over her shoulders, and be running about again. Tired as she was, she must instantly repair to the hotel, to investigate the truth and offer her services.—

CHAPTER 11

IT WOULD NOT DO.—Not all that the whole Parker race could say among themselves, could produce a happier catastrophe than that the family from Surry and the family from Camberwell were one and the same.—The rich West Indians, and the young ladies' seminary had all entered Sanditon in those two hack chaises. The Mrs. Griffiths who, in her friend Mrs. Darling's hands, had wavered as to coming and been unequal to the journey, was the very same Mrs. Griffiths whose plans were at the same period (under another representation) perfectly decided, and who was without fears or difficulties.—All that had the appearance of incongruity in the reports of the two, might very fairly be placed to the account of the vanity, the ignorance, or the blunders of the many engaged in the cause by the vigilance and caution of Miss Diana Parker. *Her* intimate friends must be officious like herself, and the subject had supplied letters and extracts and messages enough to make everything appear what it was not.—

Miss Diana probably felt a little awkward on being first obliged to admit her mistake. A long journey from Hampshire taken for nothing—a brother disappointed—an expensive house on her hands for a week—must have been some of her immediate reflections, and much worse than all the rest must have been the sort of sensation of being less clearsighted and infallible than she had believed herself.—No part of it however seemed to trouble her long. There were so many to share in the shame and the blame, that probably when she had divided out their proper portions to Mrs. Darling, Miss Capper, Fanny Noyce, Mrs. Charles Dupuis and Mrs. Charles Dupuis's neighbour, there might be a mere trifle of reproach remaining for herself.—At any rate, she was seen all the following morning walking about after lodgings with Mrs. Griffiths—as alert as ever.—

Mrs. Griffiths was a very well-behaved, genteel kind of woman, who supported herself by receiving such great girls and young ladies, as wanted either masters for finishing their education, or a home for beginning their displays.—She had several more under her care than the three who were now come to Sanditon, but the others all happened to be absent.—Of these three, and indeed of all, Miss Lambe was beyond comparison the most important and precious, as she paid in proportion to her fortune.—She was about seventeen, half mulatto, chilly and tender, had a maid of her own, was to have the best room in the lodgings, and was always of the first consequence in every plan of Mrs. Griffiths.—

The other girls, two Miss Beauforts, were just such young ladies as may be met with, in at least one family out of three, throughout the kingdom; they had tolerable complexions, shewy figures, an upright decided carriage and an assured look;—they were very accomplished and very ignorant, their time being divided between such pursuits as might attract admiration, and those labours and expedients of dexterous ingenuity, by which they could dress in a stile much beyond what they *ought* to have afforded; they were some of the first in every change of fashion—and the object of all, was to captivate some man of much better fortune than their own.—

Mrs. Griffiths had preferred a small, retired place, like Sanditon, on Miss Lambe's account—and the Miss Beauforts, though naturally preferring anything to smallness and retirement, yet having in the course of the spring been involved in the inevitable expence of six new dresses each for a three days' visit, were constrained to be satisfied with Sanditon also, till their circumstances were retrieved. There, with the hire of a harp for one, and the purchase of some drawing paper for the other, and all the finery they could already command, they meant to be very economical, very elegant and very secluded; with the hope, on Miss Beaufort's side, of praise and celebrity from all who walked within the sound of her instrument, and on Miss Letitia's, of curiosity and rapture in all who came near her while she sketched—and to both, the consolation of meaning to be the most stylish girls in the place.—The particular introduction of Mrs. Griffiths to Miss Diana Parker, secured them immediately an acquaintance with the Trafalgar House family, and with the Denhams;—and the Miss Beauforts were soon satisfied with "the circle in which they moved in Sanditon" to use a proper phrase, for every body must now "move in a circle",—to the prevalence of which rotatory motion, is perhaps to be attributed the giddiness and false steps of many.—

Lady Denham had other motives for calling on Mrs. Griffiths besides attention to the Parkers.—In Miss Lambe, here was the very young lady, sickly and rich, whom she had been asking for; and she made the acquaintance for Sir Edward's sake, and the sake of her milch asses. How it might answer with regard to the baronet remained to be proved, but as to the animals, she soon found that all her calculations of profit would be vain. Mrs. Griffiths would not allow Miss Lambe to have the smallest symptom of a decline, or any complaint which asses' milk could possibly relieve. "Miss Lambe was under the constant care of an experienced physician;—and his prescriptions must be their rule—" and except in favour of some tonic pills, which a cousin of her own had a property in, Mrs. Griffiths did never deviate from the strict medicinal page.—

The corner house of the Terrace was the one in which Miss Diana Parker had the pleasure of settling her new friends, and considering that it commanded in front the favourite lounge of all the visitors at Sanditon, and on one side, whatever might be going on at the hotel, there could not have been a more favourable spot for the seclusions of the Miss Beauforts. And accordingly, long before they had suited themselves with an instrument, or with drawing paper, they had, by the frequency of their appearance at the low windows upstairs, in order to close the blinds, or open the blinds, to arrange a flower pot on the balcony, or look at nothing through a telescope, attracted many an eye upwards, and made many a gazer gaze again.—A little novelty has a great effect in so small a place; the Miss Beauforts, who would have been nothing at Brighton, could not move here without notice;—and even Mr. Arthur Parker, though little disposed for supernumerary exertion, always quitted the Terrace in his way to his brother's by this corner house, for the sake of a glimpse of the Miss Beauforts—though it was half a quarter of a mile round about, and added two steps to the ascent of the hill.

CHAPTER 12

CHARLOTTE HAD been ten days at Sanditon without seeing Sanditon House, every attempt at calling on Lady Denham having been defeated by meeting with her beforehand. But now it was to be more resolutely undertaken, at a more early hour, that nothing might be neglected of attention to Lady Denham or amusement to Charlotte.—

"And if you should find a favourable opening my love," said Mr. Parker (who did not mean to go with them)—"I think you had better mention the poor Mullins's situation, and sound her ladyship as to a subscription for them.—I am not fond of charitable subscriptions in a place of this kind—it is a sort of tax upon all that come—yet as their distress is very great and I almost promised the poor woman yesterday to get something done for her, I believe we must set a subscription on foot—and therefore the sooner the better,—and Lady Denham's name at the head of the list will be a very necessary beginning.—You will not dislike speaking to her about it, Mary?—"

"I will do whatever you wish me," replied his wife—"but you would do it so much better yourself. I shall not know what to say."—

"My dear Mary," cried he, "it is impossible you can be really at a loss. Nothing can be more simple. You have only to state the present afflicted situation of the family, their earnest application to me, and my being willing to promote a little subscription for their relief, provided it meet with her approbation."—

"The easiest thing in the world"—cried Miss Diana Parker, who happened to be calling on them at the moment—. "All said and done, in less time than you have been talking of it now.—And while you are on the subject of subscriptions Mary, I will thank you to mention a very melancholy case to Lady Denham, which has been represented to me in the most affecting terms.—There is a poor woman in Worcestershire, whom some friends of mine are exceedingly interested about, and I have undertaken to collect whatever I can for her. If you would mention the circumstance to Lady Denham!—Lady Denham *can* give, if she is properly attacked—and I look upon her to be the sort of person who, when once she is prevailed on to undraw her purse, would as readily give ten guineas as five. And therefore, if you find her in a giving mood, you might as well speak in favour of another charity which I, and a few more, have very much at heart—the establishment of a charitable repository at Burton on Trent.—And then,—there is the family of the poor man who was hung last assizes at York, though we really *have* raised the sum we wanted for putting them all out, yet if you *can* get a guinea from her on their behalf, it may as well be done.—"

"My dear Diana!" exclaimed Mrs. Parker.—"I could no more mention these things to Lady Denham—than I could fly."—

"Where's the difficulty?—I wish I could go with you myself—but in five minutes I must be at Mrs. Griffiths'—to encourage Miss Lambe in taking her first dip. She is so frightened, poor thing, that I promised to come and keep up her spirits, and go in the machine with her if she wished it—and as soon as that is over, I must hurry home, for Susan is to have leeches at one o'clock, which will be a three hours' business,—therefore I really have not a moment to spare—besides that (between ourselves) I ought to be in bed myself at this present time, for I am hardly able to stand—and when the leeches have done, I dare say we shall both go to our rooms for the rest of the day."—

"I am sorry to hear it, indeed; but if this is the case I hope Arthur will come to us."—

"If Arthur takes my advice, he will go to bed too, for if he stays up by himself, he will certainly eat and drink more than he ought;—but you see Mary, how impossible it is for me to go with you to Lady Denham's."—

"Upon second thoughts Mary," said her husband, "I will not trouble you to speak about the Mullins's.—I will take an opportunity of seeing Lady Denham myself.—I know how little it suits you to be pressing matters upon a mind at all unwilling."—

His application thus withdrawn, his sister could say no more in support of hers, which was his object, as he felt all their impropriety and all the certainty of their ill effect upon his own better claim.—

Mrs. Parker was delighted at this release, and set off very happy with her friend and her little girl, on this walk to Sanditon House.—It was a close, misty morning, and when they reached the brow of the hill, they could not for some time make out what sort of carriage it was, which they saw coming up. It appeared at different moments to be everything from the gig to the phaeton,—from one horse to four; and just as they were concluding in favour of a tandem, little Mary's young eyes distinguished the coachman and she eagerly called out, " 'Tis Uncle Sidney mama, it is indeed." And so it proved.—Mr. Sidney Parker driving his servant in a very neat carriage was soon opposite to them, and they all stopped for a few minutes.

The manners of the Parkers were always pleasant among themselves—and it was a very friendly meeting between Sidney and his sister in law, who was most kindly taking it for granted that he was on his way to Trafalgar House. This he declined however.

"He was just come from East Bourne, proposing to spend two or three days, as it might happen, at Sanditon—but the hotel must be his quarters.—He was expecting to be joined there by a friend or two."—The rest was common enquiries and remarks, with kind notice of little Mary, and a very well-bred bow and proper address to Miss Heywood on her being named to him—and they parted, to meet again within a few hours.—

Sidney Parker was about seven or eight and twenty, very good-looking, with a decided air of ease and fashion, and a lively countenance.—This adventure afforded agreeable discussion for some time. Mrs. Parker entered into all her husband's joy on the occasion, and exulted in the credit which Sidney's arrival would give to the place.

The road to Sanditon House was a broad, handsome, planted approach between fields, and conducting at the end of a quarter of a mile through second gates into the grounds, which though not extensive had all the beauty and respectability which an abundance of very fine timber could give.—These entrance gates were so much in a corner of the grounds or paddock, so near one of its boundaries, that an outside fence was at first almost pressing on the road—till an angle *here*, and a curve there threw them to a better distance. The fence was a proper park paling in excellent condition; with clusters of fine elms, or rows of old thorns following its line almost every where.—*Almost* must be stipulated—for there were vacant spaces—and through one of these, Charlotte, as soon as they entered the enclosure, caught a glimpse over the pales of something white and womanish in the field on the other side;—it was a something which immediately brought Miss Brereton into her head—and stepping to the pales, she saw indeed—and very decidedly, in spite of the mist—Miss Brereton seated, not far before her, at the foot of the bank which sloped down from the outside of the paling and which a narrow path seemed to skirt along;—Miss Brereton seated, apparently very composedly—and Sir Edward Denham by her side.—

They were sitting so near each other and appeared so closely engaged in gentle conversation, that Charlotte instantly felt she had nothing to do but to step back again, and say not a word.—Privacy was certainly their object.—It could not but strike her rather unfavourably with regard to Clara;—but hers was a situation which must not be judged with severity.—She was glad to perceive that nothing had been discerned by Mrs. Parker; if Charlotte had not been considerably the tallest of the two, Miss Brereton's white ribbons might not have fallen within the ken of *her* more observant eyes.—Among other points of moralising reflection which the sight of this tete a tete produced, Charlotte could not but think of the extreme difficulty which secret lovers must have in finding a proper spot for their stolen interviews.—Here perhaps they had thought themselves so perfectly secure from observation!—the whole field open before them—a steep bank and pales never crossed by the foot of man at their back—and a great thickness of air, in aid.—Yet, here, she had seen them. They were really ill-used.—

The house was large and handsome; two servants appeared, to admit them, and every thing had a suitable air of property and order.—Lady Denham valued herself upon her liberal establishment, and had great enjoyment in the order and importance of her style of living.—They were shown into the usual sitting room, well-proportioned and well-furnished;—though it was furniture rather originally good and extremely well kept, than new or showy—and as Lady Denham was not there, Charlotte had leisure to look about, and to be told by Mrs. Parker that the whole-length portrait of a stately gentleman, which, placed over the mantlepeice, caught the eye immediately, was the picture of Sir Harry Denham—and that one among many miniatures in another part of the room, little conspicuous, represented Mr. Hollis.—Poor Mr. Hollis!—It was impossible not to feel him hardly used; to be obliged to stand back in his own house and see the best place by the fire constantly occupied by Sir Harry Denham.

NOTES TO 'SANDITON'

ADVERTISING ('puffing')

Advertisements for goods and services were published in newspapers and magazines and on placards. The *Morning Post* was a London daily paper read by the rich and fashionable; it included **lists of genteel arrivals and departures** not only in London but also in Bath, Weymouth, Cheltenham, Brighton and Ramsgate during their various social seasons. Its advertisements were aimed at a national as well as London readership. The *Kentish Gazette* came out twice weekly and was aimed at people in Kent and nearby counties including Sussex; it regularly carried **advertisements by medical men** looking for assistants and business investors. Many newspapers and pamphlets also promoted **cures** and health services.

Houses with accommodation to let in a resort would put advertising bills in their windows.

The development of **seaside resorts** depended on the eighteenth-century fashion for combining medical treatments with leisure activities as in the older spa towns such as Bath or Tunbridge Wells. Soon **Brighton** and some other coastal resorts developed 'seasons' and were promoted in **pamphlets** that stressed amenities and quality of air. Competition was fierce and, as well as the benefits of the promoted resort, the drawbacks of rivals were pointed out: some, for example, had a problem with smelly seaweed and putrid stagnant water, both of which were thought to cause malignant fevers.

Access from London was a strong selling point for seaside resorts and *A Guide to All the Watering and Sea Bathing Places*, edited by John Feltham (1803–1825), included a table of distances.

CARRIAGES

It was expensive to **keep a coach** and needed an income of at least £800–£1,000. Besides the coach, a coachman was required, along with a groom, horses and stabling. Even keeping **a single horse** for riding was beyond a small income, requiring about £20 for stabling and an extra servant, as Elinor Dashwood points out in *Sense and Sensibility*. For economy, an old carriage could be renewed by having new lining fitted over the old woodwork. **Equipage** referred to carriage, horses, related accessories and servants.

A **chaise** was a substantial four-wheeled close carriage drawn by two or four horses, carrying two or three passengers, four at most. Open carriages usually owned by young affluent men included the **gig**, a light two-wheeled carriage with a single horse for one or two people; the two-wheeled **tandem**, drawn by two horses harnessed one behind the other; and the larger **phaeton** with four wheels drawn by a pair of horses.

Sometimes a traveller would use his own carriage but hire horses and a driver at inns on the way. A **post-chaise** was available with horses for hire to people with sufficient money who wanted speed (hence to 'post' was to hurry). A **hack** was a vehicle for hire.

With a network of **turnpike roads** (toll roads administered by private trusts but paying fees to the government) travel to the seaside resorts had become speedier. Local roads were maintained by the parish or local landowners and could be in poorer condition, like the one leading to the Heywoods' house.

CLOTHES AND ACCESSORIES

Young ladies in the Regency period often wore fashionable white, especially in muslin, a material which suited the Empire style with its light long flowing shape. **Pendant lace** refers to any piece of special lace hanging out for display.

Blue shoes for ladies were fashionable from the 1790s, replacing the more serviceable black ones. **Nankin boots** (advocated by Lord Osborne in 'The Watsons') were half boots for gentle walking: they reached above the ankle, were fastened by front laces, and could be made of 'nankin' or nankeen, pale yellow cotton originally from Nanking, China.

Genteel young ladies would usually have been taught music as one of their accomplishments, with the **pianoforte** the most common instrument; the **harp** was also popular and had the advantage of allowing the lady to be seen in a graceful posture. It is the chosen instrument of attractive Mary Crawford in *Mansfield Park*.

HOUSES

The original houses of coastal villages from which the south-coast resorts were being developed would usually be slightly inland for protection from the sea and bad weather. Tom Parker has left his inherited mansion, built in a sheltered valley like most old manor houses, and built himself a new home on a cliff in Sanditon, positioned to take advantage of the fine view of coast and sea but also attracting a buffeting from wind and rain.

Newbuilt resort houses were often named patriotically for recent battles. In the decisive naval battle of Trafalgar in 1805 Lord Nelson defeated the French and Spanish fleets; in 1815 the Duke of Wellington, leading an Anglo-Dutch army assisted by the Prussians, defeated Napoleon at the Battle of Waterloo, and the name was thus more current in 1817 than Trafalgar. Other house names like Prospect and Bellevue advertised a view.

Terraced houses in a crescent shape were associated with superior accommodation in spas and resorts like Bath and Brighton. Other terraces formed a line of houses raised up from the natural street level to provide a wide walkway as a formal promenade. A **mall** (the name originating in a London alley where pall-mall – a form of putting – was played) was a term used for a fashionable walkway.

In new Georgian houses, the living rooms were often on the first floor, with large or full-length **windows** through which occupants could see and be seen. Frequently there was a small balcony outside. The elegant **Venetian window** had three openings, the central one being arched and larger than the others.

With eyes trained by **picturesque theory** as taught by **William Gilpin** in his books of tours through Britain (such as *Observations on the*

NOTES TO 'SANDITON'

Western Parts of England, Relative Chiefly to Picturesque Beauty [1798]), Tom Parker mistakes a rundown double tenement (a house divided and let to two separate tenants) for a picturesque rural cottage. The ***cottage ornée***, designed specifically to be picturesque and seem rural, was a detached mock rustic dwelling built for the gentry. In Sanditon Sir Edward is erecting one for letting out to genteel visitors.

LITERARY ALLUSIONS

References are to Austen's usual authorities, **William Gilpin** on the sublime and picturesque and the poet **William Cowper** on nature and rural life, both authors alluded to throughout her works. The line 'She never heard of half a mile from home' is taken from Cowper's poem, 'Truth' (1782), in which a simple Christian peasant woman is contrasted favourably with the famous philosopher Voltaire, regarded by many as a dangerous atheist.

Most of the literary allusions in 'Sanditon' occur in Sir Edward's jumbled speeches. He refers to lines of current poetry expressing exaggerated emotions, especially those taken from the popular Romantic works of **Walter Scott** and **Robert Burns**. The quotation 'O, Woman! in our hour of ease' comes from Scott's *Marmion* (1808), where the maiden Clara rushes to the aid of the fatally wounded knight (Scott's character shares her name with Lady Denham's interesting companion, young Clara Brereton). The lines from *The Lady of the Lake* (1810) celebrate the selfless love of a father for his daughter. In neither *Marmion* nor *The Lady of the Lake* are there many lines about the sea, although *Marmion* has an account of a sea voyage. Burns wrote love poems to and about several women including Mary Campbell ('Highland Mary'). His known promiscuity and love of alcohol shocked some of his primmer readers.

William Wordsworth was at this time known primarily for *Lyrical Ballads* (1798), *Poems in Two Volumes* (1807) and *The Excursion* (1814). **James Montgomery**'s poetry included *The Wanderer of Switzerland* (1806) and *The West Indies* (1807), the latter accompanying a series of pictures published to commemorate the abolition of the slave trade. **Thomas Campbell** wrote *The Pleasures of Hope* (1799), a lengthy meditation on hope in a world of war, tyranny and injustice, from which Sir Edward quotes the line, 'Like angel visits, few and far between'.

Sir Edward regards **novels from circulating libraries** as 'trash', a common opinion among the educated at the time. The Austens, however, found reading such works an amusing pastime, see the spoof 'Letter to Mrs Hunter' in this volume. Sir Edward quotes the facetious phrase 'fair questioner' from **Frances Burney**'s *Camilla: or, a Picture of Youth* (1796), a serious novel admired by Jane Austen. Charlotte Heywood also refers to *Camilla* as she contemplates spending money in Sanditon: Burney's heroine overspends her small allowance in the spa of Tunbridge Wells and faces much social embarrassment. Both Sir Edward and Charlotte are aware of the clichés of 'modern literature': the stock figures of popular romance include the aristocratic seducer and the impoverished heroine. For Sir Edward and Charlotte, the latter role is taken by Lady Denham's companion, the beautiful Clara.

The novels of **Samuel Richardson** have sunk deeply into Sir Edward's addled mind, especially *Clarissa* (1747–8), in which the virtuous heroine is pursued and ultimately raped by the villainous Lovelace, who then dies in a duel. Despite his best efforts, Richardson found many readers admiring Lovelace for his wit, humour and inventiveness, and the character was copied by a large number of novelists, including Burney with Sir Clement Willoughby in *Evelina* (1778). Sir Edward is eager to emulate Lovelace by abducting and seducing Clara.

Timbuktu, an ancient city on the southern edge of the African Sahara, largely unvisited by Europeans, was often used to signify the most distant place imaginable. A similar use is made of the Russian area Kamchatka in 'Plan of a Novel'.

MONEY AND INCOME

In the landowning classes, the eldest son inherited the family estate with home farm and tenanted farms; before he inherited, he would usually receive an allowance from his father. Younger sons might possess an individual 'collateral' inheritance from a relative with no direct heir. Without inherited income or expectations, young men would often enter the professions: the Church, law or military.

The **solicitor** listed in the Sanditon library subscription is from Gray's Inn, one of the London Inns of Court; he would have lower social standing than a barrister. The **lieutenant** from the Royal Navy is of modest rank, while the **captain** from Limehouse would be from the Merchant Navy, so of lesser status than a Royal Navy captain. **Half-pay officers**, from army or navy, were not on active service and were receiving reduced pay.

Beyond the professions, men might make money from **investments** in the City of London and in government **bonds** which paid dividends. They might also be involved in **mining** land for various substances from coal to gold, in trade or in speculative **entrepreneurial projects** such as the development of resorts. British merchants and **plantation owners** might amass substantial fortunes from the West Indies if they survived the tropical diseases; when they returned with their riches to Britain, they were regarded as both indolent and passionate as a result of living in a hot climate.

A final way of making a fortune needed luck: winning the **lottery**, either a private one or more usually the state lottery, which lasted from 1694 to 1826.

Women were of course barred from the professions, their main outside roles being limited to **governess, teacher** and **companion**. Below these was the uneducated **nursery maid** who looked after young children and kept a nursery clean. Her wage would be as low as £6 or £8 a year, where an educated governess might expect £40. Lady Denham is in the unusual position for a widow of having command of her original substantial fortune of £30,000 and her first husband's wealth. More commonly a widow subsisted on a **jointure**, usually a proportion of the estate agreed for her maintenance in the original marriage settlement.

Although there was some organized parish poor relief, much assistance for the poor had to come from private charity. Hard economic times followed the end of the Napoleonic Wars in 1815 and **charitable subscriptions** abounded. For these, well-off people would agree to make a specific contribution to a worthy cause; if prominent people subscribed, others would be encouraged to follow suit. Usually subscriptions would be local; Diana Parker reveals her absurdity by the distant nature of her charitable activities – in **Worcestershire, York** and **Burton-on-Trent** in Staffordshire, all far from England's south coast. **Charitable repositories** in part resembled charity shops, where donated goods were sold for the benefit of the poor. Sometimes they also offered schooling and lodging for the poor. **Putting a child out** required an initial premium so that the young person could enter an apprenticeship or be shown some other way of earning a living.

Throughout 'Sanditon' there is discussion of **political economy**: whether the market should simply be left to take care of itself or be regulated to avoid huge inequalities of wealth in society. Another debate was whether consumption by rich visitors actually benefited the poorer classes or disturbed the original economy of a region.

PLACES

Sanditon and Brinshore are fictional resorts on the Sussex coast. Their real-life rivals were developed in the eighteenth and early nineteenth centuries out of old fishing villages, **Brighton** being the largest and most fashionable, having been patronised by the Prince of Wales from the 1780s. **Worthing**, visited in 1798 by Princess Amelia, George III's youngest daughter, is about ten miles west of Brighton. **Tonbridge**, about thirty miles south of London, was on one of the main coach roads to the coast from the capital; the road divided at the spa town of Tunbridge Wells, with one branch going south-east to **Hastings** and the other south-west to **Eastbourne**, both resorts on the south coast.

A resort's **amenities** could include **assembly rooms, a bathing house, a hospital, billiard rooms,** and **shops**. The **library** would sell stationery, perfume, jewellery and ornaments as well as lending books. In smaller towns, the subscription book of the library could act as a kind of **social register** listing visitors arriving in the town. The holiday **season** for seaside resorts ran from May to October, with August and September usually being the most expensive months.

Surrey was at this time a rural county south of London; it included **Camberwell**, then a country village near the capital.

Shropshire is a county in the west Midlands, therefore far from Sanditon. **Battle** is a small town seven miles inland from Hastings, the name being short for 'Battle Abbey' after the church built by William the Conqueror to commemorate the Battle of Hastings. **Hailsham** is about six miles north of Eastbourne. **Chichester** is a small cathedral city five miles inland from the south coast. **The Isle of Wight** is a large island off the south coast of England. **South Foreland** near Dover to **Land's End** at the tip of Cornwall comprises the full length of England's south coast.

SEA CURES

Sea air and salt water were believed to have healing properties and were much promoted by enthusiastic treatises. **Immersion** might occur in the sea or a sea-water bath.

Bathing (not swimming but 'dipping' for a minute or two in the cold sea) was promoted for a huge variety of ailments from the 'lax fibred' to those with gout and dropsy. For a shilling the patient would enter a horse-drawn wooden box or **machine** (for ladies the box had a canvas modesty hood) and be trundled into the sea. A man might dip naked but a lady would put on a flannel bathing costume and be urged into the water by a **dipper**. Some medical men tried to moderate the fantastic claims for sea water, for example **Dr Thomas Trotter**, who accused doctors (the 'medical tribe') of exploiting illness for gain.

SICKNESS AND MEDICINES

Nervous diseases of all sorts were blamed on the self-indulgence or **hypochondria** of the leisured: '*Nervous* Disorders are the Diseases of the Wealthy, the Voluptuous, and the Lazy . . . mostly produced, and always aggravated, by *Luxury* and *Intemperance*,' declared **George Cheyne** in *The English Malady: or, a Treatise on Nervous Diseases of All Kinds* (1733). Others believed a 'languid' way of life could affect and corrupt the liver.

It was thought that **bile**, the bitter fluid secreted by the liver, would, in excess or if obstructed, make a person **bilious**, suffering pain, spasms or nausea. **Headaches** might suggest a hot bilious state; to ameliorate this the skin would be blistered and leeches applied to the temples and behind the ears.

A **decline** could refer to general debility or a specific disease such as consumption/tuberculosis.

Hysterical fits or convulsions were associated mainly with women; they probably occurred more in fiction than in life.

Perspiration, so feared by Arthur Parker, was usually seen as healthy.

The Parkers' self-medicating is alarming. To have **teeth extracted or pulled** was a drastic remedy since there was no way properly to dull the pain. Applying **leeches** for three hours would be weakening even to the healthy (leeches inject a blood-thinning agent with their bite; once leeches were removed, pressure had to be applied to the wound so the flow of blood would be stopped). **Friction or vigorous chafing** or rubbing was not usually recommended for sprains or strains.

A common domestic remedy was **bitters** (either quinine [bark of the Peruvian cinchona tree] or native herbs such as camomile and tansy) boiled to a concentrate, then used for fevers and upset stomachs. **Poultices** for sprains were made from stale beer or vinegar, brandy, oatmeal, camphorated spirits of wine and volatile aromatic spirit. Serious bruises could be treated with a poultice from boiling breadcrumbs, elderflower and camomile.

Cocoa, a chocolate drink made from sweetened and flavoured cacao beans, was regarded as a stimulant. **Butter** was potentially harmful to weak stomachs since it could easily go rancid. **Green and black tea** and their properties were much discussed at the time; one authority considered green tea relaxing to delicate people and depressive to melancholy ones, so causing many nervous ailments. Moderation was recommended. **Asses' milk** was seen as particularly suitable for asthmatics and consumptives.

Smelling salts, usually of ammonium carbonate, were used against faintness. **Drops** could be an opiate like laudanum or elixir of vitriol.

The **chamber horse** was an early exercise machine which simulated the experience of riding a horse.

JANE AUSTEN ON FICTION

PREFACE TO JANE AUSTEN'S WRITINGS ON FICTION

THROUGHOUT her life, Austen was fascinated by the craft of fiction. She minutely considered her own work and the literary habits of others. As she had in her childhood, she continued to entertain her family with comic pieces mocking the absurdity of the English novel as written by the sillier writers of her generation.

Her niece Anna, daughter of her eldest brother James, described how she fetched books from the circulating library, which she and her aunt Jane then enjoyed reading and ridiculing for their improbable stories and sensational characters. One of these was *Lady Maclairn, the Victim of Villany* (1806), 'an exceedingly lengthy affair' written by 'Mrs Hunter of Norwich'. Presumably Anna had composed a letter as from Mrs Hunter, to which Jane Austen replied in a note, 'To Mrs Hunter of Norwich', describing the tears the novel brought to her eyes.

Their aunt's success as a published author prompted Anna and her half-siblings Caroline and James Edward to write fiction of their own; all asked Jane Austen for views on their work. The most sustained creative attempt was made by Anna during the summer and autumn of 1814 before her marriage to Benjamin Lefroy ('Ben' in the letters) and the pregnancy that swiftly followed. During these months Anna sent draft chapters from her home in the rectory at Steventon to her aunts Jane and Cassandra and grandmother Mrs Austen, now living at the cottage in Chawton, for their comments. As courier, she used members of the Digweed family, who were friends and neighbours of the Austens. Although fond of the Digweeds, Jane Austen enjoyed parodying the speech habits of Mrs Digweed, noting her favourite phrase, 'beyond everything'.

The letter extracts printed here are taken from Jane Austen's replies to Anna's letters and drafts. Austen helped Anna by providing much needed advice on the right amount of descriptive minuteness in fiction, on the paring down of detail, on adroit characterization and on social verisimilitude. People in a novel should act as closely as possible to how real people would act in life, she counselled. As well as aiding her niece's work, these extracts form a commentary on Jane Austen's own practice of fiction.

The burlesque 'Plan of a Novel' is undated but was probably written during or shortly after the exchange of correspondence in 1815–16 between Jane Austen and James Stanier Clarke, chaplain and librarian to the Prince Regent. His absurd suggestions were first that Austen describe a clergyman remarkably like himself, and then, noting the approaching marriage of the Prince Regent's daughter Charlotte to the German Prince Leopold, that she write a 'Historical Romance illustrative of the History of the august house of Cobourg'. This correspondence with Clarke provided a major impetus for the 'Plan', but the little work also derives much hilarity from the sensational plots of contemporary novels including Frances Burney's *The Wanderer* (1814) and Mary Brunton's *Self-Control* (1811). In the latter the perfect heroine starves herself for the benefit of others and is pursued by an obsessive lover who abducts her to the wilds of Canada.

The speed with which everything happens in 'Plan' is reminiscent of the fast condensed stories in the childhood writings, 'Evelyn' for example, where the hero gains a young wife, estate and money in a few pages. Included in 'Plan' are Jane Austen's marginal notes, here identified by lower-case letters, indicating the 'various quarters' from which 'hints' for the mock-novel are derived.

TO MRS. HUNTER OF NORWICH[1]

MISS JANE AUSTEN begs her best thanks may be conveyed to M[rs.] Hunter of Norwich[2] for the Threadpaper[3] which she has been so kind as to send her by M[r.] Austen,[4] & which will be always very valuable on account of the spirited sketches (made it is supposed by Nicholson or Glover[5]) of the most interesting spots, Tarefield Hall, the Mill, & above all the Tomb of Howard's wife,[6] of the faithful representation of which Miss Jane Austen is undoubtedly a good judge having spent so many summers at Tarefield Abbey the delighted guest of the worthy M[rs.] Wilson. Miss Jane Austen's tears have flowed over each sweet sketch in such a way as would do M[rs.] Hunter's heart good to see; if M[rs.] Hunter could understand all Miss Jane Austen's interest in the subject she would certainly have the kindness to publish at least 4 vols more about the Flint family, & especially would give many fresh particulars on that part of it which M[rs.] H. has hitherto handled too briefly; viz, the history of Mary Flint's marriage with Howard.

Miss Jane Austen can not close this small epitome of the miniature abridgment of her thanks & admiration without expressing her sincere hope that M[rs.] Hunter is provided at Norwich with a more safe conveyance to London than Alton can now boast, as the Car of Falkenstein which was the pride of that Town was overturned within the last 10 days.

NOTES TO 'TO MRS. HUNTER OF NORWICH'

1 This spoof letter was recorded in a letter which Austen's niece Anna Lefroy wrote to her half-brother James Edward Austen-Leigh in 1864.

2 **Norwich**: a county town 100 miles from London, much further than the distance from Alton to London, which was served by Collier's or Falkner's

coach. The name presumably came from the current owner or driver; here it is comically replaced by the 'Car of Falkenstein' in imitation of contemporary literary-Gothic language.

3 **Threadpaper**: a strip of thin soft paper folded in creases to keep threads separate.

4 **Mr Austen**: here, Anna's father and Jane's brother, James.

5 **Nicholson or Glover**: Francis Nicholson (1753–1844) and John Glover (1767–1849), British artists best known at the time for romantic landscapes.

6 **Mr Howard**: in Mrs Hunter's novel, a curate married to the beautiful and better born Mary Flint. Because of the downwardly mobile marriage, Mary is disinherited and dies in undeserved poverty. The Wilsons are good, modest farmers living at Tarefield Abbey, where Mrs Wilson takes in paying lodgers. The 'Tomb of Howard's wife' does not appear in Mrs Hunter's novel.

LETTERS ON FICTION
TO ANNA LEFROY

Postscript to a letter from Mrs Austen, ?c. mid-July 1814
?Chawton to Steventon

My dear Anna—I am very much obliged to you for sending your MS. It has entertained me extremely, all of us indeed; I read it aloud to your G. M.—& A! C!—and we were all very much pleased.—The Spirit does not droop at all. Sir Tho:—Lady Helena, & S! Julian are very well done— & Cecilia continues to be interesting inspite of her being so amiable.—It was very fit that you should advance her age. I like the beginning of D. Forester very much—a great deal better than if he had been very Good or very Bad.—A few verbal corrections were all that I felt tempted to make—the principal of them is a speech of S! Julians to Lady Helena— which you will see I have presumed to alter.—As Lady H. is Cecilia's superior, it w^d not be correct to talk of <u>her</u> being introduced; Cecilia must be the person introduced—and I do not like a Lover's speaking in the 3^d person;—it is too much like the formal part of Lord Orville,[2] & I think is not natural. If <u>you</u> think differently however, you need not mind me.—I am impatient for more—& only wait for a safe conveyance to return this Book.—Yours affec^{ly}, J. A.

Wednesday 10–Thursday 18 August 1814
Chawton to Steventon

My dear Anna
    I am quite ashamed to find that I have never answered some questions of yours in a former note.—I kept the note on purpose

to refer to it at a proper time, & then forgot it.—I like the name "Which is the Heroine?" very well, & I dare say shall grow to like it very much in time—but "Enthusiasm" was something so very superior that every common Title must appear to disadvantage.[3]—I am not sensible of any Blunders about Dawlish. The Library was particularly pitiful & wretched 12 years ago, & not likely to have anybody's publication.—There is no such title as Desborough— either among the Dukes, Marquisses, Earls, Viscounts or Barons.—These were your enquiries. —I will now thank you for your Envelope, received this morning.—I hope M.̣ W. D. will come. —I can readily imagine M.ṛ ͅ H. D. may be very like a profligate Young Lord—I dare say the likeness will be "beyond every thing".—Your Aunt Cass:—is as well pleased with S.ṭ Julian as ever. I am delighted with the idea of seeing Progillian again.

Wednesday 17.—We have just finished the 1.ṣṭ of the 3 Books I had the pleasure of receiving yesterday; I read it aloud—& we are all very much amused, & like the work quite as well as ever.—I depend upon getting through another book before dinner, but there is really a great deal of respectable reading in your 48 Pages. I was an hour about it. —I have no doubt that 6 will make a very good sized volume.—You must be quite pleased to have accomplished so much.—I like Lord P. & his Brother very much;—I am only afraid that Lord P.—'s good nature will make most people like him better than he deserves.—The whole Portman Family are very good—& Lady Anne, who was your great dread, you have succeeded particularly well with.—Bell Griffin is just what she should be.—My Corrections have not been more important than before; —here & there, we have thought the sense might be expressed in fewer words—and I have scratched out Sir Tho: from walking with the other Men to the Stables &c the very day after his breaking his arm—for though I find your Papa did walk out immediately after his arm was set, I think it can be so little usual as to appear unnatural in a book—& it does not seem to be material that Sir Tho: should go with them.—Lyme will not do. Lyme is towards 40 miles distance from Dawlish & would not be talked of there.—I have put Starcross indeed.—If you prefer Exeter, that must be always safe.[4]—I have also scratched out the Introduction between Lord P. & his Brother, & M.[r] Griffin. A Country Surgeon (dont tell M.[r] C. Lyford) would not be introduced to Men of their rank.—And when M.[r] Portman is first brought in, he w.[d] not be introduced as the Hon[ble]— That distinction is never mentioned at such times;—at least I beleive not.[5]—Now, we have finished the 2.[d] book—or rather the 5.th—I do think you had better omit Lady Helena's postscript;—to those who are acquainted with P. & P.[6] it will seem an Imitation.—And your Aunt C. & I both recommend your making a little alteration in the last scene between Devereux F. & Lady Clanmurray & her Daughter. We think they press him too much—more than sensible Women or well-bred Women would do. Lady C. at least, should have discretion enough to be sooner satisfied with his determination of not going with them.—I am very much pleased with Egerton as yet—. I did not expect to like him, but I do; & Susan is a very nice little animated Creature—but S.[r] Julian is the delight of one's Life. He is quite interesting.—The whole of his Break-off with Lady H. is very well done.—

Yes—Russel Square is a very proper distance from Berkeley S.[t]—We are reading the last book.—They must be two days going from Dawlish to Bath; They are nearly 100 miles apart.[7]

Thursday. We finished it last night, after our return from drinking tea at the G.[t] House.[8]—The last chapter does not please us quite so well, we do not thoroughly like the Play; perhaps from having had too much of Plays in that way lately.—And we think you had better not leave England. Let the Portmans go to Ireland, but as you know nothing of the manners there, you had better not go with them. You will be in danger of giving false representations. Stick to Bath & the Foresters. There you will be quite at home.—Your Aunt C. does not like desultory novels, & is rather fearful yours will be too much so, that there will be too frequent a change from one set of people to another, & that circumstances will be sometimes introduced of apparent consequence, which will lead to nothing.— It will not be so great an objection to me, if it does. I allow much more Latitude than she does—& think Nature & Spirit cover many sins of a wandering story—and People in general do not care so much about it—for your comfort. I should like to have had more of Devereux. I do not feel enough acquainted with him.—You were afraid of meddling with him I dare say.—I like your sketch of Lord Clanmurray, and your picture of the two poor young girls enjoyments is very good.—I have not yet noticed S.! Julian's serious conversation with Cecilia, but I liked it exceedingly;—what he says about the madness of otherwise sensible Women, on the subject of their Daughters coming out, is worth it's weight in gold.—I do not see that the language sinks.—Pray go on.

Yours very affec:^{ly} J. Austen

[Postscript]
    Twice you have put Dorsetshire for Devonshire. I have altered it.—Mr Griffin must have lived in Devonshire; Dawlish is half way down the County.—

Friday 9–Sunday 18 September 1814
Chawton (to Steventon?)

My dear Anna
    We have been very much amused by your 3 books, but I have a good many criticisms to make—more than you will like.—We are not satisfied with M^{rs}. F.'s settling herself as Tenant & near Neighbour to such a Man as Sir T. H. without having some other inducement to go there; she ought to have some friend living thereabouts to tempt her. A woman, going with two girls just growing up, into a Neighbourhood where she knows nobody but one Man, of not very good character, is an awkwardness which so prudent a woman as M^{rs}. F would not be likely to fall into. Remember, she is very prudent;— you must not let her act inconsistently.—Give her a friend, & let that friend be invited to meet her at the Priory, & we shall have no objection to her dining there as she does; but otherwise, a woman in her situation would hardly go there, before she had been visited by other Families.—I like the scene itself, the Miss Lesleys, Lady Anne, & the Music, very much.—Lesley is a noble name.—Sir T. H. you

always do very well; I have only taken the liberty of expunging one phrase of his, which would not be allowable. "Bless my Heart."—It is too familiar & inelegant. Your G. M. is more disturbed at Mrs F.'s not returning the Egertons visit sooner, than anything else. They ought to have called at the Parsonage before Sunday.—

You describe a sweet place, but your descriptions are often more minute than will be liked. You give too many particulars of right hand & left.—

Mrs F. is not careful enough of Susan's health;—Susan ought not to be walking out so soon after Heavy rains, taking long walks in the dirt. An anxious Mother would not suffer it.—I like your Susan very much indeed, she is a sweet creature, her playfulness of fancy is very delightful. I like her as she is <u>now</u> exceedingly, but I am not so well satisfied with her behaviour to George R. At first she seemed all over attachment & feeling, & afterwards to have none at all; she is so extremely composed at the Ball, & so well satisfied apparently with Mr Morgan. She seems to have changed her Character.—You are now collecting your People delightfully, getting them exactly into such a spot as is the delight of my life;—3 or 4 Families in a Country Village is the very thing to work on— & I hope you will write a great deal more, & make full use of them while they are so very favourably arranged. You are but <u>now</u> coming to the heart & beauty of your book; till the heroine grows up, the fun must be imperfect—but I expect a great deal of entertainment from the next 3 or 4 books, & I hope you will not resent these remarks by sending me no more.—We like the Egertons very well, we see no Blue Pantaloons, or Cocks & Hens;—there is nothing to <u>enchant</u> one certainly in Mr L. L.—but we make no objection to him, & his inclination to like Susan is pleasing.—The Sister is a good contrast—but the name of Rachael is as much as I can bear.—They are not so much like the Papillons[9] as I expected. Your last chapter is very entertaining—the conversation on Genius &c. Mr St J.—& Susan both talk in character & very well.—In some former parts, Cecilia is perhaps a little too solemn & good, but upon the whole, her disposition is very well opposed to Susan's—her want of Imagination is very natural.—I wish you could make Mrs F. talk more, but she must be difficult to manage & make entertaining, because there is so much good common sense & propriety about her that nothing can be very <u>broad</u>. Her Economy & her Ambition must not be staring.—The Papers left by M^{rs}. Fisher is very good.—Of course, one guesses something.—I hope when you have written a great deal more you will be equal to scratching out some of the past.—The scene with M^{rs}. Mellish, I should condemn; it is prosy & nothing to the purpose—& indeed, the more you can find in your heart to curtail between Dawlish & Newton Priors, the better I think it will be.—One does not care for girls till they are grown up.—Your Aunt C. quite enters into the exquisiteness of that name. Newton Priors is really a Nonpareil.—Milton w^d have given his eyes to have thought of it.—Is not the Cottage taken from Tollard Royal?[10]—

Sunday 18.th—I am very glad dear Anna, that I wrote as I did before this sad Event[11] occurred. I have now only to add that your G. Mama does not seem the worse now for the Shock.—I shall be very happy to receive more of your work, if more is ready; & you write so fast, that I have great hopes M^r. D. will come freighted back with such a Cargo as not all his Hops or his Sheep could equal the value of.

Your Grandmama desires me to say that she will have finished your Shoes tomorrow & thinks they will look very well;—and that she depends upon seeing you, as you promise, before you quit the Country, & hopes you will give her more than a day.—Y^{rs}. affec:^{ly}

J. Austen

Wednesday 28 September 1814
Chawton to Steventon

My dear Anna

I hope you do not depend on having your book back again immediately. I keep it that your G: Mama may hear it—for it has not been possible yet to have any public reading. I have read it to your Aunt Cassandra however—in our own room at night, while we undressed—and with a great deal of pleasure. We like the first chapter extremely—with only a little doubt whether Ly Helena is not almost <u>too</u> foolish. The matrimonial Dialogue is very good certainly.—I like Susan as well as ever—and begin now not to care at all about Cecilia— she may stay at Easton Court as long as she likes.—Henry Mellish I am afraid will be too much in the common Novel style—a handsome, amiable, unexceptionable Young Man (such as do not much abound in real Life) desperately in Love, & all in vain. But I have no business to judge him so early.—Jane Egerton is a very natural, comprehendable Girl—& the whole of her acquaintance with Susan, & Susan's Letter to Cecilia, very pleasing & quite in character.—But <u>Miss</u> Egerton does not entirely satisfy us. She is too formal & solemn, we think, in her advice to her Brother not to fall in love; & it is hardly like a sensible Woman; it is putting it into his head.—We should like a few hints from her better.—We feel really obliged to you for introducing a Lady Kenrick, it will remove the greatest fault in the work, & I give you credit for considerable forbearance as an Author in adopting so much of our opinion.—I expect high fun about Mrs Fisher & Sir Thomas.—You have been perfectly right in telling Ben of your work, & I am very glad to hear how much he likes it. <u>His</u> encouragement & approbation must be quite "beyond everything".—I do not at all wonder at his not expecting to like anybody so well as Cecilia <u>at first</u>, but shall be surprised if he does not become a Susan-ite in time.—Devereux Forester's being ruined by his Vanity is extremely good; but I wish you would not let him plunge into a "vortex of Dissipation". I do not object to the Thing, but I cannot bear the expression;— it is such thorough novel slang—and so old, that I dare say Adam met with it in the first novel he opened.— Indeed I did very much like to know Ben's opinion.—I hope he will continue to be pleased with it, I think he must—but I cannot flatter him with there being much Incident. We have no great right to wonder at his not valueing the name of Progillian. <u>That</u> is a source of delight which he hardly ever can be quite competent to.—Walter Scott[12] has no business to write novels, especially good ones.—It is not fair.—He has Fame & Profit enough as Poet, and should not be taking the bread out of other people's mouths.—I do not like him, & do not mean to like Waverley if I can help it—but I fear I must.—I am quite determined however not to be pleased with M^rs. West's[13] Alicia de Lacy, should I ever meet with it, which I hope I may not.—I think I can be stout against any thing written by M^rs. West.—I have made up my mind to like no Novels really, but Miss Edgeworth's, Yours & my own.—

What can you do with Egerton to increase the interest for him?—I wish you c^d. contrive something, some family occurrence to draw out his good qualities more—some distress among Brothers or Sisters to releive by the sale of his Curacy—something to take him mysteriously away, & then heard of at York or Edinburgh—in an old great Coat.—I would not seriously recommend any thing Improbable, but if you c^d. invent something spirited for him, it w^d. have a good effect.—He might lend all his Money to Captn. Morris—but then he w^d. be a great fool if he did. Cannot the Morrises quarrel, & he reconcile them?—Excuse the liberty I take in these suggestions.—

Your affect^te. Aunt J. Austen

Wednesday 30 November 1814
London, Hans Place, to Hendon

My dear Anna

I have been very far from finding your Book an Evil I assure you; I read it immediately—& with great pleasure. I think you are going on very well. The description of D^r. Griffin & Lady Helena's unhappiness is very good, just what was likely to be.—I am curious to know what the end of them will be: The name of Newton-Priors is really invaluable!—I never met with anything superior to it.—It is delightful.—One could live upon the name of Newton-Priors for a twelvemonth.—Indeed, I do think you get on very fast. I wish other people of my acquaintance could compose as rapidly.—I am pleased with the Dog scene, & with the whole of George & Susan's Love; but am more particularly struck with your serious conversations &c.—They are very good throughout.—S^r.

Julian's History was quite a surprise to me; You had not very long known it yourself I suspect—but I have no objection to make to the circumstance—it is very well told—& his having been in love with the Aunt, gives Cecilia an additional Interest with him. I like the Idea:—a very proper compliment to an Aunt!—I rather imagine indeed that Neices are seldom chosen but in compliment to some Aunt or other. I dare say Ben was in love with me once, & w^d never have thought of <u>you</u> if he had not supposed me dead of a Scarlet fever.—Yes, I was in a mistake as to the number of Books. I thought I had read 3 before the 3 at Chawton; but fewer than 6 will not do.— I want to see dear Bell Griffin again.—Had not you better give some hint of S^t. Julian's early [history in the beginning of your story?][14]

NOTES TO LETTERS ON FICTION

1 'G. M.' is Mrs Austen, Anna's grandmother and Jane's mother. 'A! C' is Aunt Cassandra, Jane's sister.

2 **Lord Orville**: the hero of Frances Burney's first and most popular novel *Evelina* (1778) which Jane Austen knew well. A formal and decorous man, he sometimes refers to the heroine in the third person when speaking to her. In *Northanger Abbey*, Austen praised both Burney and Maria Edgeworth, whose *Patronage* was published in 1814.

3 The early nineteenth century saw a vogue for one-word titles indicating the moral nature of the novel, e.g., Mary Brunton's *Self-Control* (1811) and *Discipline* (1815), Maria Edgeworth's *Ennui* (1809) and *Patronage*—and Austen's *Persuasion*, a title provided posthumously for the novel by Jane's brother Henry. Less common were titles posing a question, e.g., Mary Meeke's *Which is the Man?* (1801) and Eleanor Sleath's *Who's the Murderer?* (1802).

4 **Lyme**: over forty miles east of Dawlish on the south coast, so too far for local gossip to travel. Starcross is only four miles away and Exeter about ten, so more suitable for the story.

5 Introductions and visits were carefully calibrated to rank, so that a lower-class country surgeon is unlikely to be introduced to a lord. The use of the title 'Honourable' for the son or daughter of a peer would be used only on formal occasions and on letters and cards, not in a casual introduction. Visits should be returned in a suitable number of days to avoid the appearance of discourtesy or carelessness, a duty Mr Watson laments in 'The Watsons'.

6 **P & P**: Austen's own *Pride and Prejudice*, which Anna knew intimately.

7 **Bath**: about 75 miles from Dawlish, nearly 110 miles by road, hence requiring a journey of two days. Equally important are distances within London: Berkeley Street in Mayfair (home of Mrs Jennings in *Sense and Sensibility*) is under two miles west of the more modest Russell Square.

8 **Great House**: Chawton House close to Jane Austen's cottage. It was owned by her wealthy brother Edward and at this time it was occupied by her brother Frank and his family.

9 **The Papillons**: John Papillon (1763–1837), rector of Chawton from 1801 to 1837, and his unmarried sister Elizabeth who acted as his hostess.

10 **Tollard Royal**: a small village in South Wiltshire, home to Ben Lefroy's sister Lucy and her husband.

11 **This sad Event**: refers to the death of Fanny Austen following the birth of her fourth daughter. She was Jane Austen's sister-in-law, wife of her youngest brother Charles.

12 **Walter Scott**'s long poems on historical, often Scottish, subjects, including *The Lay of the Last Minstrel* (1805) and *The Lady of the Lake* (1810), had been much acclaimed. Scott was celebrated as a poet before he became a hugely popular novelist. His first novel, *Waverley, or 'Tis Sixty Years Since*, came out in July 1814 and went through four editions before the year's end. Scott published his early novels anonymously, but Austen was aware of his authorship.

13 **Jane West**: a popular didactic writer of historical tales such as *Alicia de Lacy: An Historical Romance* (1814).

14 This unsigned letter is incomplete.

PLAN OF A NOVEL, ACCORDING TO HINTS FROM VARIOUS QUARTERS

Scene to be in the Country, Heroine the Daughter of a [a]Clergyman, one who after having lived much in the World had retired from it, & settled on a Curacy, with a very small fortune of his own.—He, the most excellent Man that can be imagined, perfect in Character, Temper & Manners—without the smallest drawback or peculiarity to prevent his being the most delightful companion to his Daughter from one year's end to the other.—Heroine a [b]faultless Character herself,—perfectly good, with much tenderness & sentiment, & not the [c]least Wit—very highly [d]accomplished, understanding modern Languages & (generally speaking) everything that the most accomplished young Women learn, but particularly excelling in Music—her favourite pursuit—& playing equally well on the Piano Forte & Harp—& singing in the first stile. Her Person, quite beautiful—[e]dark eyes & plump cheeks.—Book to open with the description of Father & Daughter—who are to converse in long speeches, elegant Language—& a tone of high, serious sentiment.—The Father to be induced, at his Daughter's earnest request, to relate to her the past events of his Life. This Narrative will reach through the greatest part of the 1st vol.—as besides all the circumstances of his attachment to her Mother & their Marriage, it will comprehend his going to sea as [f]Chaplain to a distinguished Naval Character about the Court, his going afterwards to Court himself, which introduced him to a great variety of Characters & involved him in many interesting situations, concluding with his

[a] Mr Gifford
[b] Fanny Knight
[c] Mary Cooke.
[d] Fanny K.
[e] Mary Cooke
[f] Mr Clarke.

opinion of the Benefits to result from Tythes being done away, & his having buried his own Mother (Heroine's lamented Grandmother) in consequence of the High Priest of the Parish in which she died, refusing to pay her Remains the respect due to them. The Father to be of a very literary turn, an Enthusiast in Literature, nobody's Enemy but his own—at the same time most zealous in the discharge of his Pastoral Duties, the model of an ^gexemplary Parish Priest.—The heroine's friendship to be sought after by a young Woman in the same Neighbourhood, of ^hTalents & Shrewdness, with light eyes & a fair skin, but having a considerable degree of Wit, Heroine shall shrink from the acquaintance.—From this outset, the Story will proceed, & contain a striking variety of adventures. Heroine & her Father never above a ⁱfortnight together in one place, he being driven from his Curacy by the vile acts of some totally unprincipled & heart-less young Man, desperately in love with the Heroine, & pursueing her with unrelenting passion—no sooner settled in one Country of Europe than they are necessitated to quit it & retire to another—always making new acquaintance, & always obliged to leave them.—This will of course exhibit a wide variety of Characters—but there will be no mixture; the scene will be for ever shifting from one Set of People to another—but all the ^jGood will be unexceptionable in every respect—and there will be no foibles or weaknesses but with the Wicked, who will be completely depraved & infamous, hardly a resemblance of Humanity left in them.—Early in her career, in the progress of her first removals, Heroine must meet with the Hero—all ^kperfection of course—& only prevented from paying his addresses to her, by some excess of refinement.—Wherever she goes, somebody falls in love with her, & she receives repeated offers of Marriage—which she always refers wholly to her Father, exceedingly angry that ^lhe sh.^d not be first applied to.—Often carried away by the anti-hero, but rescued either by her Father or the Hero—often reduced to support herself & her Father by her

^g Mr Sherer.

^h Mary Cooke

ⁱ Many Critics

^j Mary Cooke

^k Fanny Knight.

^l Mrs Pearse of Chilton-Lodge.

Talents, & work for her Bread;—continually cheated & defrauded of her hire, worn down to a skeleton, & now & then starved to death.—At last, hunted out of civilised Society, denied the poor Shelter of the humblest Cottage, they are compelled to retreat into Kamschatka where the poor Father, quite worn down, finding his end approaching, throws himself on the Ground, & after 4 or 5 hours of tender advice & parental Admonition to his miserable Child, expires in a fine burst of Literary Enthusiasm, intermingled with Invectives against Holders of Tythes.—Heroine inconsolable for some time—but afterwards crawls back towards her former Country—having at least 20 narrow escapes of falling into the hands of Anti-hero—& at last in the very nick of time, turning a corner to avoid him, runs into the arms of the Hero himself, who having just shaken off the scruples which fetter'd him before, was at the very moment setting off in pursuit of her.—The Tenderest & completest Eclaircissement takes place, & they are happily united.—Throughout the whole work, Heroine to be in the most [m]elegant Society & living in high style. The name of the work not to be [n]Emma—but of the same sort as [o]S & S. and P & P.

[m] **Fanny Knight**
[n] **Mrs. Craven**
[o] **M.̲ H. Sanford**

NOTES TO 'PLAN OF A NOVEL'

Mr Gifford, a rather unexpected source, was presumably William Gifford, chief reader for and associate of the publisher and bookseller John Murray. Gifford read and approved *Emma* before Murray offered to publish it in 1815. Austen and he may have corresponded but are unlikely to have met.

Fanny Knight was the eldest daughter of Jane Austen's brother Edward of Godmersham Park, whose family took the name Knight in 1812. Austen advised her niece on her romantic dilemmas.

Mary Cooke was the daughter of Jane Austen's godfather, Reverend Samuel Cooke, and his wife Cassandra (née Leigh), first cousin to Mrs Austen, Jane and Cassandra's mother. Mrs Cooke was author of the Gothic novel *Battleridge* (1799).

Mr Clarke was James Stanier Clarke, domestic chaplain and librarian to the Prince of Wales, and, for a short time, correspondent of Jane Austen (see Preface, p. 214).

Mr Sherer was Reverend Joseph Sherer, vicar of Godmersham, the Knights' parish.

Mrs Pearse of Chilton-Lodge was Anne, wife of John Pearse, Director and then Governor of the Bank of England. The Pearses lived at Chilton Lodge in Chilton Foliat, a few miles from Kintbury, where the Austens' friends the Fowles lived in the rectory.

Mrs Craven was Catherine, second wife of Reverend John Craven (James Austen's uncle-in-law), a longstanding friend of the Austens. The Cravens lived at Chilton Foliat.

Mr H. Sanford was Henry Sanford, friend and business associate of Jane Austen's brother Henry in London. Like Mr Gifford, he is an unexpected source for a spoof novel.

Kamschatka: now commonly Kamchatka, an area of present-day Russia little known in the West. Like Timbuktu in 'Sanditon', the name mainly signified remoteness for English readers.

POEMS AND CHARADES

PREFACE TO THE POEMS AND CHARADES

GEORGE HENRY LEWES told Charlotte Brontë that Jane Austen was 'not a poetess' and that she had 'none of the ravishing enthusiasm of poetry'. She would probably have agreed, but, like many in the leisured gentry and middle class, she enjoyed the pastime of writing light verses and taking part in rhyming games. One of these demanded verses rhyming with 'Rose'. Jane's contribution is one of four; the others were written by Jane's sister Cassandra, their mother Mrs Austen and their sister-in-law Elizabeth, Edward's wife.

Austen was a skilled needlewoman and sewed little gifts for family members and friends, often accompanied by a few lines, as with the little bag made for Mary Lloyd and the hand-embroidered handkerchiefs for Catherine Bigg. Other occasional poems were inspired by jolly family events like homecomings, the birth of children or Christmas festivities, as well as by absurdities gleaned from local gossip or newspapers.

In all her light verse Austen showed her delight in words and names and in the comic possibilities of rhyme and abrupt conversational phrases, a delight that continued into her last days. After laying aside her pen before finishing 'Sanditon', she wrote or dictated a final comic poem. The skit 'When Winchester races first took their beginning' was composed less than three days before her death.

POEMS

'This Little Bag'

The clergyman's widow Mrs Martha Lloyd with her daughters Martha and Mary rented the parsonage at the small village of Deane from the Reverend George Austen. The two families of Austens and Lloyds became great friends and in 1792, when the Lloyds left Deane for Ibthorpe, about fourteen miles away, Jane Austen made a 'housewife' ('hussif') or sewing kit for Mary. A tiny pocket of the housewife hid a slip of paper on which the following poem was written.

> This little bag I hope will prove
>   To be not vainly made—
> For, if you thread & needle want
>   It will afford you aid.
>
> And as we are about to part
>   T'will serve another end,
> For when you look upon the Bag
>   You'll recollect your freind.
>   Jan:^{ry} 1792.

'Miss Lloyd has now sent to Miss Green'

Jane Austen sent these lines from Bath to her sister Cassandra, who had travelled to Ibthorpe to help nurse Mrs Lloyd during her final illness. Mrs Lloyd died on 16 April 1805, so the verses must have been written shortly afterwards. Professional dressmakers, presumably like Miss Green mentioned here, would make up material provided by the customer. As the daughter of the deceased, Martha Lloyd would need to wear full mourning, probably of black crape, and would want the clothes sewn speedily.

> Miss Lloyd has now sent to Miss Green,
> As, on opening the box, may be seen,
> Some yards of a Black Ploughman's Gauze,
> To be made up directly, because
> Miss Lloyd must in mourning appear—
> For the death of a Relative dear—
> Miss Lloyd must expect to receive
> This license to mourn & to grieve,
> Complete, e're the end of the week—
> It is better to write than to speak—

'Happy the Lab'rer'

Part of a family game, this poem required words to rhyme with 'rose'. The labourer is imagined in a coat of a light brown cloth, in his buttonhole a 'Cabbage rose' (a large, round, double rose with a strong scent). People of low status might sit in specific pews in a country church but not in the box-pews reserved for the upper orders.

Miss J. Austen

> Happy the Lab'rer in his Sunday Cloathes!—
> In light-drab coat, smart waistcoat, well-darn'd Hose
> And hat upon his head to Church he goes;—

As oft with conscious pride he downward throws
A glance upon the ample Cabbage rose
Which stuck in Buttonhole regales his nose,
He envies not the gayest London Beaux.—
In Church he takes his seat among the rows,
Pays to the Place the reverence he owes,
Likes best the Prayers whose meaning least he knows,
Lists to the Sermon in a softening Doze,
And rouses joyous at the welcome close.—

'Oh! Mr Best'

In July 1806 Jane Austen was on holiday in Clifton spa near Bristol, with her mother, sister Cassandra and close friend Martha Lloyd. Evidently Martha wanted to visit the Yorkshire spa town of Harrogate, famed for its sulphur wells which were thought to purge the system or provide a general tonic. Since it was unusual for genteel women to travel alone, Martha needed an escort—hence the plea to 'Mr Best'. The assumption was that they would hire a carriage or post-chaise and teams of horses. In company, this long journey of 200 miles would seem as short as the one-mile distance between the town of Newbury and Speen Hill.

Oh! Mr Best, you're very bad
    And all the world shall know it;
Your base behaviour shall be sung
    By me, a tuneful Poet.—

You used to go to Harrowgate
    Each summer as it came,
And why I pray should you refuse
    To go this year the same?—

The way's as plain, the road's as smooth,
    The Posting not increased;

You're scarcely stouter than you were,
    Not younger Sir at least.—

If e'er the waters were of use
    Why now their use forego?
You may not live another year,
    All's mortal here below.—

It is your duty Mr Best
    To give your health repair
Vain else your Richard's pills will be,
    And vain your Consort's care.—

But yet a nobler Duty calls
    You now towards the North.
Arise ennobled—as Escort
    Of Martha Lloyd stand forth.

She wants your aid—she honours you
    With a distinguish'd call.
Stand forth & be the friend of her
    Who is the friend of all.—

Take her, & wonder at your luck
    In having such a Trust.
Her converse sensible & sweet
    Will banish heat & dust.—

So short she'll make the journey seem
    You'll bid the Chaise stand still.
T'will be like driving at full speed
    From Newb'ry to Speen Hill.—

Convey her safe to Morton's wife
    And I'll forget the past,

And write some verses in your praise
    As finely & as fast.

But if you still refuse to go
    I'll never let you rest,
But haunt you with reproachful song
    Oh! wicked Mr Best!—

                    J.A.
              Clifton 1806

'See they come'

Francis or Frank, Jane Austen's fifth brother, a Royal Navy officer, married Mary Gibson in Ramsgate in Thanet, Kent, in July 1806; the couple then spent their honeymoon at Godmersham Park, the home of Austen's third brother, the rich landowner Edward.

Fanny, Edward's eldest daughter, records that she received a letter from 'Aunt Jane, with some verses of hers'. These are written from the point of view of Fanny, who imagines the happy couple coming in their carriage 'post haste', i.e., with the speed of fast mail coaches. The couple pass through the city of Canterbury and the village of Chilham, then enter Godmersham Park, where Fanny's five brothers rush out to the main gate to greet them.

See they come, post haste from Thanet,
    Lovely Couple, side by side;
They've left behind them Richard Kennet
    With the Parents of the Bride!

Canterbury they have passed through;
    Next succeeded Stamford-bridge;
Chilham village they came fast through;
    Now they've mounted yonder ridge.

Down the hill they're swift proceeding,
  Now they skirt the Park around;
Lo! the Cattle sweetly feeding,
  Scamper, startled at the sound!

Run, my Brothers, to the Pier gate!
  Throw it open, very wide!
Let it not be said that we're late
  In welcoming my Uncle's Bride!

To the house the chaise advances;
  Now it stops—They're here, they're here!
How d'ye do, my Uncle Francis?
  How does do your Lady dear?

On Sir Home Popham's sentence—April 1807

A controversial naval officer and Tory Member of Parliament, Sir Home Popham was praised for his part in the daring capture of Buenos Aires from the Spanish in summer 1806, but subsequently, in March of the following year, he was court-martialled at Portsmouth for achieving this success by withdrawing troops from the Cape of Good Hope, thus leaving Cape Town unprotected from the enemy. Although Popham was found guilty, his career was undamaged, for in time he became a knight and a rear-admiral. His trial and resultant 'severe reprimand' attracted much publicity in the press, with many regarding Popham as vindicated.

The 'Ministry' Jane Austen vilifies here was the coalition government known as the 'Ministry of all the Talents', presided over by Lord Grenville and including the Whig politician Charles James Fox. It achieved the abolition of the slave trade but was regarded as ineffective in its negotiations to end the long war with France.

Of a Ministry pitiful, angry, mean,
A Gallant Commander the victim is seen;

For Promptitude, Vigour, Success—does he stand
Condemn'd to receive a severe reprimand!
    To his Foes I could wish a resemblance in fate;
That they too may suffer themselves soon or late
The Injustice they warrant—but vain is my spite,
<u>They</u> cannot so suffer, who never do right.—

To Miss Bigg previous to her marriage, with some pocket hand[kerchie]fs. I had hemmed for her.—

Jane Austen evidently wrote two different poems to accompany the cambric (white linen) handkerchiefs she had embroidered with Catherine Bigg's name or initials. The Bigg family of Manydown Park, Wootton St Lawrence, about five miles from Steventon, were old friends of the Austens; the friendship survived Jane Austen's retraction of her acceptance of a marriage proposal from Harris Bigg-Wither in December 1802.

Harris's fifth sister Catherine married Reverend Herbert Hill on 25 October 1808 and Austen's little poems were written during the wedding preparations.

Cambrick! with grateful blessings would I pay
    The pleasure given me in sweet employ:—
Long may'st thou serve my Friend without decay,
    And have no tears to wipe, but tears of joy!
               J. A.—Aug.st 26.—1808—

On the same occasion—but not sent.—

Cambrick! Thou'st been to me a Good,
And I would bless thee if I could.
Go, serve thy Mistress with delight,
Be small in compass, soft & white;
Enjoy thy fortune, honour'd much

To bear her name & feel her touch;
And that thy worth may last for years,
Slight be her Colds & few her Tears!—

To the memory of M^rs. Lefroy, who died Dec:^r
16.—my birthday.—written 1808.—

Of the surviving verses by Jane Austen, this is the only one with a serious intent. It was written to elegise her friend and mentor, Anne Lefroy, who died from a horse-riding accident in 1804 on Austen's twenty-ninth birthday. Anne Lefroy was the wife of the rector of Ashe, two miles from Steventon. Known as 'Madam Lefroy', by all accounts she was a cultured philanthropic lady of wide literary knowledge; she became a friend and mentor to the young Jane Austen, who greatly esteemed her.

The comparison with the eminent man of letters Dr Samuel Johnson was high praise; in his *Life of Johnson* (1791) James Boswell quoted William Gerard Hamilton's remark, 'No man can be said to put you in mind of Johnson.'

The day returns again, my natal day;
What mix'd emotions with the Thought arise!
Beloved friend, four years have pass'd away
Since thou wert snatch'd forever from our eyes.—

The day, commemorative of my birth
Bestowing Life & Light & Hope on me,
Brings back the hour which was thy last on Earth.
Oh! bitter pang of torturing Memory!—

Angelic Woman! past my power to praise
In Language meet, thy Talents, Temper, Mind,
Thy solid Worth, thy captivating Grace!—
Thou friend & ornament of Humankind!—

At Johnson's death, by Hamilton t'was said,
"Seek we a substitute—Ah! vain the plan,
No second best remains to Johnson dead—
None can remind us even of the Man."

So we of thee—unequall'd in thy race
Unequall'd thou, as he the first of Men.
Vainly we search around thy vacant place,
We ne'er may look upon thy like again.

Come then fond Fancy, thou indulgent Power,—
—Hope is desponding, chill, severe to thee!—
Bless thou, this little portion of an hour,
Let me behold her as she used to be.

I see her here, with all her smiles benign,
Her looks of eager Love, her accents sweet.
That voice & Countenance almost divine!—
Expression, Harmony, alike complete.—

I listen—'tis not sound alone—'tis sense,
'Tis Genius, Taste, & Tenderness of soul.
'Tis genuine warmth of heart without pretence
And purity of Mind that crowns the whole.

She speaks; 'tis Eloquence—that grace of Tongue
So rare, so lovely!—Never misapplied
By <u>her</u> to palliate Vice, or deck a Wrong,
She speaks & reasons but on Virtue's side.

Her's is the Energy of soul sincere.
Her Christian Spirit, ignorant to feign,
Seeks but to comfort, heal, enlighten, chear,
Confer a pleasure, or prevent a pain.—

Can ought enhance such Goodness?—Yes, to me,
Her partial favour from my earliest years
Consummates all.—Ah! Give me yet to see
Her smile of Love—the Vision disappears.

'Tis past & gone—We meet no more below.
Short is the Cheat of Fancy o'er the Tomb.
Oh! might I hope to equal Bliss to go!
To meet thee Angel! in thy future home!—

Fain would I feel an union in thy fate,
Fain would I seek to draw an Omen fair
From this connection in our Earthly date.
Indulge the harmless weakness—Reason, spare.—

              J.A.

'Alas! poor Brag, thou boastful Game!'

The verses refer to a debate related by Cassandra to Jane Austen in a letter of January 1809 written from their brother Edward's mansion of Godmersham Park about which card game they should play, 'brag' or 'speculation'. Jane Austen at Chawton composed the burlesque comic verses for her young nephew Edward as a monologue mainly spoken by the game of speculation. It comically echoes the soliloquy in *Hamlet* beginning, 'Alas, poor Yorick!'

> "Alas! poor Brag, thou boastful Game!—What now avails thine empty name?—
> Where now thy more distinguish'd fame?—My day is o'er, and Thine the same.—
> For thou like me art thrown aside, At Godmersham, this Christmas Tide;
> And now across the Table wide, Each Game save Brag or Spec: is tried."—

"Such is the mild Ejaculation, Of tender hearted Speculation."—

'My dearest Frank'

The verses celebrate two events: the birth of a boy (Francis William) on 12 July 1809 to Mary and Frank Austen, Jane's fifth brother, and the move on 7 July into their new home in Chawton Cottage of Jane Austen, her mother, sister Cassandra and friend Martha Lloyd. The women were having some alterations made to the house.

Mary Austen had had a hard time with the birth of her first child named Mary Jane in April 1807, and would die after the birth of her eleventh child in 1823.

Frank had been a precocious temperamental child and, aged seven, reputedly bought a donkey or pony, rode it, then sold it for a profit.

Jane had not yet met Fanny, wife of her youngest brother Charles, but she imagined the pair settled opposite to her Chawton cottage, 'over-right' in Hampshire dialect. Fanny died in 1814; see 'Letters to Anna' in this volume (p. 222).

Chawton, July 26.—1809.—
My dearest Frank, I wish you joy
Of Mary's safety with a Boy,
Whose birth has given little pain
Compared with that of Mary Jane.—

May he a growing Blessing prove,
And well deserve his Parents Love!—
Endow'd with Art's & Nature's Good,
Thy name possessing with thy Blood,
In him, in all his ways, may we
Another Francis William see!—

Thy infant days may he inherit,
Thy warmth, nay insolence of spirit;—
We would not with one fault dispense
To weaken the resemblance.
May he revive thy Nursery sin,
Peeping as daringly within,
His curley Locks but just descried,
With "Bet, my be not come to bide."—
   Fearless of danger, braving pain,
And threaten'd very oft in vain,
Still may one Terror daunt his Soul,
One needful engine of Controul
Be found in this sublime array,
A neighbouring Donkey's aweful Bray.
So may his equal faults as Child,
Produce Maturity as mild!
His saucy words & fiery ways
In early Childhood's pettish days,
In Manhood, shew his Father's mind
Like him, considerate & kind;
All Gentleness to those around,
And eager only not to wound.
   Then like his Father too, he must,
To his own former struggles just,
Feel his Deserts with honest Glow,
And all his self-improvement know.—
A native fault may thus give birth
To the best blessing, conscious worth.—

   As for ourselves, we're very well;
As unaffected prose will tell.—
Cassandra's pen will paint our state,
The many comforts that await
Our Chawton home, how much we find
Already in it, to our mind;
And how convinced that when complete

It will all other Houses beat
That ever have been made or mended,
With rooms concise, or rooms distended.
You'll find us very snug next year,
Perhaps with Charles & Fanny near,
For now it often does delight us
To fancy them just over-right us.—
                              J.A.

'In measured verse'

These light comic verses most likely concern Austen's niece Anna, daughter of her eldest brother James and future recipient of the letters on fiction. As a child, Anna often stayed at Chawton Cottage with her grandmother and aunts. The geographical references probably allude to Mary Brunton's 1811 novel *Self-Control*, which describes the heroine's abduction to the exotic parts of Canada. Jane Austen had found its plot especially improbable and mocked it in 'Plan of a Novel' (see p. 227f).

1

In measured verse I'll now rehearse
   The charms of lovely Anna:
And, first, her mind is unconfined
   Like any vast savannah.

2

Ontario's lake may fitly speak
   Her fancy's ample bound:
Its circuit may, on strict survey
   Five hundred miles be found.

3

Her wit descends on foes and friends
   Like famed Niagara's Fall;

And travellers gaze in wild amaze,
    And listen, one and all.

4

Her judgment sound, thick, black, profound,
    Like transatlantic groves,
Dispenses aid, and friendly shade
    To all that in it roves.

5

If thus her mind to be defined
    America exhausts,
And all that's grand in that great land
    In similes it costs—

6

Oh how can I her person try
    To image and portray?
How paint the face, the form how trace
    In which those virtues lay?

7

Another world must be unfurled,
    Another language known,
Ere tongue or sound can publish round
    Her charms of flesh and bone.

'I've a pain in my head'

Maria Beckford was the daughter of Francis Beckford of Basing Park, Hampshire. After the death of her sister in 1803, Maria managed the household of her brother-in-law John Middleton. In 1808 Middleton rented Chawton House, owned by Jane Austen's rich brother Edward, and Maria and Jane Austen, living in nearby Chawton Cottage, became acquainted. Maria had frequent ailments requiring consultations with Mr Newnham, the Alton apothecary. For her relief he might prescribe 'calomel', mercury chloride, much used as a purgative.

> I've a pain in my head
>   Said the suffering Beckford,
> To her Doctor so dread.
>   Oh! what shall I take for't?
>
> Said this Doctor so dread,
>   Whose name it was Newnham.
> For this pain in your head,
>   Ah! what can you do Ma'am?
>
> Said Miss Beckford, Suppose
>   If you think there's no risk,
> I take a good Dose
>   Of calomel, brisk.—
>
> What a praise-worthy notion.
>   Replied Mr Newnham.
> You shall have such a potion,
>   And so will I too Ma'am.—
>   Feby. 1811.—

On the marriage of Mr Gell of East Bourn to Miss Gill.—

These comic verses playing on words in the way so many in the Austen family enjoyed were prompted by a notice in *The Hampshire Telegraph and Sussex Chronicle*, 25 February 1811: 'On Saturday was married, Mr. Gell, of Eastbourn, to Miss Gill, of Well-street, Hackney'.

Of Eastbourn, Mr Gell
    From being perfectly well
Became dreadfully ill
    For the Love of Miss Gill.
So he said with some sighs
    I'm the slave of your i.s
Ah! restore if you please
    By accepting my e.s.

'I am in a dilemma'

These two lines form part of a letter to Austen's sister Cassandra in Godmersham, written on 30 April 1811 from London where Jane was staying with her brother Henry. Evidently, they relate to a family in-joke resulting from gossip concerning Cassandra and Fanny, brother Edward's eldest daughter.

Emma Plumptre, Fanny's friend, was a daughter of John Plumptre, whose estate neighboured Godmersham. In September 1811, Emma became engaged to Henry Gipps, a member of the local militia from a Kent banking family; he was ordained in the Church of England in 1815.

"I am in a Dilemma, for want of an Emma,"
"Escaped from the Lips, Of Henry Gipps."—

'Between Session & Session'

These lines were also copied in the letter of 30 April 1811 to Cassandra Austen and again concern matters at Godmersham.

In the late eighteenth and early nineteenth centuries many canals were cut through the English countryside to promote trading and industrial traffic. Proposals for these huge projects, usually supported by investors, had to be approved by Parliament in a 'session'. A proposal for a Weald of Kent canal, a 28-mile waterway linking the Rivers Medway and Rother was first made in 1800, with an expanded scheme brought before Parliament in 1811.

The Austens' hostility to the Bill was based on the unfounded fear that the canal would cross Edward's Godmersham Park. Jane Austen was hoping that a deferral would frustrate 'Wicked Men', presumably the commercial entrepreneurial interests promoting the Bill, along with the Members of Parliament supporting them. The 'nation' would of course never have been consulted since such decisions were taken by a small number of propertied men. The Weald of Kent project was not carried out.

"Between Session & Session"   "And the Villainous Bill"
"The just Prepossession"   "May be forced to lie still"
"May rouse up the Nation"   "Against Wicked Men's will."

'When stretch'd on one's bed'

Headaches were a perennial problem (cf. 'I've a pain in my head' concerning Maria Beckford). They were exacerbated by bad lighting and limited use of spectacles. If the headache persisted, the main treatment was leeches to remove what was perceived as a harmful excess of blood in the head.

    When stretch'd on one's bed
    With a fierce-throbbing head
Which precludes alike Thought or Repose,
      How little one cares
      For the grandest affairs
That may busy the world as it goes! —

    How little one feels
    For the Waltzes & reels
Of our dance-loving friends at a Ball!
      How slight one's concern
      To conjecture or learn
What their flounces or hearts may befall.

How little one minds
If a company dines
On the best that the Season affords!
How short is one's muse
O'er the Sauces & Stews,
Or the Guests, be they Beggars or Lords! —

How little the Bells,
Ring they Peels, toll they Knells
Can attract our attention or Ears! —
The Bride may be married,
The Corse may be carried,
And touch nor our hopes nor our fears.

Our own bodily pains
Ev'ry faculty chains;
We can feel on no subject beside.
'Tis in health & in Ease
We the Power must seize
For our friends & our Souls to provide.

Oct.! 27. 1811.

J.A

'Camilla, good humoured, & merry, & small'

Jane Austen wrote these comic lines when in November 1812 she learnt that her friend Camilla Wallop was to marry Reverend Henry Wake. Camilla was thirty-eight, a mature age for marriage.

Camilla, good humoured, & merry, & small
For a Husband was at her last stake;
And having in vain danced at many a Ball
Is now happy to jump at a Wake.

'When Winchester races first took their beginning'

Jane Austen wrote this poem on 15 July 1817 in Winchester where she had come for medical treatment. The previous day the *Hampshire Chronicle and Courier* advertised the Winchester Races for 29–31 July to be held on the flat ground at Worthy Down; perhaps Austen saw the advertisement and it prompted her into light verse.

Horse racing was a popular pastime and the Austen family often attended race meetings. These meetings were accompanied by much betting, eating and drinking. Enjoyment very much depended on the weather. The joke in Winchester was that St Swithin, patron saint of the city (Latin *Venta*) was also associated with rain. The popular belief is that, if it rains on his day, 15 July, the rain will continue for the next forty days.

St Swithin's shrine had long been demolished, as had the old bishop's palace, a new one having been erected in the late seventeenth century.

When Winchester races first took their beginning
It is said the good people forgot their old Saint
Not applying at all for the leave of S^t: Swithin
And that William of Wykham's approval was faint.

The races however were fix'd and determin'd
The company met & the weather was charming
The Lords & the Ladies were sattin'd & ermin'd
And nobody saw any future alarming.

But when the old Saint was informed of these doings
He made but one spring from his shrine to the roof
Of the Palace which now lies so sadly in ruins
And then he address'd them all standing aloof.

Oh, subjects rebellious, Oh Venta depraved
When once we are buried you think we are dead

But behold me Immortal.—By vice you're enslaved
You have sinn'd & must suffer.—Then further he said

These races & revels & dissolute measures
With which you're debasing a neighbouring Plain
Let them stand—you shall meet with your curse in your
    pleasures
Set off for your course, I'll pursue with my rain.

Ye cannot but know my command o'er July.
Henceforward I'll triumph in shewing my powers,
Shift your race as you will it shall never be dry
The curse upon Venta is July in showers.

CHARADES

The Austen family much enjoyed composing and circulating charades, a popular domestic amusement of the time. The three printed here have been identified as by Jane Austen.*

1.

When my 1st is a task to a young girl of spirit
And my second confines her to finish the piece
How hard is her fate! but how great is her merit
If by taking my whole she effect her release!

Jane

2.

Divided, I'm a Gentleman
In public Deeds and Powers
United, I'm a Man who oft
That Gentleman devours.

Jane

3.

You may lie on my first, by the side of a stream,
And my second compose to the Nymph you adore
But if when you've none of my whole, her esteem
And affection diminish, think of her no more.

Jane

---

* The solutions are Hemlock, Agent and Banknote.